DIARY OF AN INVASION

ALSO BY ANDREY KURKOV
IN ENGLISH TRANSLATION

Death and the Penguin
The Case of the General's Thumb
Penguin Lost
A Matter of Death and Life
The President's Last Love
The Good Angel of Death
The Milkman in the Night
The Gardener from Ochakov
Ukraine Diaries: Dispatches from Kiev
The Bickford Fuse
Grey Bees

Andrey Kurkov

DIARY OF AN INVASION

MOUNTAIN LEOPARD PRESS
WELBECK · LONDON & SYDNEY

First published in Great Britain in 2022 by
Mountain Leopard Press
an imprint of
Welbeck Publishing Group
London & Sydney
www.mountainleopard.press

9 8 7 6 5 4 3 2 1

A CIP catalogue record for this book is available from the British Library

ISBN (HB) 978-1-914495-84-7
ISBN (PB) 978-1-914495-91-5

Map © Emily Faccini

Excerpt from *The Long Shadow of the Past: Memorial Culture and Historical
Politics* reproduced here with the permission of Verlag C.H. Beck
© Assmann, Aleida, Der lange Schatten der Vergangenheit.
Erinnerungskultur und Geschichtspolitik. Monografie.
Verlag C.H. Beck. München 2021

Designed and typeset in Haarlemmer by Libanus Press, Marlborough
Printed and bound in Great Britain by
CPI Group (UK) Ltd, Croydon, CRO 4YY

The publishers acknowledge with gratitude the original
sources of Andrey Kurkov's texts within this volume.

B.B.C. Radio Four
B.B.C. World Service
Dag og Tid
Kyiv Post
La Reppublica
Daily Mail
The Economist
Financial Times
Grid
Guardian
New Statesman
New Yorker
Observer
Sunday Times
The Author

CONTENTS

For the soldiers of the Ukrainian army

Preface

On February 24, 2022, I wrote hardly anything. Woken by the sound of Russian rocket explosions in Kyiv, I stood at the window of my apartment for about an hour and looked out into the empty street, aware that the war had begun, but not yet able to accept this new reality. I did not write anything for the next few days either. The car journey, first to Lviv and then on to the Carpathian Mountains, was unimaginably long due to endless traffic jams. A sea of cars from all the other regions of the country poured into the narrow funnel of roads leading to the west. Everyone was trying to escape to save their families from the outrage of war.

Only when we reached Uzhhorod and had been welcomed into the home of our friends, did I sit down at someone else's desk and open my computer – not to write but to read the notes and texts that I had written over the past two months. I was trying to find in them a premonition of this war. I found in them much more than I expected.

Ukraine has given the world many first-class chess players. Good players see the game many steps ahead. Probably Ukrainians have this ability in their genes because of the county's turbulent history and their need to foresee and plan for the future of their country and for that of their family, for many years to come.

A dramatic experience makes for a dramatic perception of the future. But, as if by some divine joke, in the Ukrainian national character, unlike in the Russian one, there is no fatalism. Ukrainians almost never get depressed. They are programmed for victory, for happiness, for survival in difficult circumstances, as well as for the love of life.

Have you ever tried to remain optimistic during catastrophe and tragedy, during bloody military operations? I have tried and will continue to try. I am an ethnic Russian who has always lived in Kyiv. I see in my worldview, in my behaviour and attitude to life, a reflection of the worldview and behaviour of the Ukrainian Cossacks of the sixteenth century, at a time when Ukraine had not yet become part of the Russian Empire, when freedom for Ukrainians was more precious than gold. That era has returned and freedom for Ukrainians is once again more important than gold.

This war pushed me and my family out of our home. I have become one of the millions of Ukrainian displaced persons. But this same war has given me the opportunity to better understand Ukraine and my Ukrainian compatriots. I have met hundreds of people, heard hundreds of stories. I have been given insights into things about Ukraine that I did not understand before. During these tragic months, Ukrainians have learned and understood a lot about their homeland and about themselves. War is not the best time for such discoveries, but without the war these discoveries would not have come to light.

This diary consists firstly of texts that I wrote in the two months before the onset of the war, followed by my wartime notes and essays. It is both a private diary and my personal history of this war. This is my story, the stories of my friends, my acquaintances and strangers, the story of my country. Taken together, this is not only a chronicle of Russian aggression in Ukraine but a chronicle of how the war imposed by Russia – and Russia's attempt to destroy Ukraine as an independent state – have contributed to the strengthening of Ukrainian national identity. The war has made Ukraine more understandable to the world – more understandable and more acceptable as one of the states of Europe.

29.12.2021

Goodbye Delta! Hello Omicron!

Goodbye Delta! Hello Omicron! This could describe the pre-New Year mood in Ukraine, and it puts us on a common trajectory with Europe and the world. Common values and enemies are the best weapons against geopolitical loneliness. But Ukraine would not be Ukraine if the New Year mood of its citizens was not enlivened with some bright and chaotic political decisions. The "orchestra" of state power – the cabinet of ministers – has been shooting new bills into the sky like fireworks, causing everyone to look up in amazement at the exhilarating spectacle.

Ukrainians always have something to talk about, to discuss and disagree with! When the Ministry of Defence decided to register almost all women between the ages of 18 and 60, the topic of a possible war with Russia came to life with renewed vigour and made its way into every kitchen. Apparently, this was the only way to revitalise Ukrainian's fear of war – people had already grown so tired of being afraid of it.

It was frightening in 2014, when, during the annexation of Crimea, the Russian State Duma voted to allow Russian troops to fight on the territory of other states. Since then, the Ukrainian–Russian war has been going on *de facto* in the Donbas.

Yet another proof of Russian military presence in the Donbas came to light when a fighter from there, under the influence of drugs, stumbled into the Ukrainian army positions. During interrogation by the Security Service of Ukraine (S.B.U.), he complained of bullying by his Russian officers.

Needless to say, the announcement by the Ministry of Defence about registering women for military service has worried Ukrainian men. And women do not like the idea either, especially since it has been clarified that both pregnant women and mothers of young children should be registered by the end of 2022. What's more, women who fail to register by then will face substantial fines. In short, far from causing a new consolidation of Ukrainian society against its enemies, this bill has provoked vigorous debate about the competence of the country's military leadership.

It was probably in order to defuse these disputes that the authorities decided to puzzle citizens yet further with another bill. It came from the Ministry of Ecology and increases the fines for damage to protected natural resources. The decree specifies the size of each fine applicable for any possible damage, including the killing of an ordinary frog (Hr.14 per frog), picking a mushroom without permission (Hr.75 per mushroom), the illegal collection of wild nuts (Hr.1,154 per kg).

Defenders of the decision concerning the military registration of women base their arguments on the example of Israel, where women serve in the army on an equal basis with men. It is a pity that the defenders of protected frogs, mushrooms and nuts have not employed similar tactics – for example, citing "the mushroom police" in Switzerland, who have the right to weigh a mushroom picker's harvest in the forest and to issue a fine if the harvest is greater than is allowed under Swiss law.

In general, I would prefer Ukraine to follow Swiss examples, rather than Israeli ones. This is what I would wish for my country for the New Year.

In the meantime, I look back and think: what do I want to transfer from 2021 to 2022? Yes, of course, I would like to transfer the old gas and electricity prices. But experience has taught me that the New Year always brings new prices for everything. So, remaining realistic, I wish that the quality of coffee in Kyiv's coffee houses will remain the same.

While not wanting a decrease in the selection of French, Italian and Spanish wines available, I would like to see wines from Ukraine's Bessarabia and Transcarpathia continue to delight us with their taste and quality in the New Year. I would also like to wish new success to Ukrainian cheese makers and to all the small, craft producers of delicious products. For Ukrainians, the taste of food is very important. Tasty food allows Ukrainians to reconcile themselves to political reality. This is our history and our mentality.

As a writer, I cannot help but share a separate piece of New Year joy. A small but high-profile "book lobby" has persuaded the government to include books in the list of goods and services that can be bought using the Hr.1,000 handouts given to every fully vaccinated citizen of Ukraine. Some 8 million virtual bank cards with these "Covid thousands" have already been issued and vaccinated Ukrainians have flocked to online bookstores to spend the money on literature. This has saved half the Ukrainian publishing houses from bankruptcy and created some new, rather pleasant problems for publishers. They urgently need to reprint books that have sold out. The only problem is a shortage of paper and a shortage of printing houses. This is both a problem and an incentive. Moreover, another Hr.18 billion has been inserted into the 2022 state budget for "Covid thousands" gifts for vaccinated Ukrainians. Soon it will be safe to say that vaccinated Ukrainians read more than unvaccinated ones.

So, handouts for the vaccinated will continue into 2022, as will the wearing of masks, the war on carefully selected oligarchs, promises to protect foreign investments and Q.R. codes – confirming our right to travel in international airspace and into restaurant premises.

Let's enjoy 2022 to the full and God bless us all!

03.01.2022

"Don't mention the war!"

Each December 31, ten to fifteen minutes before the onset of the New Year, the president congratulates Ukrainian citizens on T.V. This Soviet tradition easily took root in Ukraine, like some other Soviet habits and rituals. Until 2015, many Ukrainians listened first to the congratulations of President Vladimir Putin to the Russian people at 10.50 p.m. and an hour later they listened to the Ukrainian president. After the outbreak of the war in Donbas and the annexation of Crimea, Russian T.V. channels in Ukraine were turned off, and with them Putin's New Year greetings. Since then, only the Ukrainian president speaks before the New Year. True, in 2018, on one of the most popular T.V. channels, owned by Ukraine's principal oligarch Igor Kolomoisky, instead of the then President Poroshenko, the Ukrainian people were congratulated by the television comedian Volodymyr Zelensky, who also announced that he was going to run for the presidency.

This year, before the onset of 2022, on the channel that used to belong to the fifth president of Ukraine, Petro Poroshenko, and which now belongs to the journalists themselves, Poroshenko congratulated Ukrainians on the New Year. They then broadcast Volodymyr Zelensky's congratulations just after midnight.

Zelensky's televised New Year's address lasted twenty-one minutes. Realising that not everyone will have the patience to listen to the whole thing, the president's office posted the full text of the speech on its website. Largely a report on the achievements and the outstanding problems, the speech included lists of the most crucial professions in the state: the military, doctors, teachers, athletes, miners, etc. Also, obviously referring to Russia, the president expressed the wish that "neighbours would come to visit with a bottle (of vodka) and jellied meat, and not barge in with weapons". This was the only mention of the war. The president did not mention the fact that, on the borders with Ukraine, Russia had assembled a huge belligerent army, along with logistic services, field hospitals and mobile refuelling bases for tanks and other equipment. But then this was common knowledge and the possibility of a Russian military offensive against Ukraine would hardly be a popular topic of conversation at the festive table.

Despite its record length, Zelensky's New Year's speech cannot be disassembled into vivid, memorable quotes. There is only one phrase with which I want to argue or at least disagree with: "We are not waiting for the world to solve our problems".

Boris Yeltsin, who firmly believed that Russia and Ukraine could only exist together, once became famous for the phrase, "I woke up in the morning and asked myself, what have you done for Ukraine?" Now, it seems to me, President Biden and the leaders of many European states are waking up with this same thought. President Biden has had his second telephone conversation with Putin in two weeks. After each such conversation he takes several days to think it over and only then does he call the President of Ukraine to talk about the content and results of the conversation. Croatia, meanwhile, signed a declaration on Ukraine's European perspective and the Estonian president promised to help Ukraine with arms. Only Germany is officially opposed to the supply of weapons to Ukraine. The German Foreign Ministry said that the sale of weapons to Ukraine could increase the chances of war. In fact, a possible war between Russia and Ukraine reduces the chances of launching the Russia–Germany gas pipeline Nord Stream 2 and Germany, and probably some other western European countries, badly want to avoid such a situation.

Of course, Ukraine is not being invited to join N.A.T.O., but the weapons of N.A.T.O. countries – both Javelins and Turkish attack drones – are already in Ukraine and already on the front line. Both Turkey and the United States are ready to sell weapons to Ukraine. Turkey is even helping to build a plant for the production of combat drones near Kyiv.

Russia does not have such drones. Immediately after the first use of Turkish attack drones – "Bayraktar" – against separatists in the Donbas and in response to the shelling of Ukraine by prohibited weapons, Russia started talking about Ukraine's plans to recapture the part of the Donbas seized by the separatists with the help of western weapons. It was under this pretext that Russia began to bring tank divisions and artillery from all over its territory to the Ukrainian border. The unrecognised president of Belarus, Lukashenko, immediately announced that his army would side with Russia in the event of a Russian–Ukrainian war. This means that the front line could stretch along the entire northeastern land border of Ukraine – more than three thousand kilometres. And this is not counting the hundreds of kilometres of the sea border along the Azov Sea, on which Russian warships could land troops. Today's front line in the Donbas is about 450 kilometres long.

In the meantime, all five thousand bomb shelters in Kyiv have been checked, as have the city's alarm sirens and the public address system for making important public announcements. But none of these actions have caused the slightest panic among the population. "We have been at war with Russia for eight years!" – say some. "Putin is bluffing and blackmailing the West!" – others say. Both are right. But it is also true that Russia refuses to give the West guarantees of non-aggression against Ukraine.

However, Kyiv remains unperturbed. Restaurants and cafés are packed. Pizza and sushi delivery couriers speed along the streets on bicycles, motor scooters, electric scooters and even on foot. Kyivites are in a hurry to celebrate. "The Golden Gate", the area of ancient Kyiv where I live, got into the list of the top one hundred "coolest" urban areas in the world, taking sixteenth place. A friend of my daughter flew out from London to celebrate New Year and really liked Kyiv and its old centre. On my short street, there are four barbers, where you can trim your beard and moustache and drink whisky, three wine bars, six cafés, a small food court with an underground floor where you can sit with a latte in what was once a swimming pool. In the building where I live there is a bar, an art gallery with a café, an art goods shop and a school of sewing and tailoring. In the ten days before New Year, using money from the city budget, a small, cosy, public garden across the street from our house was turned into a cool – not to say cold – concrete-clad memorial park named after Pavel Sheremet. Pavel Sheremet was a Belarusian journalist who fled from Moscow to Ukraine and lived in a nearby street until he was killed on July 20, 2016 on the street where he lived. They simply attached a bomb to the underside of his car. He drove away from the house and the car exploded.

My wife and I heard this explosion. It was early on a summer morning in the third year of the war in the Donbas, which in Ukraine is called the Russian–Ukrainian war, but that explosion is the only one I have heard in Kyiv in my entire life.

Remaining residents of the small town of Stanytsya Luhanska, which was partially destroyed by separatist artillery at the beginning of the war, have lived there more or less calmly since 2015, despite the fact that the entire town, in which twelve thousand people lived before the war, is located right on the demarcation line, immediately beyond which is separatist-held Luhansk. And this autumn, for the first time in six years, shells once more fell on the roofs of civilian residences in Stanytsya Luhanska. This happened even before Russia began to send military echelons with tanks and guns to the Donbas and its borders with Ukraine.

Exacerbations and local escalations in hostilities are commonplace in the Donbas, but, usually, the artillery of the separatists and their Russian commanders aim to destroy Ukrainian army military positions, not the dwellings of civilians.

In the front-line zone, the attitude towards a possible war is not as it is in Kyiv. They know the war better, and therefore they are genuinely afraid of it. During the 2019 presidential elections, residents voted for Volodymyr Zelensky, who promised to end the war with Russia in one year and return stability and prosperity to Ukraine. In the third year of Volodymyr Zelensky's presidency, a "big war" seems much closer than before.

But it would seem that the majority of Ukrainians have little fear of anything – of Russia, or of Covid (less than half of adults have been vaccinated, although vaccines have been widely available since the summer). Judging by opinion polls, Ukrainian citizens are mostly afraid of poverty. That is why more than one million of them have moved to live and work in Poland. Hundreds of thousands more live and work in the Czech Republic, Spain, Portugal and Italy. Hardworking Ukrainians have even trodden a path to Denmark. Thousands of Ukrainian citizens now work on Danish farms. Millions of Ukrainians live abroad and are constantly transferring their salaries to their loved ones in Ukraine. Several times Zelensky's government has announced plans to tax these transfers. After all, we are talking about billions of euros.

Half of western Ukraine lives on money earned by relatives abroad. And apparently, they live so well (and so far away from daily shellings) that the inhabitants of eastern Ukraine, who traditionally went to work in Russia, have also switched to Western Europe. In Russia there are now many fewer Ukrainian guest workers than there once were. And if eastern Ukraine, a bastion of pro-Russian sentiment, has started to turn to the West, then this is another reason for Russia to be nervous.

———

Vladimir Putin once said that the Germans invented Ukraine in 1918 in order to divide the Russian Empire, but, at the end of last year, he changed his mind and said that Ukraine had been created by Vladimir Lenin. Apparently, he said this to show that Russia has more claim to Ukraine than Europe has. Ukraine, for the President of Russia, is an *idée fixe* which keeps him awake at night and occupies his every waking hour. His political comrades-in-arms on Russian television daily suggest either bombing Kyiv, or dividing Ukraine into three states, or seizing the entire territory, except for western Ukraine, or seizing the coastal territory from Odesa city to Transnistria. Chechen President Ramzan Kadyrov proposed seizing Ukraine on his own and annexing it to Chechnya. True, he later added that he would only do this if Putin ordered him to do it.

Will Putin order his troops to go on the offensive? This will become clear by early February. At least this is the time frame given by military and political experts. By then Americans and Russians will have met three times and discussed the situation, the future of their relationship and the future of Ukraine. The meetings will take place without representatives of Ukraine.

"We are not waiting for the world to solve our problems," President Zelensky said in his New Year's greetings.

Personally, I am waiting for that and rather banking on it.

05.01.2022

Merry Christmas!

Christmas is not white this year! It is rather greyish and, in some places, even green – at least around the town of Brusyliv in Zhytomyr oblast* where winter wheat is springing up in the fields.

Still, the mood of Ukrainians is snowy and joyful. In this kind of mood, children usually go sledging or have snowball fights. In the villages, the onset of evening reveals which houses are inhabited by young families. Electric Chinese garlands, thirty or fifty metres in length, have become popular and they light up the facades of houses in otherwise dark streets. Many homes have decorated spruce trees in their courtyards, and those who do not have evergreens have hung Christmas decorations on apple and pear trees.

The festive season in Ukraine lasts one month – from St Nikolaus' Day – December 19 – to Epiphany on January 19. To celebrate for a whole month you must have enviable health. Those whose constitutions are less robust reduce the festive period to a mere two weeks: from the Ukrainian Christmas to the "European" one, that is from December 24

* Oblast is roughly the equivalent of an English county.

to January 7. True, for genuine believers, preparations for the Orthodox Christmas include a forty-day fast. First, you live courageously for more than a month without meat or alcohol. Then, on Holy Eve, January 6, you put twelve meat-less dishes on the table and wait for the appearance of the first star in the sky. Ukrainians are not big fans of restrictions, no matter where they spring from – the church or the government – how can you fast on New Year's Eve? What about the jellied meat and Olivié salad with Champagne! So, it is fair to say that Christmas is a very high peak in the mountain range of festive season celebrations rather than the main and only winter festival.

At Christmas you cannot clean the house, you cannot refuse to help if asked and you cannot hunt or fish. Traditionally, it is the housewives who monitor the implementation of these rules, which their husbands know nothing about. And when, at the Christmas table, a usually strict housewife generously allows her husband some vodka or wine, it does not mean that she has decided to let him get drunk on Christmas Day. It is simply a way of ensuring that the thought of hunting and fishing will not even occur to anyone.

There has always been a big difference between New Year and Christmas celebrations. New Year is a noisy, mass holiday, with fireworks and Champagne. Christmas is a quiet, family time. Both holidays have been victims of political repression. In 1915, Tsar Nicholas II banned celebration of the New Year, declaring it a "negative German influence". The Bolsheviks, having thrown off the tsar, allowed the "Holiday of the Christmas tree" to re-emerge and even came up with a new name for the holiday, *Krasnaya Yolka* – "Red Christmas tree". It was to this *Krasnaya Yolka* festival that

Vladimir Lenin was travelling from Moscow to see the children in the village of Sokolniki on January 6, 1919, when he and his guards were robbed by the then infamous Moscow bandit Yakov Koshelkov. Lenin was left without a Browning, money, or even a car, but he still managed to reach the children in Sokolniki. For peasant children at that time, the New Year's holiday was something exotic and foreign. Christmas was more familiar. If you noticed that Lenin was on his way to see the children on December 31, not on January 6 – that is, not on the Holy Eve of Christmas – then it immediately becomes clear that the Bolsheviks' plan was to replace Christmas with the New Year.

If in Russia the Bolsheviks' war against Christmas and all religious holidays in general was more or less successful, then the 1917 revolution and the end of the World War I gave a new impetus in Ukraine to the national liberation movement. The hope for an independent Ukraine had become a powerful incentive for the revival of folk traditions, including that of Christmas. The Ukrainian composer and lecturer at Kyiv University, Mykola Leontovych, spent twenty years arranging and re-arranging the old Ukrainian carol, "*Shchedryk*". In January 1919, in Kyiv, at the request of the government of the Ukrainian People's Republic, the Ukrainian Republican Choir was created to acquaint Europe and the world with Ukrainian music and culture. "*Shchedryk*" became the choir's principal success. They went on tour to Europe in March 1919. In September 1922, the conductor and founder of the choir, Oleksandr Koshits, left Poland with some of the singers to tour the U.S.A., from where they never returned.

On October 5, 1922, the Ukrainian Christmas carol

"*Shchedryk*" was performed for the first time in America at New York's Carnegie Hall. The English version, "Carol of the Bells", was first performed in New York at Madison Square Gardens in March 1936 by a choir under the direction of Peter Wilchousky, an American conductor of Ukrainian origin. It was Wilchousky who wrote the English text of this Christmas carol. This is how the Ukrainian carol became a worldwide Christmas hit. The history of this song and the story of the Ukrainian choir's eternal tour of the U.S.A. under the direction of Oleksandr Koshits is now being made into a book by the researcher and writer Tina Peresunko as the topic of her Fulbright visiting scholar project. Personally, I am really looking forward to reading it. I think that it will be the perfect gift for Christmas 2023!

Until the book is published, you may find "*Shchedryk*" on YouTube and other platforms and can listen to it in Ukrainian or English. It creates the perfect Christmas mood.

14.01.22

Ukrainian T.V. series: producers and actors

The highest mountain in Ukraine is in the Carpathians and is called Hoverla. Its height is 2,061 metres. But Ukraine's most important mountain is located in Kyiv, this is the Pechersky Hill, with a height of only 195 metres. The Pechersk district of Kyiv, located on the hill of the same name, is the political heart of Ukraine. Here, in the space of one or two blocks, we find the Cabinet of Ministers, the Parliament, the Office of the President and many other important government institutions. Among all these ministries and other state offices, the Pechersk District Court has enjoyed a particularly negative reputation for more than twenty years. It was the judge of this court, Rodion Kireev, who, in October 2011, on the direct orders of the administration of President Viktor Yanukovych, sentenced Yulia Tymoshenko to seven years in prison with a fine of 150 million euros for causing damage to Ukraine when signing a gas agreement with Russia. Former Ukrainian President Viktor Yanukovych had two strong feelings about Yulia Tymoshenko – fear and hatred. After the victory of the Euromaidan protests, judge Rodion Kireev fled from Ukraine to Moscow and now works there as a lawyer. At the same time, Yanukovych fled to Moscow along with his "personal" prosecutor, prosecutor general Viktor Pshonka, along with several hundred other officials, judges and military leaders. But the Pechersk District Court remained and once again has a connection with the office of the current president, Volodymyr Zelensky.

On January 6, Christmas Eve, while President Zelensky was skiing in the Carpathian mountains, the Pechersk District Court confiscated the property and assets of the fifth president of Ukraine, Petro Poroshenko. The war between the sixth president and the fifth president is coming to a head. An arrest warrant was also issued against Petro Poroshenko himself. True, in order to avoid personally signing this order, the prosecutor general of Ukraine, Irina Venediktova, went on vacation for one day. The arrest warrant for Poroshenko was signed by her deputy, who will remain responsible for his signature. Poroshenko himself is still in Poland but promises to return in the second half of January. As an experienced politician, Poroshenko understands that not to return is to admit guilt. Even today, Poroshenko is the leader of the opposition and the head of the second most popular political party, European Solidarity. So, the task for him is to make an impressive return to Ukraine and to use his possible arrest to advance his political struggle for a return to power. Officially, Poroshenko is accused of high treason and more specifically, of financing terrorism. This accusation is based on the fact that he approved the direct purchase of coal for Ukrainian power plants by the Donbas separatists at a time when these power plants were in dire need of fuel. After the annexation of Crimea and the outbreak of war in the Donbas, almost all Ukrainian coal mines ended up in the territories seized by the separatists. The separatists' coal was delivered by train through Russian territory while hostilities continued on the front line.

The story of the issuance of an arrest warrant against Poroshenko reminds us of the story of the trial and arrest of Yulia Tymoshenko. There is, however, a slight difference. Back in 2011, it was Yanukovych alone who feared and hated Tymoshenko, whereas Poroshenko has, simultaneously, three high-ranking enemies: Volodymyr Zelensky, the oligarch Igor Kolomoisky and the President of the Russian Federation, Vladimir Putin, who flatly refused not only to meet but even to speak on the telephone with Poroshenko.

Former Ukrainian ambassador to the U.S.A. in 2015–19, Valeriy Chaly, suggested in an interview that Poroshenko's arrest is one of the Kremlin's conditions for organising a meeting between Putin and Zelensky. So far, none of President Zelensky's attempts to arrange a telephone conversation, let alone a meeting with Putin have got anywhere. But Poroshenko has not been arrested yet. In any case, a new episode of the series "The Fifth President's Persecution" will soon be on all Ukrainian television channels.

In the meantime, Ukrainians are watching the events in Kazakhstan wide-eyed, eagerly discussing developments. The protests in Kazakhstan have raised the revolutionary spirit in Ukraine and the most radical sofa-based analysts began to predict a Euromaidan for Kazakhstan, with further democratisation and a victorious fight against corruption. However, Russia's immediate reaction stalled all talk of victory and a brilliant future for the great Central Asian nation. At the request of the President of Kazakhstan, the "peacekeeping forces" of the Collective Security Treaty Organisation, which includes Russia, Belarus, Kazakhstan, Armenia, Kyrgyzstan and Tajikistan, entered Kazakhstan and this has made everybody think more deeply about what is happening in Almaty and Astana. Many complaints against the Ukrainian authorities have already been voiced in Kyiv, asking why Ukraine has still not issued an official statement of support for the Kazakh revolution. Neither President Zelensky nor any other representative of the country's leadership has yet so much as commented on the events taking place there. On the other hand, Yevgeny Shevchenko, a member of parliament, who is little known outside Ukraine, went to the Kazakh capital and said that he was there waiting for the introduction of Russian troops, since he did not believe in the likelihood of President Tokayev's taking control of the situation. Shevchenko not only entered parliament with the Servant of the People party of Volodymyr Zelensky but, during the 2019 presidential elections, he was a confidant of presidential candidate Zelensky. He never really concealed his pro-Russian and anti-American views. Last year, he became notorious in Ukraine when, in the midst of Belarusian protests, he went to Minsk and appealed to Belarusians to forgive Alexander Lukashenko's sins. There in Minsk he met with Lukashenko in the presidential palace and expressed support for him. This puzzled many Ukrainians and Belarusians. Ukrainian society asked some pointed questions: "Who sent him to Lukashenko? Whose support did he express: was it on behalf of the parliament or on behalf of the president?" Shevchenko was expelled swiftly from the parliamentary faction of the Servant of the People party and the party also stated that he had organised the meeting with Lukashenko on his own initiative. He is now an independent, non-partisan parliamentary deputy and, as it turns out, the head of a group advocating inter-parliamentary ties with Kazakhstan.

There are more than enough such "pro-Russian" James Bonds in Ukraine. It is not a crime to have pro-Russian or anti-American views – after all, we are a democratic country. However, to declare these views publicly after the annexation of Crimea and the outbreak of war in Donbas is not strictly *comme il faut*. According to the latest ratings, up to twenty per cent. of voters are still prepared to vote for pro-Russian parties in Ukraine. And this during the build-up of Russian troops on Ukrainian borders!

By the way, the introduction of Russian troops in Kazakhstan was met with relief by some Ukrainians. They thought that now Russia would forget about Ukraine – at least for the time being. Geopolitical naivety is one more misfortune afflicting Ukrainian society. On the same day, when the dispatch of Russian paratroopers to Kazakhstan began, the communist party of the Russian Federation submitted to the State Duma a bill for the recognition of the "Donetsk People's Republic" and "Luhansk People's Republic". State Duma deputy Kazbek Taisayev, member of the Central Committee of the Communist Party of the Russian Federation, said that he was confident about the approval of this bill and that, like South Ossetia and Abkhazia, the occupied part of the Ukrainian Donbas would soon become a territory officially controlled by Russia.

Ukrainian mass media hardly reacted to this news from the Russian Duma. During the tradition New Year and Christmas holidays, which last a whole month from St. Nicholas Day, December 19 to Epiphany, January 19, Ukrainians, like Russians, visit friends and family, arrange merry feasts and watch T.V. This time, both Ukrainians and Russians were entertained and made happy by the Kvartal 95 Studio, created in 2003 by president-to-be Volodymyr Zelensky. T.V. viewers on both sides of Russian–Ukrainian front are delighted with the seventh season of the super-popular T.V. comedy "Matchmakers", which stars famous Ukrainian and Russian actors. In 2017, this series was banned in Ukraine when the leading actor in the series, Fyodor Dobronravov, voiced his approval of the annexation of Crimea. Both Dobronravov and two other actors from the series were banned from entering Ukraine. Volodymyr Zelensky was the producer of the series at the time and criticised the bans and the decisions made by the Security Service of Ukraine (S.B.U.). After Zelensky became president in May 2019, the ban on Dobronravov's entry into Ukraine was lifted, as was the ban on showing the series on Ukrainian T.V. channels.

The seventh season of "Matchmakers" was filmed on

"neutral territory" – in Belarus. In Russia, it is shown on the Russia-1 T.V. channel, which is banned in Ukraine for its anti-Ukrainian propaganda. In Ukraine, the series is shown on the 1 + 1 channel, owned by the oligarch Igor Kolomoisky. The Russian channel bought the rights to broadcast this Ukrainian series from a foreign intermediary. Direct trade of T.V. content with Russia is prohibited in Ukraine.

While Ukrainian and Russian television viewers laugh in front of their screens, the first of a series of talks on Ukraine between the U.S.A. and Russia took place in Geneva. The parties once again restated the positions they had announced previously. Few believe that the U.S.A. or Russia will make concessions. The three planned meetings between N.A.T.O. and the Russian Federation are likely simply to prolong the "time for diplomacy" and postpone possible military action.

In the meantime, the Ukrainian leadership is once again worried about the absence of Ukrainian representation in the negotiations on Ukraine. The head of the office of the President of Ukraine, Andriy Yermak, said that in the near future he was going to meet with the main Russian negotiator, the deputy head of the presidential administration of Russia, Dmitry Kozak. He also mentioned a possible meeting between Putin and Zelensky in Beijing during the Olympics. This news caused concern among a number of Ukrainian political scientists. After all, the United States and some European countries have declared a political boycott of the Beijing Olympics, which means that any possible meetings between the Russian and Ukrainian presidents are bound to follow the Russian scenario, especially if this happens in the absence of representatives from Germany, France or the U.S.A. Without their participation, negotiations between

Russia and Ukraine about Ukraine are much more dangerous than negotiations between Russia and our western allies without the participation of Ukraine.

Surely, the president of Ukraine is thinking about this too while he is skiing and snowboarding in the Carpathians in the Ukraine's best mountain resort, Bukovel, thirty kilometres from Hoverla.

15.01.2022

January Evening by Candlelight

Recently a strong wind of up to 70 k.p.h. has been blowing across Ukraine. A strong wind usually changes the weather and cuts off electricity simply by breaking the power cables. No electricity supply usually means a break in communication with the outside world – no Wi-Fi or T.V. and no way to charge a mobile telephone. All that remains is a candle and a book, just like two hundred years ago. As was the case then, a candle is more important than a book. And cheaper!

When the electricity went off that night in hundreds of villages because of the wind, tens, if not hundreds of thousands of Ukrainians burrowed into the drawers of their tables and sideboards looking for candles. Everyone's world was reduced to the space that can be illuminated by a candle. Forced romance won out over high-tech reality.

The darkness brought by the wind found me visiting friends in Obukhovsky district, sixty-five kilometres from Kyiv, in the historical village of Hermanivka, which has been in existence since at least the eleventh century. We were sitting at the table, drinking wine and talking about books. It seems to me, more than ever, that books exist not to be read but to be talked about. Of course, T.V. series are talked about more often than books but books are more pleasant as a topic of conversation. Books are more soulful than T.V. And, again, you can read without electricity. Unless it is an e-book.

This time the conversation was about a book that those born in the U.S.S.R. were required to read at school in the course on Russian literature and those born in independent Ukraine read and continue to read but do so now in the section for foreign literature – the novel in verse *Eugene Onegin* by the Russian poet and writer Alexander Pushkin (1799–1837).

At the table, lighted by candles, sat two charming young women, Dasha and Katya – both refugees from Donetsk — along with our hosts, Julietta and Arie. The mistress of the house, Julietta, is Afro-Ukrainian. Her father was from Africa. He came to the U.S.S.R. as a student. Having graduated, he returned to his homeland, leaving his daughter and her mother in Kyiv. Julietta's husband, Arie van der Ent, a citizen of Holland, is a famous Slavist, publisher and translator. He moved to Ukraine a couple of years ago to be with Julietta. It was Arie, the translator of many Russian and Ukrainian poets, including the works of the most famous grand dame of Ukrainian literature, Lina Kostenko, who first spoke at the table about *Eugene Onegin* and Pushkin.

Arie had recently received a Russian grant provided through a publishing house for a new Dutch translation of this work. Russia still spares no expense in promoting its classical culture. Russia's powerful cultural image is considered the best argument against its extremely negative and aggressive political image. In Holland, Russia's image is much worse than in neighbouring Germany or France. After several years of investigation, a trial began in March 2020 that is still ongoing into the case of the shooting down by a Russian Buk missile over the Donbas of flight MH17, which was flying from Amsterdam to Kuala Lumpur.

All the poetry of Alexander Pushkin has already been translated into Dutch. The latest translations of *Eugene Onegin*, *The Bronze Horseman* and other works were made by one of the most famous Russianists in Holland, Hans Boland, who spent years preparing an almost complete collection of Pushkin's poetic works. At the presentation of Boland's translations in 2013, Dutch Foreign Minister Frans Timmermans said, "This is a huge gift for the Dutch reader. And a huge gift for the Dutch language". In August 2014, Boland refused to accept the Pushkin medal from the Russian state for his efforts to popularise Russian literature, saying, "I would have accepted the honour done to me with great gratitude, if [it were] not for your president, whose behaviour and way of thinking I despise. He poses a great danger to the freedom and peace of our planet. God grant that his 'ideals' will be completely destroyed in the near future. Any connection between him and me, his name and the name of Pushkin is disgusting and unbearable".

Pushkin, like that most famous of Ukrainian poets, Taras Shevchenko, was during his lifetime, to use today's terminology, a dissident and a political prisoner. For his satirical anti-monarchist poems, the tsar sent him into exile to fight locusts in Chisinau and Odesa. It was in Chisinau that Pushkin began to work on the novel *Eugene Onegin* and it was in Odesa that he continued this work. So Ukraine seems quite a logical place to work on the new Dutch translation of his novel.

In the ancient village of Hermanivka, in a cosy house on Taras Shevchenko Street, work is now in full swing on a new translation of *Eugene Onegin* into Dutch. Work also continues on translations of Ukrainian poetry, an activity which Arie van der Ent does without grants or support from the Ukrainian state. His work is fuelled by sheer enthusiasm. I am sure that Arie would also refuse the Pushkin medal if the Russian state offered it to him. He, like Hans Boland, loves Pushkin and does not like Putin. And besides, he loves his wife Julietta and Ukraine very much – enough to sell his apartment in Rotterdam and buy a house in a Ukrainian village!

I like this paradoxical situation in which Pushkin "supports" the popularisation of Ukrainian poetry in the Netherlands and in Europe.

At the table, our conversation about books, with glasses in hand, continued even after the lights in the house came back on. Just in case, we did not extinguish the candles, so that later we would not have to look for matches.

Lately, in the Ukrainian mass media, they seem almost afraid to discuss books. On the T.S.N. website of T.V. channel 1 + 1, in an article on New Year's gifts, readers were advised not to give books to their relatives and friends. Moreover, readers were warned of the terrible consequences of presenting such a gift: if you do not want quarrels and misunderstandings in the family, it is better not to give such a thing as a book to your husband. And giving a book as a gift to your wife for the New Year can be the reason for her marital betrayal. It should be added, that after heated discussion of these tips on Facebook, this part was cut from the article about New Year's gifts. Now books are not mentioned at all.

And finally, I want to draw your attention to the village of Hermanivka. Here you can find most interesting examples of nineteenth century architecture, an art gallery, a historical museum rich in exhibits. Here, until 1919, a large Jewish colony lived its stormy life, the history of which ends with two bloody pogroms. The border between Poland and the Russian Empire once ran next to the village. Here, in the eleventh century, there was a protected settlement, as discovered by Ukrainian archaeologists in late 1990s. And here, in 1663, the "Black Council" took place, a meeting that attempted to negotiate between the two opposing Cossack clans of Hetman Ivan Vyhovsky on the one hand and Hetman Yuri Khmelnitsky's on the other. Ivan Vyhovsky was considered a pro-Polish politician and statesman and Yuri Khmelnitsky was considered pro-Russian. The meeting ended in bloodshed. From that moment on began a period in Ukrainian history that is called in school history textbooks "The Ruins". This is the era of internecine wars, which only strengthened the political influence of Moscow in the territory of today's Ukraine.

21.01.2022

"Nothing Personal!"

Around midnight, on the day we visited our good friends Julietta and Arie, the two women from Donetsk, Dasha and Katya, started getting ready to go home to Kyiv. I was surprised: "Is it possible to get a taxi to come out here at this time of night?" It turned out that it was possible. Julietta called several private taxi drivers in Obukhiv and one of them agreed to take her guests to Kyiv for Hr. 1,000 – about thirty-three euros. Pretty cheap for an hour's journey, you might think. But you have to remember that the minimum pension in Ukraine is Hr. 2,500, and the minimum wage Hr. 6,500. So, for a taxi driver, who might spend Hr. 250 on petrol, this is a very good wage, even if you consider that he will have to make the return journey without passengers.

The next morning, Saturday, gusts of wind were still trying to blow the taxi off the road as we travelled home. We had left our friends in a house that was once more without electricity. As we drove back to Kyiv we were listening to the radio. The radio host was making fun of a recent interview with President Zelensky in which the President had said "the Soviet Union had its pluses and minuses".

There followed a report about a high-ranking policeman who was caught drink-driving. His conversation with the officer who apprehended him was recorded and we heard the drunken voice of the offender explaining to the officer that, "Colleagues must support each other, otherwise where would we be?" When my wife and I go to visit people by car, our usual plan it to stay overnight with our hosts. What is the point of coming to visit and not drinking some good wine? Sadly, I cannot say that all drivers think like this. There are still far too many drunk drivers on the roads of Ukraine, drunken policemen among them.

The next item of news was about the hackers who had the day before carried out the most substantial attack of the past four years on the websites of the Ukrainian Cabinet of Ministers and many other government agencies. Russia immediately stated that it had nothing to do with the attack and at the request of the U.S.A., even went so far as to arrest fourteen Russian hackers who had been accused of attacks on businesses in America.

Once back in Kyiv, I went to meet my acquaintance from Kharkiv, a city with a million inhabitants, thirty kilometres from the border with Russia.

"What do you think?" he said. "Will there be a war?"

"I hope not," I said.

"I think there will be," he said sadly. "But they will not enter Kharkiv. There will be no attack on Kharkiv."

He went on to explain that the Russian troops gathered near Rostov-on-Don, together with the separatists from the Donbas, were preparing to capture the city of Mariupol and, possibly, to break through and create a land corridor to the Crimea. The troops massing near Voronezh would also target the Donbas and the eastern part of Kharkiv region, while the troops massed near Bryansk would target Chernihiv and Sumy, which are within easy reach of Kyiv.

The coffee in that café is usually excellent but this conversation made it seem very bitter indeed.

I went home and decided to take my mind off the war by looking at Facebook. In the Ukrainian segment, there have always been more posts about cats than about war. My expectations proved correct, but I still got into a heated discussion about school meals. It turned out that on January 1, 2022, a radical reform of school food was introduced in Ukraine. Sweet buns, sausages, cream cakes, sugar and salt, along with a long list of other tasty things, have been banned. The author of the reform is the extremely popular T.V. chef Yevgen Klopotenko. Moral support for the difficult task of reforming school meals was provided by Elena Zelenskaya, a screen-writer for the Kvartal 95 Comedy studio founded by her husband Volodymyr Zelensky, now the Ukrainian president.

Ukrainian society, on Facebook and beyond, is now divided into two equal halves – those who support the reform of school meals and those who rant about it, or write saying that their children are refusing to eat the new healthy food and demand that they return to the old, less healthy but popular stuff. The new school menu, consisting of 160 dishes, as well as recipes for all the new dishes, can be found on the websites of the Ministry of Health and the Ministry of Education – when their websites are not paralysed by hackers, that is.

Now Klopotenko is finishing work on a new menu for kindergartens and vocational schools. His other plans include changing the curricula of catering colleges. The scope of his activities is amazing and, pleasantly, he is very tolerant of the wave of hatred against him, simply declaring that all the criticism helps him to focus even more effectively on the tasks at hand. It must be added that before this reform of school meals in Ukrainian schools, children were fed according to the standards, norms, and recipes approved in the U.S.S.R. in 1956. So perhaps some good can come from T.V. celebrities.

After two weeks of holidaying, the country is gradually returning to sober reality. During our dinner in Hermanivka, the two female refugees from Donetsk told us that they attend territorial defence courses near where they live now, in Kyiv. There they are being trained in military first aid and civil defence tactics. They are ready to respond in the case of attack. Since January 1, 2022, it is not only school meals that have changed. The country's defence system was also transformed. This is the day that Ukraine's territorial defence forces were activated. A new law had already increased their contingent by up to eleven thousand people in May 2021.

We are talking about volunteers who will have to use weapons to defend their villages, towns, and cities. Member of Parliament, Fyodor Venislavsky, who deals with security, defence and intelligence issues, said that by February all members of the territorial defence units would receive weapons and be informed of their deployment positions in the event of hostilities. Members of this territorial defence force living on the border with Russia should already be in receipt of their weapons and be ready to use them. At the same time, the Kremlin has started transferring from the Far East of Russia to the border with Ukraine Iskander missile systems, capable of destroying targets on enemy territory at a distance of up to 500 kilometres.

I think it is safe to say that the flashpoint in this geopolitical conflict, which has long been creating sparks on the border of Ukraine, will be reached within a month. I already see clearly that Russia will not simply withdraw its troops from the Ukrainian borders. The fruitless negotiations with N.A.T.O. are over, having achieved not the slightest result. Russia will continue to raise the stakes, believing that a possible military strike on Ukraine would be a blow to N.A.T.O.'s reputation. After all, at the start of any hostilities in Ukraine, N.A.T.O. will take three steps back and simply observe what is happening. It is possible that for Vladimir Putin a blow to N.A.T.O.'s reputation is even more important than biting off another piece of Ukraine. Perhaps he will even apologise to Ukraine later, after the war. He will say "Nothing personal!" – as Mafiosi sometimes say in American gangster films, before killing their victim.

Between Virus and War

On Tuesday, I left Kyiv to spend a day or two at our little house in the village. As usual, I had two goals for this trip: to work in silence and to check if our boiler was working. The weather is temperamental this winter. Once a week the temperature drops to around minus twelve Celcius, then returns to zero. In such weather, you need to either keep the heating on and, of course, be ready to pay for the gas you use, or turn off the boiler, drain the water from the pipes and radiators and then close the house until spring.

Our older son called me that same evening and told me that he had coronavirus. Just in case, I decided not to return to Kyiv too soon. The window of my "rural" office overlooks the neighbour's yard. Every day, several times a day, my retired neighbour Tolik goes to the gate to smoke. He likes to greet the villagers passing along the street. Some stop for a couple of minutes to talk. He never goes beyond the gate – his old legs do not allow it. Sometimes I go and talk to him over the fence. Yesterday, while we were talking, a fellow villager from the far end of our street passed by. "Good news!" was his business-like greeting. "Now we can carry our hunting rifles without a case! The Cabinet of Ministers has approved the law! Because of the military threat!"

"I wish I had an air rifle!" Tolik responded dreamily. "I'd use it to scare the stray dogs away. They are so noisy!"

Tolik has three kennels in his yard. Two for their own dogs, Dolka and Baloo, and one for Pirate, the ginger dog of a neighbour who died two years ago. Tolik and his wife took Pirate in when his master died, but every day he still runs next door to guard his old house, only returning to Tolik's yard for food and shelter at night.

"They are not reporting about Poroshenko!" was Tolik's parting shot as he put his cigarette butt out on the green metal fence. Leaning heavily on his cane, he set off slowly down the path to the door of his house.

The fact that Poroshenko is hardly ever mentioned in the news on the country's main T.V. channels does not surprise me. This does not mean they do not think about him in the Presidential Office. Quite the opposite! He did return to Ukraine last week in order to become the leader of the united opposition; at least, that was his own scenario for his return. However, according to the scenario of the Office of the President, he returned to go to jail with the possibility of being released on bail of Hr. 1 billion ($37 million).

It took the judge a full three days to release Poroshenko, with no bail demanded. However, his passports were taken away and he has been forbidden from travelling outside the Kyiv region. This is clearly not the result expected by the Office of the President and probably explains why political experts are now commenting on the fact that President Zelensky is looking for a new prosecutor general and another team of investigators in order to make another attempt to put the fifth president behind bars.

Actually, Poroshenko has failed to unite the scattered opposition around himself and is unlikely ever to succeed in this endeavour. None of the leaders or prominent politicians of other opposition parties even went to meet him at the airport as a sign of support in his troubles with Zelensky. But fans of his party did come from all over Ukraine, undeterred by the police who, on instructions from the authorities, tried to prevent their buses from reaching the capital. Similarly, eight years ago, on instructions from Kyiv, the police tried to stop buses with people travelling to the Maidan protests. At that time, the actions of the authorities were more blatant and aggressive – they punctured the tyres of the buses, beat up and arrested activists and fabricated criminal cases against them. We saw nothing like that this time.

Russian politicians regularly claim that Ukraine is in the midst of a civil war, not a war with the Russian Federation. If there is some kind of civil war going on in Ukraine, then it is most likely a war between the current president and the former president. Such wars have become a kind of tradition for Ukrainian politicians, only now this political civil war is taking place against the backdrop of Russian preparations for a real war against Ukraine. And although Ukraine appears to be preparing for possible Russian aggression, it sometimes seems that for the current president, the war with Poroshenko remains the priority.

Poroshenko himself called on all political forces to unite in the face of Russian aggression. But he seems not to have received any positive response. Neither Yulia Tymoshenko nor Arseniy Yatsenyuk have any desire to strengthen the already strong position of Poroshenko's political party, European Solidarity. Recently, in opinion polls, European Solidarity has been gaining on Zelensky's Servant of the People party – and sometimes even overtaking it. This, of course, cannot but disturb the Office of the President.

In my village, as probably in other villages too, the locals scold the current government and are silent about the previous incumbents. While no-one discusses the war between the sixth president and the fifth in the village, people are loudly indignant at Germany's attitude towards Ukraine. Anti-German sentiment rose sharply following statements by Ukrainian politicians criticising Germany for refusing to supply Ukraine with weapons and even forbidding Estonia from transferring to the Ukrainian army howitzers it had purchased from Germany.

While I was self-isolating away from my family in a house between Kyiv and Zhytomyr, my publisher, Alexander Krasovitsky, the owner of one of Ukraine's largest publishing houses, Folio – also the publisher of Ukrainian editions of works by the Norwegian authors Jo Nesbø and Erlend Loe – went to Odesa on business and fell sick there. A coronavirus test showed positive. A mighty wave of Omicron is now covering the whole of Ukraine. Alexander is stuck in a hotel in Odesa, waiting to recover and trying to use this time to solve on his mobile telephone several production problems, the most important of which is the acute shortage of paper that is crippling Ukraine's publishing industry. While the "Covid thousands" helped Ukrainian publishing back from the brink of collapse, publishing houses have run out of books to sell. Reprinting books is problematic because the price of paper has risen by two hundred per cent. Even at this high price, there is still no paper available on the market.

Finnish paper mills, which in the past supplied Ukrainian publishers, have changed to the production of paper for commercial packaging. This is understandable because, a few years ago, economists predicted a fall in demand for paper for books in connection with the growing popularity of e-books. There are only two paper mills in Ukraine. They can produce up to five thousand tonnes of paper, but Ukrainian publishing houses need sixty thousand tonnes. Ukrainian publishers have never been major players in the international paper market because of the recurring crises in the Ukrainian book market.

The publishing house Folio has its own printing house. It is located in a small town Derhachi, between the city of Kharkiv and the Russian–Ukrainian border, only twenty-five kilometres away. Supposing Alexander can find enough paper and is able to buy it at the new high price and bring it to the printing house, is there any guarantee that the printing house, along with the paper, would not be seized by Russian troops?

The word "guarantee" has become very popular nowadays. Russia demands written guarantees from the U.S.A. that Ukraine will not be accepted into N.A.T.O. Russia has asked the U.S.A. for written responses to their demands for guarantees about Ukraine remaining in the Russian sphere of influence. Russia refuses to give guarantees of non-aggression against Ukraine and China refuses to give guarantees of non-aggression against Taiwan. For some reason, it seems to me that these two hot spots on the world map – Ukraine and Taiwan – are connected. In both regions, "former masters" are laying claim to the independent countries that they once controlled. In both cases, the U.S.A. is on the side of the independent countries. Bloomberg recently reported that Xi Jinping asked President Putin not to attack Ukraine until after the Beijing Olympics. This indicates that there will be no attack on Taiwan before the end of the Olympics either. But what will happen after the Olympic Games? "Synchronized swimming" by the armies of Russia and China in foreign waters?

This evening, having finished his cigarette, my retired neighbour Tolik firmly declared that there would be no war. "How do you know?" I said.

"He is afraid! On T.V., every day they show planes with weapons arriving in Kyiv from England and America!"

"On the contrary!" I told him. "That could make him attack all the faster, so that the United States and Great Britain have less time to supply Ukraine with stocks of weapons."

My neighbour did not argue with me. Instead, he invited me to come in for coffee. I politely declined. I do not drink coffee in the evening, so as to be able to sleep.

Before going to bed, I called my son, and he said he was feeling better. Then I called my publisher friend in Odesa and asked how things were with the paper. "I found a couple of tonnes!" he told me. "They should soon arrive at the printing house. I have four volumes of Ibsen ready for printing there. I want them ready in February."

I wanted to ask whether he thought he would have time to print his Ibsen before the end of the Beijing Olympics, but I did not. His voice was indeed too cheerful for a man with coronavirus. And why ask? If he found the paper, then he should certainly have time to print the books before February 20. Whether he will be able to move them from the printing house in time is another matter. But it is too early to judge. At the moment, life goes on as usual. President Zelensky just opened a new bridge over the River Dnipro in the industrial city of Zaporizhzhia. My good friend, the poet and psychiatrist Boris Khersonsky, has been nominated for the Taras Shevchenko State Prize for literature – the result will be announced on March 9. The governor of Odesa, Sergey

Grinevetsky, together with the head of the Ukrainian National Space Centre, Vladimir Prisyazhny, have announced that a piece of land on the border of the Odesa and Mykolaiv regions has been selected for the construction of a spaceport.

There is plenty to look forward to and plenty of justification for thinking that Ukraine has a bright future. As far as space travel is concerned, Ukraine is proud that the founder of Soviet space science, Sergei Korolev, was born in Ukraine. What is more, he was born in Zhytomyr, a city fewer than seventy kilometres from my village home.

30.01.2022

Choosing Your Words
The Language Question in Ukraine

Do you know the rules for corresponding with political prisoners? I do. I am corresponding with Nariman Dzhelyal, a Crimean Tatar political prisoner, a politician who has never hidden his negative attitude towards the annexation of Crimea but who is considered very moderate by his colleagues. He was arrested in September of last year, after returning from Kyiv, where he had taken part in the first meeting of the international "Crimean Platform", an organisation that seeks to return Crimea to Ukraine through diplomatic means. According to Russian practice, those who do not agree with Putin's policies have drugs or grenades planted on them and are then accused of drug trafficking or terrorism. Nariman Dzhelyal, like the vast majority of arrested Crimean Tatars, was charged with terrorism. He and the Akhmetov brothers are accused of attempting to blow up a rural gas pipeline – that is, of planning an attack on the omnipotent Russian gas.

When I write a letter to Nariman Dzhelyal with pen and paper, I take a picture of it and send it via WhatsApp to his wife Leviza. She prints it out, passes it through a lawyer to her husband in prison. He writes an answer, sends it to his wife through a lawyer and she, having photographed the answer, sends it to me on WhatsApp. Many people from Ukraine and other countries write to Nariman Dzhelyal in prison. Not all the letters reach him because most people send letters to the address of the prison. There the letters are opened and it is decided which letters to pass on to him and which not. The main rule for Russian prisons is that letters can only be written in Russian. Otherwise they are destroyed and they certainly do not reach the addressee. This also applies to foreigners in Russian prisons, including those who do not know Russian. I write letters in Russian, which is my native language. Nariman's native language is Crimean Tatar, but, like all residents of Crimea, he is fluent in Russian.

They want to keep him in jail for twenty years. For some reason, Russian courts are very fond of jailing Crimean Tatars – and others who do not agree with the annexation – for exactly twenty years. The first Crimean resident charged with terrorism was Oleg Sentsov in 2014. He too was given twenty years, for allegedly plotting to blow up the monument to Lenin in Simferopol. He served five years before he was exchanged for a Russian prisoner.

Maybe the Russian leadership believes that twenty years is long enough to make sure that no-one will even remember about the annexation of Crimea? Or is this the maximum prison term that a judge can give the accused according to

Russian law? I have not studied Russian criminal law and do not intend to. But I will support Nariman Dzhelyal until he is released. More than 130 Crimean Tatar activists are now in Russian prisons. And there will probably be more of them there soon.

Against the backdrop of what is happening in Crimea and against the backdrop of the growing numbers of Russian troops and military equipment on the borders with Ukraine, the well-known Ukrainian T.V. presenter Snezhana Yegorova shocked the country with a post on Facebook. "YES!!! I support PUTIN!!! And I'm not going to change my mind about the fact that it's TIME TO RETURN COMMON SENSE TO UKRAINE!!!" In the same post, she advises viewers to watch a Russian propaganda video about U.S.A. covert operations to destroy Russia and take over Ukraine and shares a link to this video on YouTube.

It was thanks to this post that I realised that Snezhana Yegorova now lives in Turkey. From there, she regularly records two-hour-long video monologues for YouTube – for everyone who does not like today's Ukraine and the European vector of development it has chosen. Her videos are watched in St Petersburg, Donetsk and Sakhalin. They are also watched in Odesa and other Ukrainian cities, although her audience there is small. Her pro-Russian worldview has long been obvious. Back in 2004 she travelled all over Ukraine as the host of concerts in support of presidential candidate Yanukovych. The 2004 elections ended with the Orange Revolution. And Yanukovych's presidency, which began in 2010, ended with the Euromaidan protests, the annexation of Crimea and the war in the Donbas.

If Snezhana Yegorova is to be remembered in years to

come, it will be only in the context of her stellar divorce from singer and writer Antin Mukharsky. They separated in 2015 and their divorce remains to this day the most famous political and show-biz divorce in Ukraine. They divorced for political reasons. Her husband, Antin, supported the Euromaidan movement and switched in daily life from speaking Russian to speaking Ukrainian. Snizhana, an ethnic Ukrainian, remained Russian speaking and spoke out publicly against the Euromaidan protests. Russian mass media happily broadcast some of her statements. For example, her fantastical allegations that, in the tents on the Maidan, illegal abortions were performed on prostitutes serving the protesters.

The fact that finally she ended up in Turkey does not surprise me at all. Before she went, she secured through the courts almost all of her ex-husband's property. Antin was also banned from travelling abroad and from meeting his children. Snizhana has five children. Mukharsky is the father of three of them: a girl and two boys. During the high-profile trial, many citizens of Ukraine took her side — firstly, she is a mother, and secondly, a television star. Now, for the majority of Ukrainians, she is the traitor who sits in Turkey and tries to persuade people to love Putin.

· The story of Mukharsky's divorce and his legal torment has a happier ending. In July 2014, he was the first Ukrainian singer to give a concert for soldiers from a venue practically in the trenches of the Donbas. Then he organised a cabaret project "Gentle Ukrainisation" to popularise the Ukrainian language. And now his new wife, art historian Elizaveta Belskaya, is actively engaged in advertising the Ukrainian language as the language of intimate communication in bed, proving that Ukrainian is much sexier than Russian. Of course, this campaign is supported by her husband.

The very idea that Ukrainian is sexier than Russian has so outraged the Russians that the activity of Elizaveta Belskaya has been discussed in a talk show on the main Russian T.V. channel. I am sure that if you said French or Italian was sexier than Russian, no-one in Russia would be outraged.

The subject of the Russian language will not disappear from the media and political space because Russia is ready to defend all Russian speakers – not just Russians alone – anywhere in the world. If a Russian has ceased to be Russian speaking, he is of no interest to Russia. In Ukraine, Russia is seen to be the protector of Russian speakers. For this reason, Ukrainian-speaking activists have a very hostile attitude towards the Russian language and towards Russian-speaking Ukrainians – who are almost half of the population. The same Antin Mukharsky who actively advocated the release of Oleg Sentsov from a Russian prison, wrote him an open letter after Sentsov's return to Ukraine, in which he expressed his indignation because Sentsov continued to speak Russian, including at international public events.

I have to say that, over the past couple of years, Sentsov has learned both Ukrainian and English rather well. His page on Facebook is in Ukrainian and he speaks publicly in Ukrainian. In everyday life, of course, he remains Russian speaking, but everyday life is a personal space in which no censorship is allowed, especially linguistic censorship.

Recently, the most famous Ukrainian Russian-speaking poet, Alexander Kabanov, who publishes books in both Russian and Ukrainian and who also edits a bilingual journal, published two books in Moscow. In an interview for the

Russian information portal Revizor.ru about the release of these books, he said, "Anyone who tells you that they are not harming the Russian language in Ukraine is either a naive fool or a scoundrel".

No, Kabanov does not call for people to love Putin. He is simply not ready for the linguistic and geopolitical changes that are inevitable in a newly independent state. In Latvia, Estonia, Moldova, and in Lithuania, while for a part of their populations the Russian language remained the language of everyday life and, to some extent, the language of culture, the majority of the Russian speakers in these countries also learned the language of the country in which they lived. This will happen in Ukraine too. In percentage terms, many more Russian-speakers will remain in Ukraine than in the Baltic states because Russification in Ukraine was much more aggressive. Kharkiv, a city with a population of one million, was the capital of Soviet Ukraine from 1919 to 1934 and was then almost one hundred per cent. Ukrainian speaking. Today it is almost one hundred per cent. Russian speaking. What it will be in fifty years, I do not know. This also depends on whether or not the 130 thousand-strong Russian-speaking army goes on the offensive in Ukraine or not. If it does not, the Ukrainian language will return in the territories that the Russian language took over. It will return very slowly and not very noticeably for many Russian-speaking Ukrainians. This will happen in step with the change of generations. After all, Ukrainian state schools no longer teach Russian, where state school education takes place only in Ukrainian. At the tertiary level, some colleges and universities use English.

In the meantime, Ukrainian-speaking parents, wives and children of Ukrainian prisoners of war and political prisoners held in Russian prisons are forced to write letters to their sons and husbands in Russian. Sometimes they write in bad Russian. But at least this increases the chances of the letter reaching their loved ones.

Reinventing History

For many people, history has long ceased to be a science and has become part of literature. It is edited just as a novel is edited before it is published. Something is added, something is thrown out, something is changed. Some concepts are polished and smoothed, some ideas are made more prominent while others are played down.

As a result of this editing, instead of comprising familiar past events, a new "formula" arises and the significance of the events is altered, as is their influence on events today.

Certain politicians are very fond of commissioning new editions of history so that the history better fits their ideology and their ideological discourse.

Sometimes a change in emphasis appears quite innocent and has no long-term consequences. I remember how President Viktor Yushchenko was fond of Trypillian culture (the Neolithic–Eneolithic culture on the territory of Ukraine and Moldova that dates back as far as 5,500 B.C.). He sincerely believed that Ukrainians are the heirs of this culture. Several amateur and professional historians began to write books about the Trypillian culture, as if it were the cradle of the Ukrainian nation. At the same time, the first private museums of Trypillian culture arose near Kyiv, at a location where archaeologists found traces of this civilisation. Since the departure of Yushchenko from Ukrainian politics, no-one talks any longer about there being a direct connection between Trypillian culture and modern Ukraine.

On the other hand, President Putin has long been fond of editing history in a way that does have an impact on contemporary life. His article dedicated to the seventy-fifth anniversary of the Soviet victory over fascism was published and read even in the U.S.A. It makes no sense to go into detail about this article, but, in our current situation, when President Putin is ready to turn three thousand kilometres of the Ukrainian border with Russia and Belarus into an endless front line, it is worth quoting from its final paragraph.

"Based on a common historical memory, we can and must trust each other. This will serve as a solid basis for successful negotiations and concerted actions for the sake of strengthening stability and security on the planet, for the sake of prosperity and well-being of all states. Without exaggeration, this is our common duty and responsibility to the whole world, to present and future generations".

Putin went on to say that Ukraine was invented by Vladimir Lenin. An earlier version of Russian history claimed that Ukraine was invented by the Germans at the end of World War I. This version was favoured both in Soviet times and in post-Soviet Russia. But now we need to focus on the words of the current president of the Russian Federation.

It was the Germans who helped Lenin to travel secretly

to Russia from exile in order to lead the 1917 revolution and overthrow the tsar. He was sent to Russia from Germany in a sealed railway carriage in the guise of valuable cargo. Under contemporary Russian law, Lenin must be considered a "foreign agent". In theory, this should be written on his mausoleum on Red Square: "Foreign agent Lenin".

You can laugh at the paradoxes of rewriting or editing history in the Russian Federation, but inside Ukraine too, history can be a thorny topic. Every now and then there are heated disputes between objectivist historians and patriotic historians. One such dispute is ongoing currently between Yaroslav Hrytsak, author of a brilliant new book on Ukrainian history, *Overcoming the Past: A Global History of Ukraine*, and Volodymyr Viatrovych, an enthusiastic historian, author of many books and former director of the National Institute of Memory. The main subject of this dispute is: can memory and history be selective? They may very well be. In fact, we live in this "selective" history.

Recently, in the very centre of Kyiv, not far from the Golden Gates, a memorial plaque appeared on the wall of the building in which the Boulangerie café is located. The board depicts a man in a military uniform of 1918–20. His name is Mykola Krasovsky. The plaque states that he was an important intelligence officer in the army of the Ukrainian People's Republic and that he lived in this house in the early 1900s. For 99.9 per cent. of Kyiv residents, his name means nothing and most of those rare people who know the name of Mykola Krasovsky are unlikely to know that he had anything to do with intelligence.

In fact, for most of his life, Krasovsky was a renowned detective who solved the most intractable and complex crimes in and around Kyiv. He was also one of the investigators in the most famous anti-Semitic case in the history of the Russian Empire – the Case of Mendel Beilis. This case was very similar to the Dreyfus Affair in France. Mendel Beilis was accused of ritually murdering an Orthodox boy in Kyiv in order to obtain "blood for making *matzah*" (the unleavened bread eaten at the Jewish festival of Pesach or Passover). The two cases show how common were anti-Semitic views among the European and Russian elites. And not only among the elite.

Krasovsky, from the outset, did not believe in the version of ritual murder. He soon also found the real killers, who turned out not to be Jews at all but local thieves. The authorities needed a Jewish version of the murder. Krasovsky was dismissed from the case. The authorities even tried to put him in jail for embezzling fifteen kopecks from the state.

It is a pity that Krasovsky's participation in the Beilis Case is not mentioned on the memorial plaque. Maybe we should ask the Kyiv police to put another on this house with the words "Legendary Kyiv detective Mykola Krasovsky"? It would also be good to ask Polish historians to look in the archives for data on his service in Polish intelligence, as well as on the date and place of his death. Sadly, Ukrainian historians do not have even these biographical details of this important figure from our history.

Ukrainian Battlegrounds: the Street, the Library and the Church

The other day, my wife returned home agitated and said that nearby, on Vladimirskaya, there was a shooting and someone had been killed. What had she actually seen? She said that a hundred metres from the main department of the S.B.U. there were a lot of police, two ambulances and a bloodied young man, very thin, lying motionless on the pavement near the currency exchange office. And next to him a man with a microphone was shouting something. "What microphone?" I said, surprised. "With a radio microphone and an amplifier on the pavement near his feet," she said. "Maybe this is some kind of protest performance?" I asked. "No, the guy lying on the ground was definitely dead! Otherwise, he would have been taken away in an ambulance!"

I decided to check the news feed on the Internet. And at that moment there appeared several headlines about an incident with machine gun fire near a cryptocurrency exchange office. It seems a fight broke out involving about thirty people, many of whom were wearing camouflage, then one of them fired a machine gun.

About a day later, the picture of what had happened became a little clearer, but not completely so. The police arrested fourteen people involved in the incident, then eleven were released and three were kept under arrest. All those arrested are members of patriotic organisations, including several veterans from the war in the Donbas. This was the second time they had tried to picket the cryptocurrency exchange office. According to these veterans, the exchange firm finances the separatist movement in Donetsk and Luhansk. The company itself is from Kharkiv and the security company that guards their office is also from Kharkiv. The activists all had legally registered hunting weapons and cartridges. The security guards who were called by the exchange company had machine guns. Both sides fired warning shots into the air. There was great panic because the shooting took place in the centre of Kyiv between the main city police department and the headquarters of the S.B.U. No-one was hurt by the bullets, but two people were sent to the hospital with injuries. One of them, the one my wife mistook for a dead man, turned out to be the Donbas war veteran and journalist, Alexei Seredyuk. I became a little more interested in this man. It turned out that he had served as the commander of the "Saint Mary" volunteer detachment, which was disbanded in 2016, when the Ministry of Defence suggested that all volunteers either join the Ukrainian army as contracted soldiers, or return home. He is also the owner of the "Iron Papa" publishing house, through which he published his book, *Confessions of a Provocateur*. In a word, he is not a typical veteran of the war in the Donbas. He is, rather, a typical radical fighter against the "Russian world".

Today there are some 400 thousand veterans from the Donbas conflict in Ukraine and their number is growing steadily. They have become such an influential force in society that at the end of 2018 the Ukrainian government was forced to establish a Ministry of Veteran Affairs.

Veterans of the ongoing war are very active and extremely close-knit. Many of them are engaged in business and they support each other economically and in other ways.

Criminals and racketeers try to avoid dealings with veterans' businesses. They understand that they might meet with armed resistance, although there have been cases in which the criminal elements have come out on top in such confrontations. In fact, some of the veterans who did not find a role in legal business went over to the other side of the law. And you often hear about convicted criminals who used to fight for Ukraine.

The most famous veteran business in Kyiv is the "Pizza Veterano" chain of pizzerias and its associated "Coffee Veterano" street kiosks. One of their pizzerias is located in the very centre of Kyiv, near the Maidan. The interior decor has a military theme and it is popular with veterans. It is a favourite meeting place, somewhere they feel comfortable. Valery Markus, the most famous writer among the Donbas war veterans goes there from time to time. His books, which are all about the war, are also mostly bought by veterans. His self-published debut novel *Footprints on the Road*, sold more than 35 thousand copies through social media. There are many such military writers, perhaps two hundred. They write almost exclusively about the war and they do not follow Ukrainian civilian literature. They are not interested in it or in non-veteran writers. Veterans are most active in big cities. In the provinces, their presence is almost imperceptible.

Last week I managed to visit a remote village in the Poltava region, close to the border with Russia. While there I did not hear a word about the war in the Donbas or meet any participants in the war.

I was invited to speak at a rural library in a village with about four thousand inhabitants. They asked me to give a lecture on the topic, "Local and national elites: their role and importance." They sent a car for the five-hour journey to and from Kozelschyna, an ancient community near the industrial city of Kremenchuk. The library is state of the art. The old building was rebuilt and turned into an educational hub with halls for lectures. There is not a single Soviet-published book in it. All its books were published in independent Ukraine. There is also an exhibition space and a small café where visitors can have free tea or coffee, or heat up their own food in a microwave. The amazing transformation of the library space was paid for by the Smart Foundation, founded by a successful young businessman born in this village but who lives between the U.S.A. and Ukraine. Behind the library, there is a convent which belongs to the Moscow Patriarchate, the Russian Orthodox Church. It has a huge cathedral, too big for a village like this.

The church, being in the territory of the Moscow Patriarchate, is, one might say, in the spiritual territory of Russian Orthodoxy. The Moscow Patriarchate has more than twelve thousand parishes in Ukraine. The number used to be higher, but since 2018 more than five hundred churches have been transferred to the Kyiv Patriarchate, the Ukrainian Orthodox Church. On the other hand, in Crimea churches that used to be Ukrainian churches of the Moscow Patriarchate have become Russian churches.

My lecture was attended by people from the villages nearby, as well as from the city of Kremenchuk, some forty kilometres away. Judging by the questions from the audience, I got the impression that people there were not happy with the current political elite of the country. They wanted to know how it would be possible to replace Ukraine's political elite with completely new people.

After the discussion, I drank tea with the organisers and was given a tour of the convent. As we approached the gate, I noticed a memorial plaque in Polish and Ukrainian. Already in the cathedral, my guide Ivan Mykolaevich Kravchenko, a local amateur historian, said that in the 1939–40 war (prior to the war between the U.S.S.R. and Germany) the N.K.V.D. used the basements of the cathedral as a prison and that for a long time five thousand Polish officers were kept there, arrested after the partition of Poland under the Molotov–Ribbentrop Pact. Historians still do not know the fate of the officers. There is a theory that they were transported to a prison in the city of Starobilsk in the Luhansk region and shot. But no evidence for this has ever been found.

In the cathedral, I was immediately struck by a large portrait of the last Russian Tsar, Nicholas II. "What is that portrait doing here?" I asked.

"He came here," Ivan Mykolaevich explained. "We have an icon of the Virgin Mary which performs miracles, so he stopped to look at the icon in Kozelschyna on his way to Odesa."

"Where is the icon?"

"The nuns keep it hidden. They only take it out once a year, on the church's festival day. Then, in the evening, they hide it away again."

It turns out that, until recently, there were two portraits of Tsar Nicholas II on display in Kozelschyna. One in the church and the other in the library. Before the renovation, a member of the radical nationalist party "Svoboda" (freedom) came regularly to the library to protest against the portrait of the tsar. The village is home to two members of this party, founded fifteen years ago in western Ukraine. One of them staged a picket for several months and refused to step inside the building where the portrait hung. Then, during the renovation work, the portrait of the tsar mysteriously disappeared. It is probably hanging in the house of one of the builders. But now the nationalist activist comes to the library for every lecture and event.

There is no Ukrainian Autocephalous Orthodox Church in Kozelschyna, only the convent and church that is subordinate to the Moscow Patriarchate. Perhaps that is why no-one today protests in front of the church in which a portrait of the last Russian tsar is hung.

In the Ukrainian churches of the Moscow Patriarchate, at the beginning of every service, they wish good health to Kirill, Patriarch of All Russia, a close associate of Putin. This is one of the reasons why many Ukrainians demand that the Ukrainian Orthodox Church of the Moscow Patriarchate be renamed the Russian Orthodox Church. But the Moscow church itself does not want to be so renamed. The priests are afraid that parishioners will leave the church if it is officially called Russian.

In 2004 and later in 2010, during their church services, Moscow Patriarchate priests called on parishioners to vote for the pro-Russian presidential candidate Yanukovych in the Ukrainian presidential elections. Since 2014, priests of the Moscow Patriarchate have refused to bury Ukrainian soldiers killed in the Donbas. As a result, the Church of the Moscow Patriarchate is often referred to as "the Moscow church". It is perceived as a political organisation. But the Moscow Patriarchate still has a very strong position in Ukraine and in three regions – Zaporizhzhia, Kherson and Luhansk – not a single congregation of the Moscow Patriarchate has transferred to the Ukrainian Orthodox Church.

In the village of Lazarivka, an hour's drive from Kyiv, where we have a house, there is also only one church and it is subordinate to Moscow. Services are in Russian, although the whole village speaks Ukrainian. People go to church only on holidays, which means that the priest has a very small income. In his spare time, the previous priest moonlighted as a taxi driver. Where the new priest earns extra money, I do not know. Around Christmastime I saw him walk along the street and, for a small fee, bless the houses of local residents and the village shops.

A year ago, President Zelensky signed the Law on Military Chaplains. Since then, for the first time, priests and worship centres have appeared in the Ukrainian army. Priests of the Moscow Patriarchate are not accepted as chaplains.

The majority of recruits start their military service as agnostics or atheists. But many of them return from the war as believers and become parishioners of the Ukrainian Orthodox Church, the church independent of Moscow, or of the Ukrainian Greek Catholic Church, which was banned in Soviet times but has since revived. I do not think that Ukraine is undergoing a religious revival, but I am sure that the Moscow Patriarchate has no future in Ukraine.

13.02.2022

Everything is Heating up, including the Sauna

Despite the persistent menace of war, things in this country must be going pretty well. How otherwise could President Zelensky have promised to give every single vaccinated person over sixty years old a smartphone? If I understand correctly, this state gift will also be given to new birthday "boys and girls" who reach the age of sixty. I quite like the idea. For ten years or more, on the birth of a child, the state has been giving the mother a parcel of useful baby-care items. For children who are starting school, the state gives a set of appropriate stationery. And now, finally, citizens who are transitioning to retirement age will be given a smartphone.

This idea is a logical step in Ukraine's digitalisation policy. Representatives of the president's office were quick to point out that the country's leadership would conduct economic and social surveys through this smartphone. It is already possible to install the application "Diya" (action) on smartphones, by which you can generate various official documents. This application has become the umbilical cord between the state and the individual. You can upload an electronic version of your passport, driving license, various certificates and, of course, a vaccination certificate. In the future, the president's team dreams of holding presidential elections through smartphones, thereby freeing pensioners and sick people from having to go to the polling station or call members of the election commission to their homes or their hospital beds.

The times they are a-changin'. Previously, candidates standing for election to parliament, as well as presidential candidates, bribed older voters with food packages or even cash rewards. Now, with the help of a donated smartphone, it will be possible to give and receive electronic gifts in the form of cheap Internet access or discount vouchers for shops.

Indeed, the possibility of issuing electronic food stamps to the poor was recently discussed in the president's office. They will also be sent through the Diya application. When news about this hit the press, journalists laughed at the president's office. It looked like an admission of failure in regulating the economy and a sign that the president's office was preparing for the worst – the appearance of a huge army of starving people. This worry subsided quickly and, when information appeared in the press that the Russian government was also developing a system of food cards for the poor, the same journalists began to laugh at the Russian government. Let us call it part of counter-propaganda. In Russia they like to talk about how poorly Ukrainians live because the country is being run by nationalists who hate Russia. Well, firstly, the president of Ukraine is not a nationalist. He is a Russian-speaking guy from a Russian-speaking industrial city and, secondly, there is not a single nationalist in the government. Not a single nationalist party member got into parliament at the last election. They simply did not get enough votes.

My neighbours in the village and other residents of Lazarivka do not live in poverty. Traditionally, Ukrainians keep large food stocks. In the courtyard of each house there is a big underground cellar filled with potatoes and other vegetables, canned food, salted lard, all preserved in big glass jars. My neighbours regularly give us either a bucket of potatoes or a three-litre jar of pickles. We too have a cellar, but it is empty. We are not villagers. Though we own a village house and a large plot of land, we do not have the time to cultivate it. True, we grow a small quantity of potatoes, carrots, onions, beets, some garlic and pumpkins. But this is more of a hobby, a type of recreation for an urban person.

Last Tuesday I went to the sauna with my friends. They go every Tuesday. I go only once a month. In fact, I don't go so much for the sauna as to hear the sauna conversation.

After all, a sauna is, first of all, two hours of communication. In addition, this time my old friend, the journalist and professor of history Danilo Yanevsky, who had recently recovered from coronavirus, was supposed to come to the sauna after a long break.

A few days earlier he had appeared on T.V. saying that he had already bought weapons and a supply of ammunition in case of war. I know that he had owned a pistol since the time of the Euromaidan protests. This is legal and not considered a military weapon. I wondered what he had invested in this time. It turned out that he had bought a machine gun and had already started going to an army practice range. While still on his sickbed, he had signed up for territorial defence by telephone.

"Do you do this training somewhere in the city?" I asked him.

"No. I have joined the regional unit!"

Danilo lives in a village that has a common border with Kyiv. For training, he travels to Hostomel, a town twenty-five kilometres from Kyiv.

"How do you get there?" I asked him, knowing that Danilo did not have a car.

"By taxi."

"It's so expensive!"

"So what?"

Our other sauna friend, Sergey Movenko, whom we once elected as President of our Steam Bath society, said that he had two hunting rifles and one carbine but not enough ammunition. He is going to buy more. He has only participated in a hunting party twice in his life and that was a long time ago. But he keeps the weapons in the correct way, in an iron cabinet, pays his membership fee to the all-Ukrainian hunting association and every three years takes his three rifles to the police, where specialists fire three shots from each of them and add bullets to the "dossier" for each gun. This is an old Soviet procedure designed to make it easier to determine which weapon was used – or, more likely, which weapon was not used – in case of an armed crime. I find it hard to understand how this system works in a country where 800 thousand members of the Hunting Association keep more than four million guns at home. And here I am only talking about officially registered weapons. How many are unregistered, especially since the start of the war in the Donbas?

Weapons are not the only things that Ukrainians like to keep at home. When, by law, M.P.s and civil servants began to file electronic declarations of their property and ordinary citizens first had access to these declarations, many were surprised to learn that M.P.s and officials had millions of dollars and euros in cash at home! Keeping two or 300 thousand dollars at home seemed to be the norm for Ukrainian V.I.P.s. I even felt scared for them, because the declarations also indicate the home addresses of these people. So almost every declaration is a tip off to the criminal world.

My friend, a former member of parliament, reassured me. "Don't worry, they don't have this money at home, and some don't have it at all. They write it like that, just in case. If they suddenly get a big bribe and want to buy a Bentley or a yacht, they can say that they bought it with money that they already had and which is recorded in the declaration. Otherwise, people from the tax service may ask them where the money for such an expensive purchase came from? This way, they have it written in the declaration, so it's all legal."

I do not know much about the life of state officials and deputies, but I have now learned to read between the lines of their declarations. Real estate in these declarations is often registered to relatives or spouses. Plots of land too.

In the meantime, my friend from the village, my namesake, Andrey, a civil servant who heads the social assistance department in the nearest town, said that since 2019, the year President Zelensky was elected, his salary has decreased by a third. Previously, he earned the equivalent of $400–500 per month, now he gets about $300.

Most officials in rural areas cannot boast in their declarations of either large sums of cash or of a prosperous life. But many of them, like Andrey, grow their own vegetables, keep chickens and rabbits, and stock up on food supplies for the winter. This makes life cheaper but deprives people of free time.

These days, when the Olympic Games continue in Beijing, none of my friends and acquaintances, either in the village or in Kyiv, are watching the competition. Ukraine is participating, but no-one expects serious results. The state has not given enough money to support athletes. The only really upsetting news from the Olympics has been the very poor result of Ukraine's biathletes. When those who should be excellent shots, shoot very badly, you cannot help feeling disappointed.

The Olympics is not even much discussed on the television news. But every day there are reports about a new European foreign minister or even a president who has decided to come to Kyiv. There is a feeling that some of the foreign dignitaries have decided to work as postmen. President Macron flew first to Putin, then flew to Kyiv to see Zelensky. He brought

Zelensky a message from Putin. Diplomatic activity has ceased to arouse interest among Ukrainians. The only thing that pleases them is that now, each night, not one plane with weapons but three or more arrive in Kyiv from the U.S.A. and Great Britain.

This help with arms serves to calm many. But others just shake their heads thoughtfully and say, "Ukraine may not have time to use the weapons sent! After all, Ukraine does not have an air defence system at all. And Russia is not going to send infantry into battle. They will use bombers and artillery".

The other day, my wife, a British citizen, received a third email from her embassy. The embassy warned that the situation could deteriorate quickly and that British citizens who chose to remain in Ukraine should not count on the embassy's help in the case of an emergency.

I do not know if the British diplomats have already left for home, or whether some of them still remain. But we are staying. There is a sauna scheduled for next Wednesday. I'm not sure I'll go, but anything is possible! And if I go it won't be for the sake of a spell in one hundred degrees Celsius in a wooden cabin, but for the sake of communication – for the sake of conversation – which can help me to understand what my friends are thinking about and what Ukraine is thinking about.

Culture under Threat

The threat of an all-out Russian attack on Ukraine, suppos-edly scheduled for the early hours of February 16, forced Zelensky to announce a new national holiday – "Unity Day". Probably, if this new national holiday had been called "The Day of Unity of the Ukrainian People in the Face of the Russian aggression", it would have been better received. But the Day of Unity turned out to be very similar to the already existing Day of Unification, which is celebrated on January 22.

On February 16, I walked the streets for an hour and a half and looked for evidence of the celebration of this new special day. After all, President Zelensky called on everyone to celebrate it by hanging Ukrainian flags in windows and on balconies. During the entire walk I saw only two Ukrainian flags and one Lithuanian flag. On the same day, February 16, Lithuania has a real national holiday, "The Day of the Restoration of Independence".

On Facebook, Ukrainians did add the blue and yellow national flag to their avatars. So did I. But we all did on January 22, as a flash-mob. There are more manifestations of patriotism on Facebook than in the real world. I do not know the reason for that.

The day before the anticipated night-time attack on Kyiv, my wife and I went to the première of Oleg Sentsov's film "Rhino". In the middle of the movie, my mobile telephone rang. I turned it off without looking to see who was calling. Then my wife's phone lit up. She looked at the name, saw that it was a friend and texted her to say that she would call back after the movie.

By the way, the sponsor of the film première was Johnny Walker Whisky. At two pop-up bars in Kyiv's House of Cinema, specially trained bartenders made cocktails and poured whisky with or without ice. A neon sign saying "Keep Walking!" glowed above the counters. For the first time, I liked this slogan. And I wasn't the only one. Several movie-goers I knew nodded at the advertisement and smiled approvingly.

After the movie, we walked home. Or rather we "kept walking" home. My wife was unhappy with the première, criticising the film for being too violent. "Why make a movie about the gangster '90s now?" she said. I said that people born in the late '90s knew nothing about the life shown in the film.

Sentsov was working hard on the project even before the Euromaidan protests. He was arrested by the F.S.B. in Crimea and spent five years in the most remote and harsh Russian prison until his release. He immediately returned to the film project. He received some funding from the Ukrainian state film commission, more money came from Europe. And finally, the film is ready. Yes, it is about life in the terribly poor and dangerous post-Soviet world, in which young men had nowhere to go but the underworld. There is a lot of violence and rough sex in the film. It is well made, although there is nothing new in it, it is true. But now that he has completed this project – interrupted by prison – Sentsov will, I hope, take on a more contemporary topic.

When we had finished debating the film, my wife called her friend back. It was Lena, a music teacher. She was very stressed and quite convinced that at three o'clock in the morning Russia would bomb Kyiv and that something had to be done. My wife told Lena that nothing like that was going to happen, but that even if they did bomb Kyiv, Lena would not be immediately affected because she lives on the quiet outskirts – nowhere near any "strategic targets". Lena was not convinced and sent us a link to the T.V. news where they announced that according to reliable sources, reported by the U.K. press, air and missile strikes on Ukraine would take place at 3.00 a.m. on February 16.

We woke up on Wednesday, February 16 and realised that the war had not started. However, on Thursday afternoon, shells did fall on the village of Maryinka and on the town of Stanytsya Luhanska, which I visited in 2015. One artillery shell pierced the ground floor wall of a kindergarten and exploded in a children's playroom. There were no children there at that moment as they were in the dining room on the second floor. But there were casualties – two care-workers, who were in the next room, had to be treated for concussion. Parents and police officers ran to evacuate the children and returned them to their homes.

I will soon be going in the direction of Stanytsya Luhanska, to the city of Sievierodonetsk, some twenty-five kilometres from the front line with the Donbas separatists. A film based on my novel *Grey Bees* is being shot there. It's about the inhabitants of the grey zone, an area of almost abandoned villages, where the remaining inhabitants survive with no electricity, no shops, no post office, and no medical care. At the beginning of the war, Stanytsya Luhanska, with its fifteen thousand inhabitants, lived without electricity for half a year. The most important commodity at that time was candlewax.

And people went outside to breathe the fresh air only in the dark, when separatist snipers could not easily see them through their viewfinders. Since that time, the mosaic of the Virgin Mary on the facade of a local government building located only two hundred metres from the river, which forms the front line, has become riddled with bullet holes. Snipers from across the river used the mosaic for target practice. The Luhansk region itself is considered very religious and almost all of the churches here belong to the Moscow Patriarchate.

Last week, Ukrainians were preoccupied not only with a possible Russian airstrike, but also with the Eurovision song contest. In fact, there were more songs on T.V. than news items about a potential war. Ukrainians were choosing a candidate to represent Ukraine at the Eurovision in Italy. In the end, based on the popular vote and that of a professional jury, Alina Pash, a singer from Transcarpathia, was announced as the official participant from Ukraine. No sooner was the announcement made than a storm arose on social media. It turned out that Alina Pash enjoys visiting Moscow and taking selfies on Red Square. What's more, she has travelled from Russia to the annexed Crimea, which is prohibited under Ukrainian law. In an attempt to defend herself, Alina Pash produced a certificate from Ukrainian border guards saying that she entered Crimea from the territory of Ukraine and submitted it to the Ukrainian Eurovision organising committee. However, the Department of Border Control stated that they had issued no such certificate to Alina Pash. It seemed that the singer had given a forged certificate to the organising committee. The poor girl is very much hated. She has refused to participate in Eurovision. But now a new problem has arisen. The second place in the competition was won by the rap group "Kalush", but some-one has unearthed and posted on Instagram a photograph of one of the band members posing in Moscow. Moscow is probably laughing at all this. Moscow loves it when Ukraini-ans take pictures of themselves on Red Square and post them on Facebook or Instagram.

Photographs from an evening of poetry with Alexander Kabanov have just appeared on Facebook. He recently pre-sented two books of poetry, published by a Moscow publishing house, at the Bulkagov House in Moscow. One of the books is called *The Police Search*. Kabanov calls himself a Ukrainian Russian-speaking poet, but he is very worried about the fate of the Russian language in Ukraine. He himself edits the Kyiv magazine *Nash* (Ours) with prose and poetry in Russian and Ukrainian, along with the works of punk artists. Until recently, there was a T.V. channel called *"Nash"* in Ukraine, but it was banned due to its obviously pro-Russian orientation. This channel was owned by Yevgeny Muraev, one of the leaders of the pro-Russian opposition bloc in the Ukrainian parliament and leader of the pro-Russian *Nashi* (Our People) political party. According to the C.I.A. and other western intelligence, if Ukraine is occupied by Russia, Moscow is going to make Yevgeny Muraev the puppet pro-Russian president of Ukraine.

In Kyiv's Bulgakov Museum, as also in Bulgakov House in Moscow, there is a literary club. It is the venue of literary evenings mostly attended by Russian-speaking intellectuals and members of the public. There are several such places in Kyiv that have always supported underground or non-popular culture. In addition to the Bulgakov Museum, the House of Scientists, which is a club of the Academy of

Sciences of Ukraine, has long been known among the Russian-speaking people of Kyiv. In 1987, when I was a sort of a dissident, I read aloud one of my first novels there. The reading lasted four hours, but the audience did not disappear. There were about a hundred listeners. By the end of the reading I was hoarse. At that time I was not yet published and such readings were the only way there was to acquaint readers with my unpublished novels. Another such liberal place was Kyiv Cinema House, where my wife and I watched the première of Sentsov's film on February 15.

In recent months, despite the dangerous situation, Ukraine remains very popular among Arab tourists. Tens of thousands of tourists from Qatar, Saudi Arabia, Kuwait and the Emirates arrive to see the Carpathians, Lviv and Odesa. The inhabitants of the Arab countries seem to have fallen in love with Ukraine. They like the Ukrainian forests, so very different from the Arabian deserts. Some residents of Arab countries have settled in Ukraine and are engaged in trade and the restaurant business. There are also those who are engaged in the smuggling of live birds, primarily falcons. The other day, employees of an N.G.O. publicly released two falcons, which were found by Ukrainian customs officers in Qatari citizens' luggage at Kyiv airport. The "tourists" had tried to smuggle out four drugged and bound falcons. Sadly, two of the falcons could not be resuscitated.

Good, non-politicised news is scarce now. The story of two falcons recovering their freedom is a welcome relief, but bad news dominates. For several days, the separatists have been shelling the positions of the Ukrainian army along the entire front line, killing and wounding several Ukrainian soldiers and officers. Both the front-line villages and the civilian population are suffering. Russia has begun evacuating women and children from separatist-controlled territories. And all men living in these territories aged eighteen and above have been drafted into the separatist army. It is impossible to predict how events will develop, but one can guess.

23.02.2022

Tension, but no panic

For three evenings in a row my telephone has rung continuously. A couple of old friends, Igor and Irina, called to say that they were leaving by car for the Carpathian Mountains. Others simply wanted to know if I thought there would be war and whether I thought the war would start immediately or in two weeks. Then the Russian President addressed the Russian people on T.V. to explain his version of the history of Russia and that of Ukraine and to change the world.

Russia recognised the two non-existent "states" on Ukrainian territory and signed treaties of friendship and military cooperation with them. Putin said that now the "borders" with Ukraine – that is the front line – would be guarded by the Russian army. This means that from now on, the Russian army will be shooting from Ukrainian territory into Ukrainian territory.

What has changed, you might ask? A great deal. Before Putin's "reorganisation", Ukrainian troops were responding with firepower to the shelling from separatists. Now, if the Ukrainian army responds to the shelling of the Russian army, it will be called a Russian–Ukrainian war. And Russian troops that surround Ukraine can invade its territory from any point along the border with Russia and Belarus.

For the first time, tension is felt in Kyiv. But still there is still no panic. Near my house, the Lebanese restaurant *Mon Cher* is building a summer terrace. After all, this year we have had a very short meteorological winter. Spring has arrived, the temperature has risen to thirteen or fourteen degrees Celsius. The sun shines, the birds sing and along the roads from the west come military trucks and military medical vehicles. They pass Kyiv and travel on to the east.

I am reminded of 2014, when armoured personnel carriers and military trucks were also driving from the west of Ukraine to the east and wrecked tanks and burned-out armoured vehicles were brought back by tractors. Now the movement is eastward only. But there is another east–west flow. Refugees from Stanytsya Luhanska, a town right on the front line near Luhansk, have reached Kharkiv. So far, only a dozen people have arrived. They abandoned their apartments and houses, calculating that soon nothing would be left of them. They survived in 2014–15, when a third of the houses in the town of fifteen thousand people were damaged by artillery shelling. Until recently, about seven thousand people remained in the town. How many are left now is hard to say, especially after a separatists' shell hit a kindergarten. Miraculously, nobody was killed.

And I lost my train tickets. I was supposed to go to Sievierodonetsk, Luhansk oblast, on March 2, returning to Kyiv on the 4th by night train. Now I will not go.

Until a couple of days ago, a film crew from Kyiv was still making their *Grey Bees* film in the semi-abandoned village near Sievierodonetsk – sixteen kilometres from the front line. A week or so ago, the military came and warned them that an evacuation could begin at any moment. "The Russians will give two hours warning before attacking!" a Ukrainian officer told the film crew. "So get ready!"

Ivanna Dyadyura, the film's producer, agreed with local drivers that they would be on standby in case of an evacuation. This insurance cost a lot of money. There is still almost no work in the area, but people have cars. There are cars, but no roads. More precisely – there is no asphalt. For a week, the cars stood idle, but then the military arrived and told them to leave urgently.

The film crew is already back in Kyiv. They had not managed to finish filming. They will have to find another location – perhaps in Chernihiv or Sumy oblast where there are many abandoned or half-empty villages. These oblasts also border with Russia. And on the Russian side of the border, stand Russian troops. How long will it be safe to film there? Nobody knows.

I do not worry about this movie anymore. Since Putin's speech, I've been thinking about something completely different. Friends kept calling and calling. Then I got another call that extinguished my anxiety.

A teacher of literature, Larisa Alekseevna, from Kyiv school number ninety-two, where all three of my children once studied, called to ask me to come the next day and teach a lesson in the history of detective literature. This request was totally unexpected. I agreed immediately. The lesson went very well. While I was talking about the difference between Australian, Japanese and British crime stories, I forgot about Russia, President Putin and their crimes. The children also seemed to forget about Russia and a possible war.

On the way home from the school, I sat down in a café to drink tea and eat a snack. I peered into the faces of the people around me to listen to their conversations, but there were no conversations to be heard. People were drinking coffee and eating their sandwiches in almost total silence.

Ukrainian politicians have been speaking louder than usual. The Foreign Ministry appealed to President Zelensky to end diplomatic relations with Russia. A former M.P. and activist, Boryslav Bereza, appealed to Zelensky with the demand to introduce martial law in the Luhansk and Donetsk oblasts. Something tells me that President Zelensky will do neither. He is on the record as saying that he still hopes Ukraine will avoid a major war.

I would like to understand his logic, but so far I have failed. The leader of the "Luhansk People's Republic", recognised by Russia, Venezuela, Cuba and Abkhazia, demanded that Ukraine "liberate" the other half of Luhansk oblast, which the separatists do not control. He wants to create a "republic" with the boundaries of the Ukrainian oblast. The head of the "Donetsk Republic" is silent for now, but, in the past, he has also threatened to take away the entire Donetsk oblast from Ukraine. The Russian Foreign Ministry stated that they recognised both "republics" within their current borders, but that in general, the borders of a "state" were the private matter of the "state" itself.

While a future war looms within this statement, it does not seem to be imminent. The pause between the recognition of the "republics" and the continuation of Russia's military operations against Ukraine could stretch for between two weeks to three months or longer. It all depends on how the world reacts to this situation. If the reaction is loud and if the new sanctions hurt the Russian economy, then the pause could stretch for six months. If the reaction turns out to be weak, then the war will not be long in coming.

Russia earns money for this war in Europe by selling oil and gas. Russia has huge financial reserves and only sanctions that halt other flows of money into Russia can curb Russia's desire to move further into Ukrainian territory.

While writing these lines, I keep checking the news feed. Now Putin has stated that he recognises the "republics" within larger borders than the territories currently controlled by the separatists. And almost immediately, I see a statement from President Zelensky that he has just signed an order drafting reservists into the army.

In recent weeks, many Ukrainians have become military experts. Me too. I already know that an advancing army loses manpower in the ratio of 10 to 1. That is, the losses of those defending territory are one tenth that of those who are advancing.

My friends sent me a screenshot from a Russian government procurement website. In the screenshot, the Burdenko – Moscow's main military hospital – is looking to buy 45 thousand body bags. In the tender, the medical term is used: pathological-anatomical bags. This number of sacks is almost in line with the opinion of one former Russian general, who said that Russia is ready to lose up to 50 thousand of its soldiers during an offensive in Ukraine. I forwarded this screenshot to a friend who understands public procurement systems. "It's a fake," he wrote back. "They have had hundreds of thousands of body bags ready for a long time!"

While writing this I see a message that Putin has recognised not only the "republics" but also their "constitutions".

These "constitutions" state that the territories of the "republics" include the entire Donetsk oblast and the entire Luhansk oblast. The moment I read this, it was if the war moved much closer.

It is already much more difficult to distract yourself from thoughts of the war. Putin spoke again and issued an ultimatum to Ukraine and the world: either the world and Ukraine recognises Crimea as Russian and Ukraine forever abandons its dreams of joining N.A.T.O., or the Russian army will advance on Kyiv.

Ukrainian news is full of forecasts of Russian attacks. The most popular suggest that Russia will first attack three cities: Kharkiv, Kyiv and Kherson. I understand that Kherson will be attacked from the Crimea, Kharkov from the Belgorod region of Russia, but from where will they attack Kyiv? The shortest way to Kyiv for the Russian army is through Belarus and the Chernobyl zone. There are very few roads, many swamps and small rivers. Yes, there are a lot of Russian tanks on the other side of the Belarusian border. Satellite imagery showed Russian military training exercises in building temporary pontoon bridges for tanks across the rivers close to Ukraine.

It is impossible to predict Putin's actions, one can only clearly see his goal, what he wants to achieve. In his latest speech, he specifically said that he did not recognise Ukraine as a state. For him, it is part of Russia. The goal is to seize Ukraine and turn it into the southwestern federal district of the Russian Federation. The State Duma can amend the Russian constitution in two hours, as it did in order to include Crimea within the Russian constitution. The executive and mindless state machine of Russia is ready to fulfil Putin's every whim.

In Ukraine, in all the churches and mosques, they pray for peace – that is, in all except the twelve thousand or so Orthodox churches of the Moscow Patriarchate where they still pray for the health of Russian Patriarch Kirill. Other churches have already asked the Moscow Patriarchate Churches to pray for peace, but the Moscow Patriarchate is silent.

In 2014, when the Ukrainian parliament held a meeting dedicated to military operations in the Donbas, to which representatives of all churches and denominations were invited, a minute of silence was declared in memory of the Ukrainian soldiers who died in the war. The entire parliament rose to its feet, except for the representatives of the Moscow Patriarchate. They remained defiantly in their chairs. The priests of the Moscow Patriarchate refused to bury Ukrainian soldiers who died in the war. Nevertheless, no-one set fire to their churches or tried to beat up the priests.

In recent days, S.B.U. officers have caught several Russian agents who had tried to mine the Moscow Patriarchate churches in Kharkiv. The agents had evidently wanted the church bombings to be one more *casus belli*.

There is nothing in the world worse than war. Even the coronavirus pandemic now seems to be something ordinary and understandable. War can never be understood or accepted.

Ukrainians continue to live as usual. Yesterday I stopped in front of a modern hipster barbershop. There, two customers were having their beards trimmed, while a third waited in line at the bar, drinking whisky. Meanwhile, a Canadian transport plane loaded with weapons was landing at Kyiv airport. This new Ukrainian reality far outdoes my writer's imagination. I cannot say that I like it. But I accept the reality.

In the meantime, my old friends Igor and Irina, who had gone by car to the Carpathians to get away from the war, called to say they were thinking of going on through Poland to Lithuania. Both Poland and Lithuania are reliable partners of Ukraine and, if necessary, will accept not only Igor and Irina, but hundreds of thousands of other Ukrainians. I only hope the need does not arise.

24.02.2022

Last Borscht in Kyiv

Between telephone conversations last evening, I was preparing Borscht for some visiting journalists. I hoped Putin would not disrupt our dinner. He did not. He decided to hit Ukraine with missiles at 5.00 a.m. this morning. The war also started in the Donbas and there were attacks in other places, including one from Belarus.

Now we are at war with Russia. But the metro in Kyiv functions and cafés are open. It has just been reported that Ukraine has severed diplomatic relations with Russia. Since the beginning of the fighting, the Ukrainian army has shot down six Russian planes and two helicopters. It is clear that we ourselves have big losses. If before the Russian aggression the situation changed every day, now it changes every hour. But I stay and will continue to write for you so that you know how Ukraine lives during the war with Putin's Russia. Stay safe wherever you are.

The Time is Now

My journalist friend from Germany could not get through today on either of my two mobile telephones. An automatic reply told her, "This number does not exist". But the Internet worked its wonders and eventually we got in touch by Zoom. After the conversation, I still remembered this phrase "this number does not exist" and then I saw on Facebook that my friend, who works at the Ministry of Foreign Affairs of Ukraine, also complained that callers could not get through to her from abroad. We need to stop being surprised by such things. As long as I exist, my telephone number also exists.

We live now with friends in western Ukraine. Nearby is a road leading to the border with Hungary. There are many cars moving along it. Sometimes they stop and the driver and passengers get out to stretch their legs. Very often, Indian and Arab students ride in old cars. I feel terribly sorry for them. I know that many of them travel from Kharkiv, from Dnipro, from Sumy, where they study medicine and other courses; students, who were supposed to receive diplomas from the university this summer. What will happen to them? What will happen to their futures? But the main thing is to survive! In Kharkiv, a student from India was killed a couple of days ago by a Russian rocket. Near Kyiv, Russian soldiers shot at a car in which an Israeli citizen was travelling. He too died.

For me, this war is already a "world war". My wife and I are very worried about our friends – a French-Japanese couple who lived in Kyiv near to us. He is a former French diplomat, 85 years old, his wife is a Japanese artist. They have always been in love with Kyiv and Ukraine, and wanted to spend the rest of their lives here. They bought an apartment near the Opera and from their windows you can see the majestic Vladimirsky Cathedral. In the first days of the war, when it was still possible to leave Kyiv without any particular problems, our French friend simply did not want to leave their house. Then, when the shelling of Kyiv became constant, his wife was worried and wanted to leave as quickly as possible. I talked to him on the telephone, arguing that they had to leave. Finally, they made up their minds. They have a car, but there is not enough petrol in the tank. At least one exit from Kyiv is safe – the exit to Odesa. There are no Russian troops on the other side. I know that they left, but they should have left with a convoy organised by the United Nations. But where they have gone, we do not yet know.

Lately our nights have become very short. I drink one hundred grams of Ukrainian cognac before going to bed, fall asleep immediately, around one in the morning. Then I wake up several times to check the news. Again, I get up and carefully read the news and start calling my friends. One of my colleagues, a good friend, ended up in Melitopol, which is occupied by the Russian army. She sits in the apartment and does not go out. I do not know how to help her. She emails me from time to time. Sometimes her telephone does not work, but it then shows signs of life again.

Another friend, a museum director, could not take the train to Lviv today. He tried to take his ninety-six-year-old semi-paralysed mother out of Kyiv. He drove her to the station and they found their carriage, but even with tickets they could not get on the train. The conductors said that tickets are not important. Today, only mothers with small children are put on the train. Trains from Kyiv to the west of Ukraine do go. People board without tickets. Whoever is able to get into the carriage becomes a passenger. There are seven or eight times more people in each carriage than there are seats.

In February 1919 something similar happened, when the Bolsheviks broke into Kyiv. They shelled the centre of the city and killed everyone they met on the way. Now history is repeating itself. The troops of the Soviet patriot Putin have surrounded Kyiv, but they cannot enter the city. The city is fiercely defended. The civilian population either hide in their apartments, or try to leave on any available form of transport, or join the territorial army to defend their beloved city.

02.03.2022

Remember Me with a Smile

I never thought that so many things could happen in a week, so many terrible things! I remember my mother's story about how, with her mother and her father, she crossed the wide Volkhov River in a dilapidated wooden boat on the first day of the war. It was the morning of June 22, 1941, the day of the German attack on the U.S.S.R. Her father was going to war. My mother never saw him again.

On February 24, 2022, the first Russian missiles fell on Kyiv. At five in the morning, my wife and I were awakened by the sound of explosions. There were three. Then, an hour later, two more explosions and then silence fell.

Silence, without which it is impossible to concentrate, will be rare now.

It was very hard to believe that the war had begun. That is, it was already clear that it had, but I did not want to believe this. You have to get used psychologically to the idea that war has begun. Because from that moment on, war determines your way of life, your way of thinking, your way of making decisions.

The day before the start of the war, our children, including our daughter who had flown in from London, had gone with their friends to the beautiful city of Lviv in western Ukraine. They wanted to visit the cafés, museums, the medieval streets of the old centre.

The day before the start of the war, I met my old friend Boris, an Armenian artist and now a citizen of Ukraine, who has been living in Kyiv for thirty years with his Ukrainian wife. He has been suffering from cancer for a while now. Boris looked confused. He had just come out of hospital, where he had had another operation.

"You know," he complained. "I have big memory problems! After the previous operation, I bought a gun to defend Kyiv. My wife forbade me to keep it at home. I gave it to a friend for safekeeping, but I don't remember which one. I've asked everyone, but they all say that I did not give them a gun!"

One of Boris' problems is that he has too many friends. Half of Kyiv loves him; he trusts everyone and is happy to talk with anyone on any topic. I don't know if he found his gun, but I am sure he is helping the military somewhere. Maybe filling sandbags for barricades, maybe digging trenches.

Another friend of mine, Valentin, is in hospital. He is himself a doctor but already retired. He has been suffering from diabetes for many years and lately fell ill with corona-virus. Complications meant that doctors first amputated his right leg, then the left. He was in intensive care on the eighth floor, where I visited him regularly. His wife was very afraid that the Russians might hit the upper floor of the hospital with a rocket or a bomb and made sure that he was trans-ferred to the fourth floor. He is still there. His wife is nearby. Every day she cooks food for him. There are almost no patients left in the hospital. And almost no medicines.

And we, having spent the first night of the war with a friend, the English writer and journalist Lily Hyde, who has been living in Kyiv for many years, decided to leave for the village. Our house in the village is not so far, just ninety kilo-metres away. When the curfew ended, I checked Google maps and saw that the way out from Kyiv to the west, in the direction of our village, was open. We packed, took food from the refrigerator and the freezer, loaded it into the car and hit the road.

Unfortunately, the situation had changed and by the time we had reached the western edge of the city, the traffic stood motionless. Among the cars there were many with number plates from other cities, Dnipro, Zaporizhzhia, Kharkiv and even Donetsk and Luhansk. I realised that these drivers had been on the road for at least two days. You could see it in their pale faces, in their tired eyes, in the way they drove.

On the way, my wife called her friend Lena, the music teacher at the Kyiv School of Arts. She asked if she would like to come with us to the village. Lena could not decide. Then she said yes, she would come with her son. They went out to the road and waited for twenty minutes before we reached our meeting place. They made their way between trucks and buses to reach our car and bundled themselves into the back seat, suitcase and all. Now the car was full.

The journey to the village, which usually takes an hour, took four and a half. We drove around abandoned, wrecked cars, peered at the guns and tanks set up for the defence of Kyiv. We saw a lot of military equipment driving in both directions on the right side of the highway, usually used by cars going to Kyiv. Very few were moving in that direction now.

It was hard on my heart. No-one said a word. I turned on the car radio and we listened to the news. The news was now from the front. The front was everywhere. The front today is three thousand kilometres long, the length of the border with Russia and Belarus. Kharkiv and Mariupol were being bombed, hundreds of tanks had entered the territory of Ukraine in several places, including from Crimea. Ballistic missiles flew from the territory of Belarus at Ukrainian cities. The news did not calm us, but it did distract us from the traffic jams.

Two Ukrainian fighter jets flew low over our car. We heard explosions. Their volume increased as we moved forward. Then, from the radio news, I realised that we were hearing the sounds of a battle in the town of Hostomel, which we were driving past. Russian troops had landed there in thirty-four helicopters. The Russians had managed to blow up the world's largest transport aircraft known as Mriya (Dream). It was built at the Kyiv's Oleg Antonov Aviation Plant. It was a one-off and was leased to the U.N. to deliver humanitarian aid to Africa. Now it is gone.

That Antonov plant was the reason my family moved from Leningrad to Kyiv. My father got a job there as a test pilot when he was demobilised from the Soviet army. Perhaps we would have moved to Kyiv anyway, to live with my grandmother, but the Antonov factory offered my father a job as a test pilot and a few years later gave us an apartment on the fifth floor of a brick building opposite the runway. The planes and the runway itself were visible from the window.

While we were crawling along the jammed highway, I thought about my childhood: how my friends and I climbed over the fence of the Antonov factory airfield and looked for pieces of aluminium in the grass. There was nothing else there. The pieces of aluminium seemed to be something valuable and surprising because of their light weight.

When we eventually arrived at the village, I turned off the radio and all became quiet. No explosions or gunfire. Birds sang, rejoicing in the coming of spring. We took our belongings into the house, showed Lena and her son to their room, made tea. I took some meat to the neighbours for their dogs – we always save the bones for them, storing them either on the balcony or in the freezer.

Our neighbours Nina and Tolik were delighted to see us. "We were expecting you yesterday!" Nina said. The day before, their son with his wife and young grandson had arrived from Kyiv.

"We would never have got here yesterday," I said. Yesterday the traffic jam was eighty kilometres long.

"Our son got here by driving through fields and villages, not along the main highway," Nina said. We agreed that I would visit several times a day to talk. We have always had very friendly relations with them.

I prepared my desk for work, set up my laptop, turned on the heating, which had been turned off a week ago when the temperature rose. Then a friend from Kyiv called me and asked, "Where are you?" I told him. He advised us to go immediately further to the west.

I looked at my workplace, thought about the heating, about the friends who came with us. "Let's go to the children in Lviv. Lena and her son can stay here. It is safer for them here than in Kyiv," I said to my wife. Elizabeth was silent, thinking.

"You had better tell them yourself," she said firmly.

I told Lena of our decision to move on and offered to show her how to regulate the heating and turn on the water pump. She flatly refused to stay. "We'll go with you," she said firmly.

We took our things out of the house again and loaded them back into the car. Elizabeth went to say goodbye to the neighbours. Nina cried and hugged my wife, her husband Tolik stood, looking pale and leaning heavily on his stick. His left hand was trembling. We said goodbye and drove back to the exit onto the Zhytomyr highway.

The journey to Lviv, 420 kilometres in distance, took twenty-two hours. The traffic jams varied in length, from ten to fifty kilometres. In the end, I began to fall asleep, so we stopped. After an hour and a half of sleep, we drove on. In the morning, we were in Lviv.

I looked at the familiar old houses and villas in those most beautiful streets and thought, "Will the Russian army come here or not? Will Putin bomb Lviv or limit himself to other regions?" In the end, I put a stop to these thoughts. They did not give me energy.

We found our children disoriented and sad. I should have taken a nap in the apartment they had rented, but I did not want to. I was painfully alert and knew that I would not be able to sleep.

Not far from the house, I noticed a gun shop. It was still closed, but there was a line of people in front of it. There were men, young boys and girls in the queue, waiting for opening time.

A friend called and asked if I had left Kyiv. I said I had. He said that now the exit along the Zhytomyr highway was impassable – the Ukrainian military had blown up the highway so that Russian tanks could not drive along the road straight into Kyiv. A little later, a message came from our friend Svetlana, who had stayed in Kyiv. "I decided to say goodbye just in case. They have warned that there will be a terrible shelling of Kyiv. I'm going to stay in my flat. I'm tired of running through the basements. If anything happens, remember me with a smile."

I realised that I had not called my older brother or my two cousins. I got through to my brother easily. He said that he was sitting at home, in the same apartment opposite the aircraft factory, and was listening to the sounds of explosions from the direction of Hostomel, which we had passed. I did not get through to my cousins. I wondered when I would see them again.

Borders

We had to get my daughter out of the country and onto a flight back to London. There was a five-day queue to get into Poland. So, we drove into the mountains towards the Hungarian border. It is a beautiful route. At first the single-lane road was relatively free-flowing. Then the traffic came to a halt. We could only edge forward hour after hour. By ten o'clock at night I realised I had to stop and get some sleep. All the hotels along the road were full, but someone told me about a simple ski hostel not far from the road. We found the place and were shown to dormitory rooms that seemed to have been decorated in better times some while ago. There was hot water but no towels. I mentioned this to the man who let us in. He immediately brought us brand-new towels with the price tags still on them. Each had cost only a little less than the price of the stay per person. My daughter came to say that there was no toilet paper in their bathroom. The caretaker apologised and said he would go and wake up the lady in the local shop in order to buy some. "No, don't do that," I told him. "We can share."

I slept well but awoke at dawn and realised that we needed to leave immediately if we were to get our daughter into Hungary that day. The road proved to be relatively clear and by 10.00 a.m. we were in sight of the border.

How Long is the Shadow of the Past?

How long is the shadow of the past? How does memory work? There are many answers to these questions, although we cannot be sure that any of the answers are one hundred per cent. correct. *De facto*, we ask our memory itself how it works. Memory, even when it becomes an interlocutor, can twist us around its little finger without any malicious intent!

I was forty years old when my back started to ache. I went to the doctor, who sent me for an X-ray. Holding the X-ray up in his hands, the doctor said to me, "You had an injury in your youth!" "No, I didn't!" I insisted. Silently, the doctor examined the picture. Then I remembered an episode from school, from the seventh or eighth grade. We were doing P.E. outside on the horizontal bars, swinging ourselves around them. At some point, I slipped and fell flat on my back. I lay there, realising that I could not move, that I had lost control of my body. Someone leaned over me and I knew they were asking me something but I could not hear them. I could still see but could do nothing. Fifteen minutes passed, perhaps, and then the sensation in my body returned. Cautiously, I got to my feet. I sat on the grass. They let me go home from school. That was all. "Yes, I have remembered now." I told the doctor. He nodded.

They say that people remember the bad things more often than the good. Not me. I remember well what has pleased and surprised me in my life, but what I did not like or what has hurt me has been forgotten, left at an almost inaccessible depth in the well of memory. In this we see the instinct of self-preservation, although it works in a special way. We protect our psyche from bad memories and support it with good memories. In our memory, we can idealise the past so that nostalgia soon sets in, even for times that we would not have wished upon our worst enemy.

I was born after the Holodomor, after World War II, after the Gulag, after the death of Stalin. My mother was born in 1931. At the age of ten, she was evacuated to the Urals with her mother, my grandmother, and her older brothers. Her father, my grandfather, was sent to the front. He was to die in 1943 near Kharkiv and is buried there.

In the evacuation trains on which they travelled, conditions were terrible and air raids were frequent. Eventually they arrived in a desolate part of the Urals in a village built by deported Ukrainian villagers. The mother and her three children were given one corner of a room in a house. The owners were told to feed the evacuees, but they gave them only leftovers, often potato peelings, from which grandmother made a kind of soup, a grey puree. The children realised quickly what hunger was. The fear of hunger remained with them and their mother all their life. Until her death, my grandmother kept every scrap of bread, drying it and storing the pieces in specially made white coarse calico bags tied with string. Thus, one historical trauma, that of forced deportation, gave rise to another historical trauma, the fear of hunger.

Grandma Taisia, for that was my grandmother's name, told me, when I was a high school student, how she had witnessed a Jewish pogrom and how, on a wooden river bridge, a Jew who had been running from the violence, was overtaken by a Cossack on a horse and chopped down by the Cossack's sabre.

My grandfather on my father's side, a Don Cossack, a communist and a Stalinist, spoke only about the war and about the exploits of Soviet soldiers. He never talked about our relatives, also communists, who had landed up in the Gulag and who had spent two decades in the camps. I heard these stories only after my grandfather died in 1980. It turned out that I was protected from the dangerous past. The stories of our suppressed relatives were known to both my father and mother, but they never talked of them to me.

It so happened that after the death of my grandfather, thanks to my elder brother, I got hold of Solzhenitsyn's forbidden book, *The Gulag Archipelago*. I read it voraciously, knowing that two of my own relatives were sent to this very Gulag. Having read it, I had a wild desire to find out the truth, to learn about the real history of the Soviet Union, not the one we studied at school and at the institute. I began to travel around the U.S.S.R., sometimes by train, sometimes hitching a lift with lorry drivers, even travelling on riverboats in the Vologda region northeast of Leningrad. During my travels I searched for the pensioners who had served in the Soviet bureaucracy. I wanted to interview them about their past, to find out what they had witnessed and what part they had played. I recorded my conversations with several of those who had agreed to speak to me. Listening to them, I sometimes felt as if I had touched a hot stove with my unprotected finger.

One of the people who agreed to talk was Alexander Petrovich Smurov. I found him in the Crimea, near the town of Sudak where he lived in quiet retirement. In the now distant 1930s, he had been one of a trio of judges there who had sentenced people without a court hearing. He spoke freely about how he had put his signature to death warrants for people about whom he knew practically nothing. To my question about the number of death sentences he had signed, he replied, "Perhaps three thousand, possibly more". This man was unafraid to recall for me what he had done. He was confident of his innocence. He spoke fondly of his youth and his enthusiasm for the Soviet cause and how he hated Khrushchev. He did not look like my grandfather or anyone else I knew of a similar age. But in some ways, he was clearly a typical representative of his time.

Observing my grandmother and mother in my youth, I could not help but notice the connection between their experiences of the famine during their evacuation in World War II and their behaviour and habits much later, in the 1970s. I might not then have known what historical memory or historical trauma were, but I could see its consequences. I understand it much better now. When I was a child, I had not understood that the attitude of local peasants towards evacuees, including towards my mother and her family, was also the consequence of another historical trauma, one in which they had been victims of forced deportation from Ukraine.

The Soviet Union managed to erase such memories from the majority of the descendants of the Ukrainians who had been deported to Siberia and the Urals. Today they are loyal citizens of the Russian Federation, fully or partially supporting the ruler of their country. They did not and do not demand an apology or compensation from their state, the heir to the Soviet Union, for the torment inflicted on their forebears by the Soviet system. Although they may still tell their family stories at home, collectively they have removed the past. Following today's events, I have the feeling that even if the great deportation has been forgotten, it nonetheless repeats itself.

Crimean Tatars know more about the meaning of this terrible word than most people. The operation to deport the Crimean Tatar population from Crimea began at 4 a.m. on May 18, 1944 and ended at 4:00 p.m. on May 20, 1944. More than 32 thousand N.K.V.D. troops were deployed to carry it out. The deportees were given from a few minutes to half an hour to get ready, after which they were transported by truck to the railway stations. From there, trains took them to their place of exile. According to eyewitnesses, those who resisted or could not walk were sometimes shot dead on the spot.

The nonviolent struggle of the deported Crimean Tatars to return to their homeland in Crimea lasted almost fifty years and ended in victory. In 1987 and 1989, by a decision of the Soviet government, the Crimean Tatar people were rehabilitated and a complex and lengthy process of repatriation began. Their historical memory turned out to be the main engine of this process. This included not only the physical return of the Crimean Tatars to Crimea but also the restoration of the Crimean Tatar way of life in the villages and towns to which the emigrants had returned from other regions of the then Soviet Union. Though the Tatars returned to a very different Crimea than the one they left, they soon started to revive the Crimea of their memory, their ways and traditions, the way of life they had lived for the centuries before their deportation.

In this new era, we see history repeating itself. In the spring of 1944, Moscow had deported an entire people with the help of military force. Seventy years later, in 2014, also in the spring and also with the help of military force, Moscow annexed the entire peninsula of Crimea, then part of Ukraine. The annexation included all the previously deported

Crimean Tatar people who had returned home after almost fifty years of forced exile.

In April 2014, almost immediately after annexation, Russian President Vladimir Putin signed decree number 268, "On measures to rehabilitate the Armenian, Bulgarian, Greek, Crimean Tatar, and German peoples and to provide state support for their revival and development". In the best Orwellian tradition, the degree "re-formulated", that is to say, downgraded, the tragedy of the Crimean Tatars. The decree, in which the peoples affected directly by the Stalinist repressions are listed in alphabetical order, is worthy of citing at least in part:

In order to restore historical justice, eliminate the consequences of the illegal deportation from the territory of the Crimean A.S.S.R., of the Armenian, Bulgarian, Greek, Italian, Crimean Tatar and German peoples and the other violations against them the following statement is issued: (As amended by the Decree of the President of the Russian Federation of September 12, 2015 N 458)

1. The Government of the Russian Federation together with state authorities of the Republic of Crimea and the city of Sevastopol:

a) will take a set of measures to restore historical justice, political, social, and spiritual rebirth of the Armenian, Bulgarian, Greek, Italian, Crimean Tatar and German peoples who were exposed to illegal deportations and political repressions on national and other grounds;

b) is to support and to promote the creation and development of national–cultural autonomies, other public associations and organisations of Armenian, Bulgarian, Greek, Italian, Crimean Tatar and German peoples, who are the citizens of the Russian Federation, living in the territory of the Republic of Crimea and the city of Sevastopol. To support and to promote basic general education in the languages of these peoples, development of their traditional crafts and forms of communal life, as well as helping to solve other issues of socio-economic development of the Armenian, Bulgarian, Greek, Italian, Crimean Tatar and German peoples;

2. This Decree shall enter into force on the day of its official publication.

President of the Russian Federation, V. Putin

Moscow Kremlin
April 21, 2014
N 268

It makes no sense to comment on a decree in which, in addition to the deported Crimean Tatar people, the allegedly deported Italian and German peoples, not individuals, are mentioned. This is political surrealism of the highest standard. I know for sure that the Italian, Bulgarian, German, and other Crimean peoples mentioned in this decree are not now subjected to repression whereas the Crimean Tatars are facing a form of deportation as I speak. Some of them are forbidden to enter their homeland, they are forbidden to enter their own homes, they are forbidden to see their families. This repression is being practiced openly in an attempt to split the people, to separate off the contingent of Crimean Tatars who are ready to collaborate with Russia from those who are not. Such a group already exists. Though this group is not large, the Kremlin's powerful propaganda machine, combined with psychological pressure on all those who speak out against the annexation, is working to increase the number of collaborators.

It would be ideal for Russia if the Crimean Tatars forgot about deportation and got rid of the oppressive burden of historical memory, which determines the Crimean Tatars' rules of conduct and their will to continue the struggle for their honour and for the honour of their ancestors. The Russian authorities understand that the Crimean Tatars' historical memory is much stronger than the historical memory of Russians. Back in the U.S.S.R., the historical memory of Russians was formatted as the "memory of heroic victors". This formula has been brought to a new level of absurdity in post-Soviet Russia. It is built on the "honour of the winner" in all possible wars, even when these wars were lost in actuality. "The honour of the winner" creates a condescending and arrogant attitude towards the "losers", that is, to those who carry, in their individual or collective experience, historical trauma. The Russian people have been deprived of their historical injuries and released from their worries about past injustice. The more than twenty million victims of the Gulag have been forgotten, which is why the Gulag and the Stalinist repressions have not become a historical trauma for the Russian people. These injuries have not changed the worldview and attitudes of the Russian people, nor did they change their identity.

When it is necessary, when there is no other way out, Russia recognises other people's injuries, but only as a tool of Russian state influence, in its struggle for territory, as part of its geopolitical interests.

The first monument to the victims of the Crimean Tatar deportation was erected in Sudak in 1994. On May 18, 2016, two years after the Russian annexation, on the anniversary of the mass deportation, the Russian authorities opened a memorial complex nearby to Suren railway station dedicated to the victims of deportation in the Bakhchysarai district of Crimea. Coincident with the opening of this complex, the National Bank of Ukraine issued a commemorative silver coin of Hr. 10 denomination, "in memory of the victims of the genocide of the Crimean Tatar people". This war, conducted in coins and monuments, will continue as a war for historical truth and historical memory.

The Tatars are not alone. Fourteen years before the deportation of the Crimean Tatars, during 1930–1, more than 1.8 million peasants were evicted from Ukraine, officially due to their resistance to collectivisation. These figures appear in Gulag documentation under the heading "special settlers". In 1947, as a result of the so-called "Operation West", another 76 thousand Ukrainians were evicted from western Ukraine to Siberia and the Far East. These people were the families of anti-Soviet underground fighters or sympathisers and people whom the leaders of the village councils of that time simply considered "unreliable".

If justice is to ever be restored, even if only formally, the historical trauma of these deportations and forced displacements needs to play a role in the lives of the heirs of these deported Ukrainians. Yet no decrees on the rehabilitation of deported Ukrainians have been adopted either during the time of the U.S.S.R. or in independent Ukraine. What has been enacted, on April 17, 1991, is the Soviet era law on the rehabilitation of victims of political repression. Ukrainian legislation at that time was still fully consistent with general Soviet legislation. Ukraine had no internal regulations of its own. The 1991 law covered the period from 1917 to April 1991 and applied to:

> "Persons who during this period were unreasonably convicted by the Ukrainian courts or repressed in the territory of the republic by other state bodies in any form, including deprivation of life or liberty, forced relocation, expulsion, and exile beyond the borders of the republic, deprivation of citizenship, forced placement in medical institutions, deprivation or restriction of other civil rights or freedoms based on political, social, class, national and religious character."

In May 2018, an improved Ukrainian version of this law came into force, although it left the list of persons covered by the law unchanged. This has left millions of the victims of mass forced relocations without specific redress in the law. This omission illustrates how the lawmakers do not want to disturb history by reminding the victims and their descendants of the crimes committed against their families. They wish to turn the page on this traumatic history, placing a symbolic full stop to the matter.

In Lithuania, there appears to be a completely different attitude to forced displacement and the deportation of its citizens. The historical memory of the tragedies of June 1941 and May 1948 are very important in shaping the Lithuanian national identity and in producing the general consensus on Lithuania's common values, in particular, the freedom of its people and the independence of the Lithuanian state.

In June 1941, almost the entire political, scientific and cultural elite of Lithuania was arrested and sent in freight trains to a camp near the town of Starobelsk in the territory of the current Luhansk region of Ukraine. From there, they were sent in freight trains to the Northern Urals and subsequently by barge to the N.K.V.D. camp in the village of Gary. The Soviet Gulag at Gary held both members of the cabinet of ministers of the Republic of Lithuania, such as Pranas Dovidaitis, Valdyamaras Vytautas Charnyatkis, Pyatras Aravičius, Antanas Endziulaitis, Kazis Yokantas, Juozas Papyachkis, Igmas Pranas Starkus and Jonas Sutkus, along with thousands of others including officers, government officials, students and public and political figures.

This operation was officially called "measures to cleanse the Lithuanian, Latvian and Estonian S.S.R.s of anti-Soviet, criminal and socially dangerous elements". It is interesting that in the document of May 16, 1941 the central committee of the All-Union Communist Party of Bolsheviks initially referred only to Lithuania. Latvia and Estonia were written into the decree by hand, that is, just prior to the signing of the document.

The loss of a people's elite cannot but become a historical trauma. Fear is inserted into the blood of the people, highlighting the fragility of the life of each ordinary person.

In May 1948, a year after "Operation West" in western Ukraine, "Operation Spring" began in Lithuania. In the course of just two days the Soviet bodies of repression deported some 40 thousand citizens to Siberia. Among this number were many women and children. This was the largest deportation of residents from Lithuania. The U.S.S.R. Ministry of State Security acted quickly and with rigour. They were in a hurry. The highest authorities demanded that the "republic be cleansed" of anti-Soviet elements. This included partisans, as well as wealthy peasants who did not agree to organise themselves into collective farms. In Siberia itself, there was an acute shortage of labour, so why not send some diligent Lithuanians there? The main goal of the operation, however, was to intimidate a population which had done its best to boycott Soviet ideological and economic reforms. This goal was largely achieved: fear remained lodged in the soul of people for decades to come. "Thousands of people were destroyed, and not just physically. Many destinies were broken," acknowledges the Lithuanian historian Arvydas Anushauskas. While the Moscow archives hold the plans and maps of this deportation from seventy years ago, they remain classified and nobody can study them.

These deportations, especially the last, the one carried out in 1948, remain in a certain sense alive, like an open wound. On their return from Siberia, after surviving for years in inhuman conditions, Lithuanians founded associations of deportees and collected much written evidence of the crimes of the Soviet regime. I met with some members of one such association in Anikschai in eastern Lithuania. For them, memory is the most important tool for preventing a repetition of such crimes against the people. But not everybody agrees that keeping the memory of these tragedies alive is a good thing. A rival theory, one of "conscious oblivion", suggests that we should forget such tragic events as it is not useful to remember them. This theory is rarely discussed in public but it is actively promoted in Russia, very successfully. The crimes of the Soviet system against its own people and against other peoples are reduced in import, or even forgotten completely. Historians work in parallel to replace the term "deportation" with terms like "internment", while also finding other ways to minimise the import of such historical tragedies.

Supporters of the "conscious oblivion" approach as an instrument for achieving peaceful coexistence of former victims and former criminals are active everywhere, not only in present-day Russia. The dispute between the "let's forget it" camp and those who fight against conscious forgetfulness continues and will continue wherever crimes have been committed against millions of people, against entire nations, against humanity. No wonder the most terrible repressions are called "crimes against humanity". This term itself indicates the impossibility of ever consigning such crimes to oblivion.

The fact that the crimes of the Gulag, despite the best efforts of Memorial activists and other democratic forces, are not a historical trauma for Russia today, proves that Russia has not yet recovered from the past, that it suffers from an analogue of the Stockholm syndrome, that Stalin's past still holds the Russian Federation hostage. It is as if they prefer the torturer they know to one they do not. They are more afraid of the imaginary, unknown, foreign torturers, ones who might attack them if they are not defended by the ones they do know.

The fact that Ukraine realises the tragedy of the Holodomor but nonetheless pushes this other tragedy, that of millions of deported peasants, a little farther to one side, probably indicates that even with an awareness of historical trauma, the people, or at least a portion of them, have a kind of filter that tries to protect the carrier of injury from the oversupply of negative past experiences.

Inevitably, historical injuries affect the construction of national identity. They can play both a positive and consolidating role, but, if they cause the victim to develop a predisposition to permanent resistance, the effect of these historical injuries can remain entirely negative. Aleida Assman, a well-known German specialist in historical trauma, writes in her book, *The Long Shadow of the Past: Memorial Culture and Historical Politics*:

> "An identity policy based on sacrificial semantics turns out to be part of the problem rather than its solution. More precisely – part of the post-traumatic syndrome, but not an attempt to overcome it. Yehuda Elkana convincingly described the devastating desire to build an Israeli identity solely based on the sacrificial experience of the Holocaust, as important cultural values are obscured and squeezed out of consciousness. He does not claim that the Holocaust should be forgotten, but he objects to the Holocaust serving as the central axis of the construction of national identity".

When a psychologist works with a person who has experienced trauma, he is looking for a way to help the victim, the carrier of the trauma, to pronounce his pain. Survivors of tragedy need to speak out in order to prevent the tragedy they have experienced from continuing to guide their actions and thoughts. Speaking out is not a way to forget, but a way to remember constructively, to make the consequences of tragedy a legacy of its own history and culture. It is this culture that helps us to understand and deal with the tragedy and to realise the reality of the historical trauma. My grandmother healed herself of her wartime wounds by making those little bags of dried bread. I was able to witness this and learn from it.

Once upon a time, historical tragedies were passed on to the next generation in folk songs and ballads. Very often, historical truth and historical trauma are returned to the people through works of art, through literature and cinema. The more powerful these mediums are, the longer the works remain relevant to the people and, in the end, the best of them fall into the cultural canon of historical experience. Tens if not hundreds of millions of people watched the film "Schindler's List". Millions watched "The Killing Fields" about the genocide in Cambodia. I hope that millions of people around the world will watch the film by Agnieszka Holland, "Mr Jones", a film about the Holodomor in Ukraine and the unwillingness of the civilised world in the 1930s to see and acknowledge the truth about what was happening in the U.S.S.R.

I hope that someday Ukrainian directors will make a film based on Vasyl Barka's novel, *The Yellow Prince*. The book is about the drama of a Ukrainian village in the 1930s, during the mass deportation of Ukrainian peasants and their future fate. Such a film is essential, both to support historical memory and to help us better understand our fundamental national values as Ukrainian people.

06.03.2022

Interview with a Cup of Coffee

In this difficult, dramatic time, when the independence of my country Ukraine is at risk, the works of the great Scottish writer Archibald Joseph Cronin, who brilliantly combined the talents of a doctor and a writer, help me a lot. I make use of all five volumes of his work, published in Moscow in 1994 by the Sytin Foundation publishing house. It does not matter what the stories are in these books. I do not read fiction now. I use the five volumes to rest my computer on, so that my Zooms and Skypes follow the rules of television, so that the laptop's camera is located at my eye level.

These are not my books and they are not from my apartment. My wife and I are now in Transcarpathia. An elderly woman, whom we do not know but whose name is Larisa, gave us the keys to her apartment while she moved in with her daughter. She is Russian-speaking, which is not uncommon in western Ukraine. All the books – and there are many of them here – are in Russian. There are both Russian and world classics and Ukrainian classics translated into Russian. She also left us a refrigerator full of food and told us to make ourselves at home.

These days, western Ukraine shows itself at its best, although the tension is palpable. When I went to the market today and wanted to buy honey, I noticed that there was honey available but that there was no-one from whom to buy it. I asked a local resident, standing nearby, "Where is the seller?" Without turning around, he answered quite sharply, "How do I know?" He then turned around and apologised to me with his eyes. I decided not to wait for the honey trader and instead bought strawberry jam from elsewhere. I just wanted something sweet. I have never eaten a lot of jam and I can drink coffee and tea without sugar – I was protecting myself from diabetes. I told everyone that my life is sweet enough. But now I want honey or jam.

War breeds death and at the same time awakens the humanity in people. Suddenly people want to help others, to help those who are in trouble. We have millions in trouble right now. Without exaggeration, we can also say that there are many millions of people who help. The humanitarian centres helping the refugees have a lot of people to help them. These centres are located mainly in schools or administrative buildings. The owners of a number of cars on our street have hung signs in them that say, "If you need to take humanitarian aid or a passenger, call me!" while adding their mobile telephone number. In the evening, the police patrol and check the cars. During the day, you often see police officers carrying machine guns.

Journalists from various countries call constantly, or send me messages. I have already learned to divide them into one of two types: those who really want to understand what is happening, to understand the feelings and the pain of Ukrainians and those who just want to make a reputation or money covering a hot topic. YouTubers have appeared who are trying to impersonate journalists from well-known publications. They also ask for video interviews. In the state in which Ukrainian public figures, writers and politicians find themselves now, it is all too easy to waste time explaining to a YouTuber with fifteen followers the complexities of the current situation. While I have known many French and English journalists for a long time, I have started to check the credentials of unfamiliar journalists through Google. This practice, as it turns out, has not been in vain and has saved me a lot of wasted time and effort.

The war has been going on for almost two weeks now. Ukraine is holding on. Many dedicated journalists, both Ukrainian and foreign, continue to work in Ukraine. Today, two of them are making their way into the combat zone near Kyiv, to Irpin. I wish them success in their work and a safe return to Kyiv. I wish good to all Ukrainians and those who are on the side of Ukraine, along with health and strength. But I ask those journalists who call Ukrainians from abroad, and who seem to want to hold the telephone in their right hand while they have a cup of coffee in their left, not to ask stupid questions. The most stupid is, "Are you ready to die for Ukraine?" Ukrainians are ready to die for Ukraine. Ukrainians die for Ukraine every day. But Ukraine itself will not die! Ukraine will survive, rebuild itself and move on, remembering this war for all subsequent centuries.

08.03.2022

Bread with Blood

Since arriving in western Ukraine, we have started eating much more bread than before. My wife and I used not to eat much bread except when we were in the village. Village bread was always tastier than the city stuff. In the Ukrainian countryside there is a long tradition of having plenty of bread on the table and of eating it with butter and salt or dipping it in milk. Bread dipped in fresh cow's milk is also given to little children – and they love it.

Our boys have always enjoyed fresh bread. They like making and eating sandwiches. In our village shop, we would buy our favourite Makariv loaf – a soft, white, brick-shaped bread. It was baked at the well-known Makariv Bakery in the town of the same name which is twenty kilometres from our village. Occasionally, you can find this bread in Kyiv, but only in small corner shops, not in supermarkets.

I have been thinking about that Makariv bread for several days now, recalling the taste. While remembering it, I taste blood on my lips, as when I was a child and someone split my lip in a fight. The Makariv bakery was bombed on Monday by Russian troops. The bakers were at work. I can imagine the fragrant smell that surrounded them the moment before the attack. In an instant, thirteen bakery staff were killed and nine more were injured. The bakery is no more. Makariv bread is a thing of the past.

I have long since run out of words to describe the horror brought about by Putin on Ukrainian soil. Ukraine is the land of bread and wheat. Even in Egypt, bread and cakes are baked using Ukrainian flour. This is currently the time when the fields are prepared for sowing, but this work is not being done. In many regions, the soil of the wheat fields is full of metal – fragments of shells, pieces of blown-up tanks and cars, the remains of downed planes and helicopters. And it is all covered in blood. The blood of Russian soldiers who do not understand what they are fighting for; the blood of Ukrainian soldiers and civilians who know that if they do not fight, Ukraine will no longer exist. In its place, there will be a cemetery with a caretaker's hut and some kind of governor general sent from Russia to sit and guard it.

Bread was mixed with blood in Chernihiv as well when Russian bombers dropped "dumb" unguided bombs onto a bread shop in the town square. People were lined up outside, waiting to buy some fresh, warm bread. Someone was just leaving the store with a bag when the bomb hit. Many people died in this bombing raid. Amnesty International has documented this crime committed by the Russian Army.

Every day the list of crimes grows longer as more and more of Putin's actions are added to the list – the shooting of young volunteers who were carrying food to the dog shelter in Hostomel, the murder of postmen who were delivering pensions to elderly residents in Sumy region, the execution of two priests on the road and the murder of employees of Kyiv's television centre. The list goes on and on. We certainly do not yet know all the crimes that have been committed but all of them will be discovered and the list will be presented at the new Nuremberg trial. It does not matter, of course, in which town the trial takes place. The main thing is to know that those who have committed these crimes will be judged!

International lawyers have already begun to collect evidence of the crimes committed.

Ukrainians are looking forward to the verdict on the murderers and war criminals. But for now, they must survive under the constant shelling of the Russian army. They spend their nights in basements, in bomb shelters, in bathrooms. The latest advice circulating on the Internet tells us that, in case of a bombing raid, if you cannot leave your apartment, the safest places to be are inside a cast-iron bathtub or in interior corridors, ones with no windows.

The people of Kyiv have grown suddenly much more attached to the metro, one of the most beautiful and deepest underground systems in the world. The metro is no longer a form of transport – it is a haven, like something from an apocalyptic movie. The stations are covered with instruction notices. There are living spaces everywhere. The platforms have been turned into cinemas where films are shown for free: children's films in the morning and films for a wider audience later in the day. Large screens have already been hung at fourteen of Kyiv's metro stations. There is a constant supply of tea and there is free Wi-Fi, though the signal is weak. Although there are insufficient toilets, people do not complain anymore about queuing for forty minutes or more. Everyone waits patiently. They are waiting for the end of the war and the beginning of the trial – a trial that the whole world will follow, as the whole world followed the Nuremberg trials.

In Russia, do they think about these future court proceedings? I am afraid they do not think about them at all. They are too busy buying dollars and euros. Sanctions targeting the banking sector have caused the value of the ruble to fall dramatically, provoking panic. Panic has also been observed on the Russian–Finnish border, via which many Russians have been leaving their homeland. They leave because they are ashamed to stay in Russia, or because they could be drafted into the army. They do not wish to die, nor do they want to kill.

Nor do not they want to be cannon fodder for the Kremlin. Some captured Russian soldiers have asked for permission to remain in Ukraine for good. "Jail awaits us if we return!" they say.

On the borders of Ukraine with Moldova, Romania, Hungary, Slovakia, and Poland, there are queues of refugees. Some Ukrainian men are trying to leave the country using fake Russian passports. They do not want to fight either. I do not judge them. Let time and history judge us all. I am glad that in this the most difficult of times, most Ukrainians have maintained their humanity and are trying to help each other. Mobilisation has been announced but no-one is taken forcibly into the army. Those who want to defend their homeland go to the nearest military registration office and enlist. Most often, they are asked to leave a telephone number and await a call. While there are many who want to fight the invaders, not all would be of use in a military operation.

In the past couple of days, I have started to dread opening Facebook. More and more often, in the news feed, I see posts by young Ukrainian women declaring their love for their recently killed husbands. I know some of these women and have met their husbands. I cannot read these cries of despair, thrown into the bottomless well of the Internet, without tears. But I cannot not read them either. I want to see and hear everything that is happening now in my country. I know that in the occupied town of Melitopol, in the south of Ukraine, arrests of Crimean Tatar activists and other active citizens have begun. I know that the workers of the Chernobyl nuclear power plant are being held prisoner by the Russian invaders and that their mobile telephones have been taken from them. Moscow television propagandists have gone there under the protection of the Russian military. I do not know what stories they tell in Russia about this war, about the capture of the

Chernobyl nuclear power plant, or about the capture of the Zaporizhzhia nuclear power plant, which is still in operation. Why do they need these atomic installations? Are they planning to blackmail Ukraine and the world? Why are they bombing children's hospitals and schools? Why do they destroy the residential areas in Chernihiv, Borodianka, Kharkiv, and Mariupol? Why are they bombing bakeries and bread shops? I do not have the answers to any of these questions.

"You can't understand Russia with your mind!" wrote the famous Russian poet of the nineteenth century, Fyodor Tyutchev. I agree with him but nevertheless I have a question: how can one understand Russia at all, if your mind cannot help you with this task?

09.03.2022

A Country in Search of Safety

My family is finding it hard to be refugees. To distract ourselves from the thought of what has been left behind and the uncertainty of the future, we try to enjoy the local scenery and take an interest in the architecture and history around us. At first, my family took photographs. They do not do this anymore. The local inhabitants, who are extremely supportive of refugees in general, take a very dim view of anyone acting like a tourist. "Don't you know there's a war on?" they shout.

This morning I went to the locksmith again. There are four of us but we have only one set of keys to the apartment. We need to make at least two more sets, but there are no key blanks available. The man in the shop says that they have been expecting a delivery any day, but that to date no key blanks have arrived. This is a new kind of shortage, one now common throughout western Ukraine. Its towns are now full of refugees. They are welcomed into homes, given rooms and apartments, settled in hostels and schools. Most of them still require keys.

The accommodation in the apartment we are in was given to us by a retired lady I had never met before, a relative of one of our friends. She went to live with her daughter and did not even take food from the refrigerator. She told us to eat it ourselves. There was no heating or hot water at first. The day before Ukraine was first attacked, the boiler broke down. At night-time, the temperature falls to minus one or two degrees Celsius. Unfortunately, we left most of our warm clothes in Kyiv. We did not expect that it would be so cold. After all, the sun was shining and we had already seen signs of spring in mid-February.

In fact, we did not really think much about what to take with us. We thought that we would go to the village, not a great distance from Kyiv and would return home quite soon. I think this is always the case at the start of war.

The owner of the apartment called the boiler repairman for us and after a few days he arrived. He inspected the heating system but said that he would need to find some parts in order to fix it. He would return as soon as he found them. Two days later he came back at around midnight and worked for about an hour. He was yawning. He wanted to stay alert, so he talked. I stood holding a torch for him, shining it onto the boiler and we talked, or rather he talked and I listened. He spoke about himself, about how he had been repairing boilers all his life, how he has sometimes been invited to rich folks' houses. He has even been chauffeur-driven to and from "posh villas". After all, boilers break down in fancy mansions too! Finally, at about one in the morning, he left. He did not charge us much. He said he would walk home, he did not want to call a taxi.

This apartment resembles the apartment of my late parents – it is like a museum of the Soviet era. Two rooms, a small kitchen, a toilet and bathroom. The living room is lined with wooden cupboards and bookcases. The owner is a Russian-speaking resident. Western Ukraine is safer for everyone, including Russian-speakers. The majority of civilians killed by the Russian army in Kharkiv, Mariupol, Melitopol, Chernihiv and other cities are Russian-speaking or ethnic Russians. This war is not about the Russian language, which I have spoken and used in writing all my life. This war is about the aging Putin's last chance to fulfil his dream of recreating the U.S.S.R. or the Russian Empire. Neither one nor the other is possible without Kyiv, without Ukraine. Therefore, blood is shed and people are dying, including Russian soldiers. This war will create an iron curtain between Ukrainians and Russians for many years to come.

Yesterday evening I called my brother in Kyiv several times. My brother is almost seventy years old. For the last thirty years he has been doing yoga and meditation. He always speaks in a calm and measured way. We have talked every day on the telephone and every day he has said that he, his wife and their cat would stay in Kyiv, despite the fact that they live next to the Antonov aircraft factory. Behind him lies Hostomel, where fierce fighting has been going on for ten days now. But yesterday they finally decided to leave. They will not go far, just to a village house, one hundred and fifty kilometres from Kyiv.

My brother, his wife, her brother and their mother set off as soon as the night curfew was lifted. The car must have been cramped. Along with the four adults and their luggage, there was Pepin the cat and Semyon the hamster. There is now only one, more-or-less safe exit from Kyiv, that to the south-west of the city.

I kept in touch with my brother on their journey. He told me that there were few cars on the roads but that they were regularly stopped at checkpoints. The soldiers did not check their documents but just looked into the car and asked about where they were going and whether they had any weapons with them.

They arrived at the village towards evening. The house was cold. There is only a wood-burning stove, an outside toilet and no running water, only a well. They quickly lit a fire in the old brick stove, but the house was still cold by the time they went to bed. Everyone slept fully dressed, covering their heads with old blankets. Several times during the night my brother got up and added firewood to the stove. Like their owners, the cat Pepin and Semyon the hamster also felt the cold. By morning, things had warmed up a little. My brother called me and asked me if there was further news during the night. They have no T.V., no radio and almost no access to the Internet where they are. But at least they were out of Kyiv, away from the constant noise of shelling that they had by then lived with for more than ten days.

Now I am waiting for two old friends to leave the capital. At the moment Valentin and Tatiana are in hospital. Valentin, a diabetic, recently had both his legs amputated. He is ninety-two-years old. They have a car and Tatiana can drive but Valentin cannot sit up. He must travel lying down. As a professor of medicine he has participated in scientific conferences all over Europe. Colleagues and friends in Germany have already invited him and his wife there. But the obstacles seemed insurmountable. The very few patients remaining in the hospital are now all together on one floor so that the small contingent of doctors and nurses still available can more easily care for them.

As of today, Tatiana is slightly more hopeful about their possible escape from Kyiv. They have been told that an evacuation train was being prepared for patients of the main children's hospital in Ukraine. The head physician had offered to take Valentin and Tatiana on this train. I am awaiting news of this as I hope they will be able to travel to western Ukraine along with the sick children.

They will leave behind in Kyiv an extraordinary apartment, filled with antiques, paintings and a huge collection of jazz records. It is located in one of Kyiv's most interesting nineteenth century buildings. Valentin has always been very fond of jazz. I can imagine the mixed feelings they will experience on their departure. And what will happen when they get to Germany? They will certainly wait for the first opportunity to return home. Of this I am sure. All the Ukrainians who have left their homes will wait for the moment when it will be safe to return. Just as I am waiting.

I am waiting for the opportunity not just to return to a peaceful Kyiv but to return to my library, to my desk, to the archives I was using to write my latest novel, to my plans for the future, to the world that I have been creating around me for decades, a world that made me happy. I could not even imagine that this happiness could be destroyed so easily. I thought that my happiness was not material but a state of mind, like the energy arising from eye contact with another person. I am someone who loves and appreciates life, the rays of the sun, the blue sky, the stars of the summer night sky.

It comforts me that I have been happy for a very long time and I feel very sad for young people. But I see how they resist the forces that wish to steal their futures from them. Young couples have been married against the barricades placed at the entrances to the city by the territorial defence forces. More than four hundred and eighty children have been born in Kyiv since the start of the war. Almost all were born underground, in bomb shelters, on metro platforms and in the basement areas of maternity hospitals. I want to imagine their futures as bright and full of sunshine. But for this, they must first survive.

Parents all over Ukraine are doing whatever they can for their children. An eleven-year-old boy from Zaporizhzhia was put on a train by his mother carrying only a plastic bag containing his passport and a piece of paper with the telephone number of friends who live in Bratislava. He travelled on his own all the way to the Ukrainian–Slovak border in Transcarpathia. His mother had to remain in Zaporizhzhia to look after her bed-ridden mother. That boy is now in Slovakia. He was welcomed there by kind people, our Slovak neighbours. I hope he will be able to return home sooner rather than later. But for that to happen, there must be an end to the atrocities perpetrated against Ukrainian people by the Russian state.

For this to happen, it will first be necessary to expel the Russians from Ukrainian territory or to agree with them to end the aggression and withdraw. Negotiations are ongoing and will probably continue for a long time. This war, conducted in the style of World War II, with its bombing of peaceful cities and murder of civilians, continues unabated. The whole world looks on and does not believe that such a war is possible in Europe in the twenty-first century. But it is possible. It continues and it will affect the whole world, not only because of the flow of refugees but also because one rogue leader of a large country has been able to destabilise everything, to destroy economies, to create universal anxiety and fear. The whole world must help Ukraine now, otherwise this war will spill further into Europe.

10.03.2022

Is it a Good Time to Look Back?

I am sitting in western Ukraine, in a small town near the mountains, in someone else's apartment. My wife and younger son are still asleep, our older son has been on duty all night at a refugee centre. In the morning, he will go on to give an English lesson to refugee children. The local library is providing space for this within a programme of activities for young ones.

It is still dark outside. I am waiting for the dawn to light up the mountains. I drink coffee with milk, although I know that after the third cup I will feel uncomfortable. Like yesterday, I think about the past. I go over in my mind what has happened to me and my family during the last thirty-four years. In my family, I am the only citizen of Ukraine. My wife was born in Surrey, she and our children are British subjects. Back in 1988, during the Gorbachev thaw, after nine months of walking around Soviet visa offices, I was allowed to leave the U.S.S.R. and travel to London for our wedding. It is a long story worthy of a book, but that book will have to wait. Ukraine became the home for my wife and the children soon after they were born.

After our wedding in Brixton, we travelled by train back to the U.S.S.R. People thought we were crazy – even the employee at the Soviet embassy in London who processed my wife's visa application. Along with the sharp and hostile expression typical of a K.G.B. representative, there was a look of bewilderment in his eyes. In the end, he even advised me to buy a V.C.R., so that I could sell it in the U.S.S.R. and have some money to live on.

Our journey to Kyiv was far from easy. We slept on the floor of the station in Berlin because there were no trains or tickets to Ukraine. When eventually we reached the Polish–Belarusian border town of Brest late one evening, we were taken off the train so that customs officers could make a thorough search of our luggage. It took hours. The train left without us. We stayed there until morning watching the customs officers rifling through our things and checking the books from Russian emigré publishers that I was bringing home to Kyiv – more than two hundred of them! Many were diaries and memoirs of twentieth century anti-Soviet politicians and public figures. In the end, the female customs officer said, "These books are no longer banned. You can take them. But if you had Khruschev's memoirs, then I would have to take that away. Khruschev is not allowed yet". She had not seen that Khruschev's memoirs were there in my case.

I had removed the book cover before leaving London. I needed that book eventually to write my novel *The Bickford Fuse* in which a half-real, half-imaginary Nikita Khruschev is one of the main protagonists.

Moving from place to place has been a tradition for generations in my family. In 1941, at the age of nine, my mother, together with her mother, two brothers and her paternal grandmother all fled Leningrad for Siberia. They were refugees until the end of the war, travelling on trains that were bombed and living in squalid quarters, not made welcome by local people who had little to eat themselves. In 1945, on the journey home, my mother caught scabies. Already a teenager, her lasting memory of that time was of a terrible sense of shame.

After the Cuban crisis, Khrushchev wanted to show that the U.S.S.R. was a peaceful country. He announced unilateral disarmament. 100 thousand officers of the Soviet army were made reservists and expected to find other work and livelihoods. My father, who had been a military pilot, was also dismissed from the army. We moved to Kyiv, to be with my grandmother. I was two years old and my older brother Misha was nine. Penguin Misha from *Death and the Penguin* is named after him.

Today my family and I are refugees, but we do not feel the hardships that many other Ukrainian refugees experience currently. We have been helped by friends and have settled into a temporary home in the Carpathian foothills. We have had a chance to find calm and carry out activities that are of use to the country. But two weeks ago, when we fled from Kyiv by car, we were refugees in every sense of the word.

Journalists from all over the world continue to call me to

ask, among other things, "the reason for this war". At first, we did not understand what war was. You can't understand it until you see it and hear it.

On February 24, we were awakened at 5.00 a.m. by the sounds of explosions. They will forever remain in my memory. We walked around the historical centre of Kyiv, near to where we live, to find the nearest bomb shelters. They are also old, almost ancient – Soviet-made, built in case of war with N.A.T.O. Before this, we had not thought about leaving Kyiv. We could not imagine that Russia would bomb the Ukrainian capital. But it had already happened. I do not think we were naive. Our shock at the actions of our eastern neighbour is evidence of modern people's unpreparedness for horrors that have no place in contemporary life. I admit I should have known better. My own compatriots, those living in the eastern areas of the country, have been experiencing attacks like these for eight years. I even wrote about it in *Grey Bees*. But still I was unprepared. And now here we are, refugees in the foothills of the Ukrainian Carpathians. In this place, nature itself calls you to reflection.

The reason for this war, simply put, is Putin's desire to re-establish a united territory just as one of which the U.S.S.R. once considered. For twenty years, he has been repeating the mantra "Ukrainians and Russians are one people," meaning "Ukrainians belong to Russia". Ukrainians do not agree with this. Putin has often stated publicly that, for him, the greatest tragedy he has experienced is the collapse of the Soviet Union. For most Ukrainians, it was not a tragedy. Rather, it was an opportunity to become a European country and to regain independence from Russia's Empire.

Ever since Putin's election, Russia has meddled in the Ukrainian economy, political life and even in its state security, always seeking to undermine the country's independence. When the dust settled after the tragedy of the Maidan, it should not have come as a surprise to discover that many leading figures in our armed forces and intelligence services had Russian passports. Such a situation would never be allowed to develop again. Putin would have to find other ways to cripple Ukraine's independence. And he did – in the annexation of Crimea and the occupation of two regions in the east of the country.

Self-imposed isolation during the pandemic seems to have dramatically aged President Putin. Perhaps he sees his end. He has decided to place himself in Russian school history books as the leader who was able to recreate the equivalent of the Soviet Union or the Russian Empire. He has no other ambition. He does not now need money; there are no banks dealing in foreign exchange in the next life and no expensive restaurants either. What he "needs" is Ukraine, Belarus and, I think, other territories previously part of the U.S.S.R. or the Russian Empire. He wants Russia to be feared. He has achieved this. He wanted total political control over the Russian Federation and he has got it. He rules a huge country with a one-party system, where any attempts at opposition are destroyed ruthlessly – just as they were in the Soviet Union.

Putin claims that Ukrainians are not a separate people and says that Ukraine was invented by Lenin. There is no basis in history for this statement. Ukraine has its own history and Russia its own. There were times when the history of Ukraine overlapped with the history of Russia and times when it did not. Just as, at other times, Ukraine's destiny overlapped with the Polish–Lithuanian state.

In the sixteenth and seventeenth centuries, while Russia continued to be a monarchy, Ukrainian Cossacks elected their commander-in-chief, or "hetman". In Ukraine, the Cossacks also elected their senior officers. Ukraine at that time had its own diplomatic service and its own justice system. Ukraine was also constantly at war, first with Poland, then with Russia, then with Turkish Crimea. Old maps from different years show Ukraine with different borders, reflecting the results of the most recent battles fought by the Cossacks. But this changed when, in 1654, the Ukrainian hetman Bogdan Khmelnitsky asked the Russian tsar for military assistance against Poland. This marked the end of Ukrainian independence. Russia gave help, but then *de facto* seized Ukraine and effectively banned the Cossack army. The Cossacks were told they must either serve in the Russian tsarist army, move to the North Caucasus and settle there, or become peasants under the control of the Russian Empire.

The Ukrainians never had a tsar and were never ready to obey one. The Russians, on the other hand, who lived for centuries under a monarchy, loved their tsars. Sometimes they killed them, but then they would adore the next one. Loyalty to the monarch remained a key feature of the Soviet era too. Of the six general secretaries of the communist party of the U.S.S.R., only one was dismissed, the Ukrainian, Nikita Khrushchev. The other five remained leaders of the Soviet state until their deaths. During the period of Putin's twenty-two-year rule in Russia, Ukraine has had five presidents.

Ukrainians are individualists, egoists, anarchists who do

not like government or authority. They think they know how to organise their lives, regardless of which party or force is in power in the country. If they do not like the actions of the authorities, they go out to protest and create "Maidans". Any government in Ukraine is afraid of the "street", afraid of its people.

Most Russians, loyal to authority, are afraid to protest and are willing to obey any rule the Kremlin creates. Now they are cut off from information, from Facebook and Twitter. But even when they have access to alternative views, they prefer to believe the official ones.

In Ukraine, there are some four hundred political parties registered with the Ministry of Justice. This underlines the individualism of Ukrainians. Ukrainians do not vote for the extreme left or the extreme right. Basically, they are liberals at heart.

The historical memory that Ukrainians have managed to regain since Soviet censorship came to an end has greatly affected their political views. Now that Ukrainians know more about the deportations of Ukrainian peasants to Siberia and the Far East in the 1920s and 1930s, they can safely say, "We and the Russians are two different peoples!" The deportations took place to punish the Ukrainians who refused to join collective farms. Ukrainians are not collective: everyone wants to be the owner of his own land, their own cow, their own crop. After the deportations, the next punishment meted out to Ukrainians for their individualism and unwillingness to become "Soviet people" was the famine, or Holodomor, of 1932–3 organised by the communists and Stalin. Officially, livestock, seed grain, animal feed, and food stocks were taken away from the Ukrainians to help the starving Russians on the Volga. The expropriation was total – everything was taken, down to the last grain, leaving Ukrainians to starve to death. To save themselves, hungry village dwellers tried to get into the cities, but the Soviet army stood guard and did not let them enter. There are no exact numbers of the deaths from starvation during that terrible time, but we are talking about many millions. During the Holodomor, there certainly were individual cases of cannibalism. However, the tragedy was turned quickly into a political tool. When the Soviet police later persecuted survivors they accused them of cannibalism, even if it was often untrue.

After World War II, Soviet propaganda set out to discredit the concept of Ukrainian nationalism once and for all. The person they used for this purpose was Stepan Bandera. The Soviet authorities worked diligently to expose Bandera as an anti-hero, but the opposite result was achieved. For many Ukrainians, Bandera became a true hero. Although there was nothing actually heroic about his story, venerating whatever the U.S.S.R. hated had become a Ukrainian habit.

After the World War I, Poland took over some parts of the Austro-Hungarian Empire, including areas of Ukrainian territory, such as Galicia where Bandera was born. A Polish citizen but ethnic Ukrainian, he organised terrorist attacks in Poland in a violent campaign for Ukrainian independence. He sent Ukrainian students to kill Polish politicians and statesmen. He was the leader of one of several nationalistic organisations campaigning at the time for Ukrainian independence. When World War II began, Bandera hoped that Nazi Germany would allow the creation of an independent Ukraine. The Nazis had no such intention and they put him in the Sachsenhausen concentration camp, where he remained until the end of the war. He never fought. After the war, he hid in Munich, where he was killed by an N.K.V.D. agent on October 15, 1959. Ukraine did have its heroes – people who were real fighters for independence – but the image of Stepan Bandera turned out to be the one that captured the imagination of those who wanted above all Ukraine's independence from the U.S.S.R. Bandera was indeed a nationalist but not a hero.

Today, the President of Ukraine, elected with seventy-three per cent. of the votes, is Volodymyr Zelensky. He is a Russian-speaking Jew from the south of Ukraine. It is ridiculous to talk about his hatred of Russian-speakers and the anti-Semitism of Ukraine. Russia, however, continues with this narrative, just as it continues to bomb the cities populated mostly by Russian-speaking Ukrainians: Kharkiv, Mariupol, Chernihiv, Akhtyrka, Kherson, and more. Inevitably, by far the majority of the victims of these atrocities are Russian speakers.

———

The Ukrainian army is successfully defending the country. Ukrainians are accustomed to freedom and value it more than stability. For Russians, stability is more important than freedom. Ukrainians have never accepted censorship. They have always wanted to say and write what they thought. That is why almost all Ukrainian writers and poets of the 1920s and 1930s were shot by the Soviet authorities. This generation of writers is known collectively as "the Executed Renaissance". If Russia takes over, there will be another executed generation of Ukrainian writers and politicians, philosophers, and philologists – those for whom life without a free Ukraine does not make sense. I know many such writers. They are my friends. I consider myself to be among that number.

It is frightening to write such words, but I will write them anyway: Ukraine will either be free, independent and European, or it will not exist at all. Then they will write about it in European history books, shamefacedly hiding the fact that the destruction of Ukraine was possible only with the tacit consent of Europe and the entire civilised world.

13.03.2022

Archaeology of War

I was born in 1961, sixteen years after the end of World War II, in which one of my grandfathers died while the other survived. Throughout my childhood I played war with my friends. We tried to divide into groups: "ours" and the "Germans". But nobody wanted to be German, so we drew lots and the losers had to become German for the duration of the game. It was clear that the Germans should lose. We ran around with makeshift wooden Kalashnikovs, "shooting" at the enemies, staging ambushes, shouting "tra-ta-ta".

When in the fourth grade we were asked to choose a foreign language for study at school, I flatly refused to go into the German language group. "They killed my grandfather Alexei," I said. No-one sought to persuade me to learn German. I studied English. The British were our allies in that war. Now the concept of "ours" has changed meaning since then, but the British are still our allies. Only now it is not "our-Soviet Union" as then but "our-Ukraine".

I am sad to think that after this war, when children will be offered Russian to study at school, they will flatly refuse and say, "The Russians killed my granddad!" or "The Russians killed my little sister!" It will surely happen. And this will be in a country where half the population speaks Russian and in which there are several million ethnic Russians, people like me.

Putin is not only destroying Ukraine, he is destroying Russia and he is destroying the Russian language. Today, during this terrible war, at a time when Russian bombers are attacking schools, universities, hospitals, I think that the Russian language is one of the least significant victims of this war. I have been made to feel ashamed many times of my Russian origin, of the fact that my native language is Russian. I have come up with different formulae, trying to explain that the language is not to blame, that Putin has no ownership of the Russian language, that many defenders of Ukraine are Russian-speaking, and that many civilian victims in the south and east of the country were also Russian-speaking and ethnic Russians. Now I just want to be quiet. I speak Ukrainian fluently. It is easy for me to move in conversation from one language to the other. I already see the future of the Russian language in Ukraine. It will soon be diminished. Just as now some Russian citizens are tearing up their Russian passports and refusing to consider themselves Russians, many Ukrainians are giving up everything Russian, including the language, the culture, even their very thoughts about Russia. My children have two native languages: Russian and English. My wife is from the U.K. Between themselves, the children have already switched to English. They still speak Russian to me, but they have no interest in Russian culture.

Not quite true – my daughter Gabriella does send me, from time to time, links to statements by some Russian rappers and rockers who oppose Putin. Apparently, she wants to support me in this way, to show that not all Russians love Putin and are ready to kill Ukrainians. I know that myself.

Among my friends and acquaintances, there is a small group of Russian writers who are not afraid to declare support for Ukraine. This includes Vladimir Sorokin, Boris Akunin and Mikhail Shishkin. These writers have long been living in exile and have long been opposed to the Kremlin. There are a few more such people who still live in Russia. They also have a good chance of becoming emigrants. I am grateful to them and put them on my list of honest and decent people. I want them to remain in history, remain in world culture, to be read and listened to. Not all of Russia is a collective Putin. The unfortunate thing is that there is within Russia no collective anti-Putin. Even Navalny was not ready to discuss the return of the illegally annexed Crimea. These thoughts mean I regularly wish to hide in memories of childhood.

As a child, I loved to travel to Tarasivka near Kyiv to the battlefields of the World War II. We travelled by train with my best friend Sasha Solovyov. We took with us folding "sapper" shovels and dug in the hills near the village. There you were very likely to dig up bullets from machine guns and rifles and even find shells. There were also fragments of grenades and buttons from uniforms. Many tons of World War II metal still lie buried around Kyiv. Not only around Kyiv but throughout Ukraine. Around the village of Lazarivka in the Zhytomyr region there is also a lot of metal and some villagers have long been engaged in treasure hunting. They have bought expensive metal detectors capable of checking the ground to a depth of one metre. In their free time, they walk through the fields and forests carrying them.

Two years ago, Slava, a tractor driver from a nearby street, found and dug out part of the barrel of a German tank gun. For a long time, he could not decide what to do with it. He usually sold some small finds on the Internet, but parts of a gun barrel – this one being about two metres long and weighing more than fifty kilograms – are not a very popular item even for collectors of military memorabilia. I do not know what he did with his barrel in the end. Most likely he sold it for scrap. I think it just lay in his yard for several months until his wife expressed her dissatisfaction. Then the barrel disappeared and I did not ask what happened to it. After the war, he will again go with a metal detector through the fields. I expect many new finds await him there. There are now thousands of tons of Russian military scrap metal both on Ukrainian soil and beneath it. Probably, after the war, Ukraine will be able to sell all this metal to China or somewhere else. But for now, Ukraine is accumulating the wreckage of tanks and burned-out armoured personnel carriers on its roads and fields.

Those inhabitants of cities not captured by the Russian army are digging trenches and building fortifications. Many civilians have become specialists in fortifications. They already know what the "first line of defence", "second line of defence", "third line of defence" mean. They are digging trenches continuously, day and night, waiting for the advance of Russian tanks and infantry. During the trench diggings, completely unexpected discoveries occur – ones not military but archaeological. Already, in two places in the trenches, the remains of ancient dwellings from the Bronze Age have been found, along with later artefacts. These amateur archaeologists, of course, wanted immediately to inform the professional archaeologists and the museums, but real archaeologists are not so easy to reach now. Museums, if they have not yet been bombed, are not ready to accept historical treasures for as long as the war continues.

A way out of the situation was quickly found: instructions appeared from museums advising anybody who comes across archaeological sites to memorise the excavation site, fix it on the map and leave it for further study and further excavation once the war is over. After the war, the ancient cultural layer will be mixed with the current one, more precisely, with the modern layer of "Russian culture". Archaeologists will be able to sort them out. Items of real historical value do not have the stamp "Made in the Russian Federation" on them.

After the war, the ruins of dozens of cities and thousands of villages will remain, along with millions of homeless Ukrainians. There will be bitterness and hatred. Children will once again play at being at war and will dig bullets and grenade fragments from out of the ground. For a long time, cars will go on being blown up by mines left near to the roadside.

A war never ends on a specific date in a specific year. A war continues as people continue to die from its consequences, from wounds received during bombing, from accidents with live munitions. Psychologically, while World War II was over by the end of the 1970s in the former U.S.S.R., the Soviet system prolonged the memory of the war and prolonged the post-war hatred through films, fiction, and school textbooks.

The school textbooks in the newly separatist "republics" say that Ukraine is a fascist state. Children are taught from birth to hate Ukraine, Europe and the U.S.A. I can only imagine how this war will be described in Russian history books. Russia has a lot of experience in rewriting history. They would like to control the history books of other countries as well. Former Minister of Education Dmitry Tabachnik, who once fled from Ukraine, told me that Russia demanded that Ukrainian school history textbooks be shown to its specialists. That was only ten years ago. During the Soviet era, the U.S.S.R. controlled the content of history textbooks published for schools in Finland. Moscow forbade Finnish historians from writing the truth about the Finnish War of 1939, the so-called Winter War, as well as a number of other events.

The independence of its history is one guarantee of the independence of a state.

I want what is written of the history of Ukraine in Ukrainian school textbooks to be the truth. Lies are beneficial only to Russia. Myths are more problematic, however. A myth becomes part of history when a country feels it needs it to raise morale, when a country is in crisis. It is then that myths become more important to a good part of the population than true history. This war has already added many myths to Ukraine's unwritten history. Some of these myths will definitely turn out to be true, some not. I just do not know which is which as yet. Although, at present, it does not matter much to me what is myth and what is true.

Today's myth is that of the pilot who protects the sky over Kyiv, "The Ghost of Kyiv" as they call it. No-one knows exactly how many Russian planes he has shot down, but he is still flying and the Ministry of Defence of Ukraine assures us that he is a real and not an invented pilot. In any case, he has fallen already into the history of Ukraine.

If his plane is shot down by the Russians and crashes somewhere, then sooner or later either a child with a sapper shovel or a tractor driver with a metal detector will stumble upon it. A piece of the aircraft's metal will end up in a museum of the history of Ukraine, where it will take its place next to Bronze Age artefacts found during the Ukrainian–Russian war when trenches were being dug near the city of Mykolaiv.

15.03.2022

"When I cry, I can't speak"

Our nights are still very short. Although the real war seems to be far away, missiles are now hitting western Ukraine with increasing frequency.

At about 2.00 a.m. here in the far west, right on the border with Slovakia, the first siren sounds – a warning of potential shelling or bombing. We do not go anywhere. We just check the news on our telephones. Sooner or later, we fall asleep again. But there will be another siren and more checking of the news before the last air raid warning of the night, which usually sounds at around 6.00 a.m. Then we get up and I start calling friends.

I want to contact my colleague, who, the last I heard, was in the now-occupied town of Melitopol by the Azov Sea. She used to send me messages via Facebook from time to time, but there has been no word from her for several days. I have also lost contact with some friends in Kyiv. They no longer answer their telephone. I do not know where they are or what has become of them.

Our friends, ninety-two-year-old amputee Valentin and his wife Tatiana, have tried to leave Kyiv several times. They could have joined an evacuation train from Kyiv's children's hospital, but they refused. A couple of days ago, they were promised a place on another evacuation train. Since then, they have not been answering their telephones. Did they get out of Kyiv? Uncertainty is the worst thing.

Many of my friends are still on the road. Traffic jams are no longer the cause of delay. Now movement is slow because of the many checkpoints manned by Ukrainian soldiers who ask you whether you have weapons with you. There are similar checkpoints in eastern Ukraine but they are manned by Russian soldiers. They check documents and search cars. Millions of Ukrainians have left their homes. Some are moving from place to place in Ukraine, looking for a place where they feel safe. Others have crossed into Europe. Mercifully, they have been met with kindness. They feel safe, but several times a day they must ask themselves, "when will we be able to return home?"

We are still in Ukraine. If there were no traffic jams, it would be forty minutes by car to the border. But there *are* traffic jams. Cars stand in line for several days at frontier crossings.

Could the whole country pour out over the border? I find the very question alarming. I think the answer is no. It is mostly city dwellers who are leaving. The villagers remain. When they hear explosions, they go down to the cellar where they store potatoes or lie down on the wooden floors of their homes and cover their ears with their hands. Like Nina, who lives in the house next to ours in the village. "If I don't answer the telephone," she told me yesterday, "it means I'm crying. And when I cry, I can't speak!"

I do not cry, but tears have often come to my eyes with the news from Kyiv, Kharkiv, Mariupol. I am not going to cry. I am only getting angrier. I have lost my sense of humour, as I did eight years ago during the time of the Maidan. Afterwards it came back. Whether it will come back this time, I am not sure.

16.03.2022

Keeping Track and Staying Positive

Another sleepless night. But no sirens. I woke up every hour and listened to the silence. Not because I was waiting for a siren to force me out of bed, in order to get dressed and run out into the yard, but because now a night without sirens somehow feels more dangerous, more ominous.

Yesterday, my youngest son installed the air-raid app on my iPhone. It is connected to my location and will wake me up whenever there is an air raid warning – broadcasting the siren directly through my telephone, even if the sound is turned off. My telephone was silent all night.

At 6.00 a.m. Stas called. He is a friend from Kyiv who is now in Lviv preparing a cargo of humanitarian aid for Kyiv. He wanted my advice about where he should send his wife and small children – to Germany or to England? I was thinking about what to say when he said that he did not want to send them to Germany. "Germany is on Russia's side." "Well, not exactly," I said, but Stas had obviously made up his mind, so I explained that they would first have to arrange some documents in Poland, but I did not know where or how to do this.

Having finished that call, I was ready to get up and get on with the day. First I took a double shower, cold and then hot, then a double coffee with milk. If I drink it without milk, my hands start to tremble and I will not be able to work at my computer.

The morning was grey and rainy. It is already springtime. On my walk, yesterday, I passed some private houses and noticed that people had already started pruning their fruit trees.

I do not want to have to spend nervous energy on mundane stuff, but I have to. Two days ago, my old MacBook Air crashed, along with the article I was writing. It was not the first time. Having rebooted, I started to write the article over again and, as if from memory, wrote it pretty quickly, in two and a half hours. I saved it onto a U.S.B. drive, translated it into English and gave it to Elizabeth. She spent a long time editing the text, clarifying the meaning of sentences. Essentially, this is now our routine from morning until late at night.

Our sons have their own routine. Together they help refugees. They are taken to various border crossings, where they prepare food and hand it out to people who are waiting to cross the border. My older son also teaches English to refugee children.

Yesterday, two of my friends told me that they were returning to Kyiv. In Kyiv, Mykola Kravchenko, a publisher friend, sits at his desk in his apartment on the ground floor of a high-rise building near the central railway station. He sits and edits the manuscript of a novel by a young writer from Lutsk. It is called *The Porcelain Doll* and it is about domestic violence. He tells me about it during one of our regular telephone conversations. I cannot help but express surprise.

"Domestic violence? Now!"

"No, I can't publish it now," he says. "But as soon as the war is over, I'll need to have it already typeset and prepared for printing." He says that he wishes he published children's books. "You know, publishers of children's books are sending typesetting to Poland now and to Lithuania, where they immediately print the books in Ukrainian and distribute them to refugee families. Some printers even pay Ukrainian publishers for these books to help them survive!"

This is true. Yesterday, I got a call, not from Poland or Lithuania but from Sweden. They are preparing free electronic children's books in Ukrainian for refugees and have asked for my fairy tales about a hedgehog that no-one strokes. I agreed to waive the rights for this edition. Children need to have a childhood, no matter where they end up living. While I was talking to the Swedish e-publisher, I was also thinking that maybe I could find the time to write a new story for children. Then I chuckled and shook my head. If I cannot even find the time to get on with my novel, how could I write a children's story? I can only write about the war, about what is happening now.

Sometimes memories catch up with me. For some reason, I find it easy to insert them into writing about the war. Maybe this is because throughout my life war has always been somewhere nearby. World War II has always been somewhere near, like the Soviet Gulag and the entire Soviet history. The German fascists killed my grandfather Alexei during World War II, another war. He was killed on the outskirts of Kharkiv near Valki station. He lies there in a mass grave. Above him, Russian soldiers are now again killing Ukrainian citizens in another war. One thought leads to another – the photographs of my grandfather as a young man, that the entire photographic archive from my side of the family is lying in Kyiv and that, if a rocket or shell hits our apartment, everything will go up in smoke – the archive, my library and collection of old vinyl records and our collection of Ukrainian art.

I wonder how I would feel if I found out that my house has been bombed? Perhaps I will not feel anything. In wartime, material things do not seem to matter. Only human life is of real value. We are ready to be left without an apartment, without a house in the village, without money. We can start over. And if we cannot, then our children can. They are younger now than Elizabeth and I were when we started to build our lives from scratch.

All day yesterday I could not get through to my friends Valentin and Tatiana. Finally, at about midnight, I heard from Tatiana, who said that they had just crossed into Poland. She explained that the journey had been very hard and that Valentin was in terrible pain. She added that when Valentin was being lifted into the carriage of the train in Kyiv, his wheelchair disappeared. "Stolen!" Tatiana sobbed, overcome with emotion. "It was an expensive wheelchair, specially designed for amputees." I imagined the crowds on the platforms, everyone pushing in order to get a place on one of the evacuation trains. I doubt that anyone stole that wheelchair. It was probably just pushed aside by people trying to clamber onto the train.

At the border, they found another wheelchair for Valentin, a simpler one. "We've been told we will have to wait ten to twelve hours," Tatiana told me. "The Poles are looking for additional carriages for the journey to Chelm." From there, they will go to Warsaw and from Warsaw to Berlin. Once in Berlin they will head towards Frankfurt, where they are awaited by Valentin's German friends and former colleagues, medical scientists whom Valentin often met at international conferences. Valentin is one of the best anaesthetists in Ukraine. Now he is in pain and without anaesthetics. His right leg was amputated a few days before the start of the war. The wound did not heal for a long time and now, due to the journey, it is bleeding again.

Near to Kyiv, in the village of Klavdiievo, a writer who fled to Kyiv from Donetsk in 2015, has been sitting with his wife in the basement of their house, listening to the shelling overhead. When a shell hit their house, they started to walk to Kyiv but soon realised this was too dangerous a thing to do, so they returned to their basement. Friends managed to organise a car to transport them to Kyiv, but just as the volunteer driver arrived in Klavdiievo, the shelling started again. Now the three of them are sitting in the basement. The car is in the courtyard. The Russian army's shelling of residential buildings in Kyiv and other cities and villages does not seem to follow any discernible schedule. Most often it happens at night and in the early morning, but in some places, bombs and shells fall at all times of day. I really hope that my colleague, his wife and the driver will manage to leave Klavdiievo and reach Kyiv safely. For now, we can only wait.

I have not heard from my friend in Melitopol for several days now. The last thing she had time to report was that Russian F.S.B. agents were going door to door with lists of people they wanted to detain. They were conducting searches and interrogations. A journalist and writer, she is undoubtedly on these lists.

It is still raining outside. Is the sky crying, or just watering the ground in preparation for the sowing of seeds? This should be under way by now but no tractors can be heard in the fields.

Russian soldiers near Kyiv have nothing to eat. They have been allowed by their commanders to rob stores and warehouses. At the beginning of the war, they had food stocks for eight days. These ran out long ago. At the same time, Russian missiles are directed at Ukrainian food depots. The largest warehouse on the outskirts of Kyiv has been blown up. Many tons of frozen meat and other products have been destroyed.

This brings to mind the Holodomor of 1932–3 and that of 1947, when the Soviet authorities killed Ukrainians in their artificial famine. This was their revenge for Ukrainians refusing to join the collective farms. The farmers did not want to give their land and their livestock for public use. Now Putin seems to want to use hunger to force Ukrainians to raise their hands and surrender, to stop defending their cities and villages. But this tactic will not work. Ukrainians did not give up even when they were not free – after World War II the partisan war against Soviet power in Ukraine continued until the early 1960s. Ukrainians will not now give up, especially after thirty years of free and independent life. Nobody here wants a return to the U.S.S.R. or to the modern Russian Gulag, where hundreds of Ukrainians and Crimean Tatars are already incarcerated.

Captured Russian soldiers say they were allowed to fire on civilians. On YouTube, there are videos of executions of unarmed people, executions of carloads of refugees, and executions of residents. The same residents whose apartment blocks were the target of the Russian rocket launchers that Russia had prepared in case of a war with the U.S.A.

Some people seem to need an extra rush of adrenaline to live a normal life. I do not need this. I would rather be in our village now, watching the onset of spring, the first flowers and cherry blossom. If I were in the village right now, I would visit my neighbours Nina and Tolik twice a day, maybe more often. We would listen to the distant explosions of shells and try to understand which side they were coming from.

The other day Nina told me that, a couple of days before, she had lain on the floor and cried when Russian planes were bombing the neighbouring village of Stavische. She is in a better frame of mind today. The explosions seem to be further away. Her sister and brother-in-law have finally escaped from Kyiv and they have already reached Khmelnytskyi. Soon they will be in western Ukraine.

It was more-or-less quiet here last night. The Russian army is trying to gain a foothold in the east of the country. The city of Mariupol is facing constant bombing, which is now practically in ruins, but there are still tens of thousands of inhabitants hiding in the rubble. Two columns of private cars, each with two thousand vehicles, are said to have been allowed to leave Mariupol. So far, this is only a rumour and there has been no official confirmation. It has been confirmed that children from Kyiv's oncology wards have already left Ukraine and are being taken to Switzerland, where they will continue their treatment.

In recent days, it seems to me that every European country has taken on a human face. I would like to say thank you to all countries that have expressed their readiness to accept

Ukrainian refugees. European and world solidarity exists. This is a nice thought for bedtime.

23.03.2022

Bills and Animals

Today I finally paid the electricity, gas and Internet bills for our village house. It is empty and there is no-one to use either the Internet or the electricity. It has been announced that there will be no fines for people who do not pay their utility bills on time, but I want to support the utility services. They must survive to see a return to normal life. If no-one pays their bills during the war, there will be no salaries for the employees of the gas service and electricity utilities, which means their life will become a double hell.

Many people now buy and pay for what they do not need because they know it helps others. Thousands of people buy online tickets to the zoo in the city of Mykolaiv. The zoo is closed, shelled by Russian artillery. There are no visitors. But the animals are there and they need to be fed. This charitable ticket-buying allows the zoo to buy animal feed at this difficult time.

Animals in Ukraine have become victims of the Russian army along with its people. In Hostomel, Russian shells hit a stable. A fire broke out inside and burned the horses alive. A rocket killed two chimpanzees and a gorilla at the Kharkiv zoo. Shells hit a small zoo near Kyiv and some of the animals escaped into the forest. Local authorities appealed to all residents not to touch the deer in the forest and, more critically, not to hunt them. Ukrainian hunters have not hunted animals for a whole month now. If they hunt, then it is only for Russian occupiers.

There are almost 700 thousand hunters in Ukraine. They have 1.5 million registered rifles and carbines in their hands. They are already in the war. One hunter in the Chernihiv region approached some Russian soldiers with a grenade in his hand and then detonated it. He died along with several Russian soldiers. Elsewhere, hunters have ambushed the Russian infantry in the forests.

While hunters go after Russian soldiers, the Russian army is busy with more sinister activities. They continue to destroy deliberately food and medicine warehouses. First it was the largest warehouse of frozen food was destroyed by Russian missiles in the Kyiv suburb of Brovary. Then the wholesale warehouse of fruits and vegetables was destroyed. In Sievierodonetsk, near Luhansk, a large food warehouse was also destroyed. Near Kyiv, in the long-suffering town of Makariv, Russian troops blew up the largest medicine warehouse. Russian planes have also bombed the bridge across the Desna River, over which the humanitarian aid was transported from Kyiv to Chernihiv.

It is beginning to feel like attempted genocide. The deliberate destruction of cities and infrastructure, the blocking of humanitarian aid, as well as the efforts to ensure an artificial famine in Mariupol, Manhush and other cities. Unlike in the 1930s, today it is impossible to kill thousands of people in secret without anyone in the world knowing about it. Now everything is being done in front of the whole world. In this situation, it is strange to hear questions from foreign, most often German, journalists who ask, "Are you already discussing with your Russian fellow writers how you will communicate after the war?"

Peace-loving Europe, it seems, has not yet realised the full horror of what is happening in Ukraine. Ukrainians have more than merely realised what is happening. The horror has passed through our blood vessels, our veins, our nerves, our bones and muscles. The horror has taken its place firmly in the minds and bodies of Ukrainians. Anything Russian now causes only hatred.

Yes. I am filled with hate too. Yet I do not give up reading my favourite Soviet writers, with whom I grew up. I do not reject Mandelstam or Andrei Platonov, Boris Pilnyak or Nikolai Gumilyov. Most of them were shot by the authorities. Today, they would probably just be thrown out of the country with the stigma of being an "enemy of the people", rather than shot.

In Russia, they print portraits of those who do not agree with Putin's policy, with Russia's aggression on Ukraine. Over these portraits, they print in bold letters, "Enemy of Russia" or "Traitor". One such "traitor" is Boris Akunin, who lives in London, another is the singer Andrei Makarevich, who is still living in Russia. A few others have also become traitors, but the majority of Russian cultural figures remain Putin patriots and support the war in Ukraine. I am not interested in them, just as I am not interested in the whole of today's Russian culture. I know who is who in today's Russia, but I do not enter into discussions on such topics. My time is now too valuable to be wasted on these matters. I do not know how much time I have left. I consider myself entitled to decide for myself which questions to answer and which questions to ignore.

Displaced Lives

A couple of days ago, I cooked a proper dinner for the first time since the start of the war. We had guests – my publisher from Kharkiv, Alexander and his driver Ivan. They were actually guests of guests and I probably should have informed the owner of the apartment that others would be staying a couple of nights with us, but, to be honest, these are not the first extra guests we have had here. A week or so ago forty-six-year-old Vladimir spent the night with us. We do not know anything about him except that he was being evacuated from Ukraine along with other people who need regular kidney dialysis. The border guards had not let him out of the country because, as a man of conscription age, he lacked the right documentation from the military enlistment office. It was already late afternoon when he was turned back at the border and Vladimir had nowhere to go. Our son, who was helping at the border crossing, brought him to our place for the night. Vladimir spent most of the next day at the military enlistment office. He managed eventually to get a certificate stating that he was not liable for military service and so could go abroad. That evening our son saw him across the border. Vladimir is already in Germany and has caught up with neighbours from his Ukrainian hospital ward.

Vladimir had slept on an air mattress on our floor and that is where my publisher and his driver slept too. We had a very good time during that dinner and even drank some wine. In the shelter of our evacuee town, it is already possible to buy beer and wine, although stronger alcoholic drinks are still prohibited. In my publisher's "shelter" village you cannot buy any kind of alcohol at all. It seems each region has its own rules on this sort of thing.

We sat around the small kitchen table talking until one in the morning. From time to time, Alexander called his wife. She is almost twelve hundred kilometres away in Dnipro, looking after her elderly parents. It is still relatively safe there, but it would be difficult for them to leave Dnipro if it did become unsafe. Their sons and their sons' families are in other cities, scattered across the country like dandelion seeds.

Our family has also been torn apart. There are just three of us now: me, my wife and our older son. We continue to keep in touch with the rest of our family.

It was still daylight when my publisher called his friend, who lives in the most dangerous district of Kharkiv where every third building has already been damaged or destroyed. The telephone connection was not very good. Alexander's friend went out onto his balcony to try and get a better connection and immediately Alexander could hear on the telephone the sounds of distant cannonade of artillery fire. "Yes," said the friend in Kharkiv, "the shelling goes on continuously and yet there are still children playing in the yard".

We called our friends in Kyiv and Ivano-Frankivsk. "How are you?" Sounds like a stupid question, but you have to ask it. Everyone is still alive – at least the ones we could get through to.

My publisher and his driver have since left for their village, in the direction of Chernivtsi. I hope they were able to relax a bit with us. Now we have a friend of my older son sleeping on the floor. He was living in a refugee centre 20 kilometres from us, but it was cold and the conditions were Spartan. I do not know how long he will stay with us, nor do I know how long we will continue to live in this small but cosy apartment. Nobody is rushing us. Our hostess, who now lives with her daughter, has not once asked us how long we intend to stay.

Last night I was awoken three times by air raid warnings. I now understand how these warnings are activated for the different regions of Ukraine. As soon as a ballistic or other missile takes off from the Black Sea, Russia or Belarus, Ukrainian electronic intelligence stations determine the direction of the flight and turn on sirens along the entire "flight path" of the missile. Nobody knows where it will fall, but all the villages and towns along its entire trajectory will hear sirens. My friends in Lviv no longer pay any attention to the warnings and no longer run out of their houses to look for bomb shelters. They are tired of being afraid.

The disappearance of fear is a strange wartime symptom. Indifference to your own destiny sets in and you simply decide that what will be will be. Still, it remains hard for me to understand the attitude of parents who allow their small children to play nearby to a multi-storey building while shells are hitting other buildings not so very far away. Is it possible to think this way about your own children too – what will be, will be?

More than one hundred and fifteen children have died already in Ukraine at the hands of the Russian military. These are the confirmed figures. The unconfirmed number is several times higher. Entire families, including their children, were killed by Russian tanks and artillery as they fled by road to western Ukraine, as they were too when fleeing from the war-torn cities in the south and east of the country. The streets of Mariupol are still littered with the corpses of civilians, both children and adults. Many bodies lie under the rubble of bombed houses. The Russian military commander responsible for the siege of Mariupol is the same colonel who only recently commanded the sieges of Syrian cities. It is therefore quite appropriate to compare the siege of Mariupol with that of Aleppo.

In the occupied territories, Russian troops only allow the civilian population to leave the city via roads leading in the direction of the separatist "republics". Those who dare to leave the ruined city through this corridor are trapped: the Russian military takes away their Ukrainian passports and other documents, puts them on buses and takes them into Russia. There they are given a paper "permit" obliging them to stay in Russia for two years and are then sent to Siberia and the Far East, where the local populations have been dwindling for years. There is no work to be had there, only dozens of empty towns and villages. In this manner, the Russian military has also "evacuated" the orphanages in the occupied parts of Ukraine, taking the children into Russia. Tracing these missing children, so that they can return home to Ukraine after the war, will be very difficult.

More and more children are travelling on their own towards Poland, Slovakia, and Hungary. They carry small backpacks and have notes sewn into their jackets, on which are written the telephone numbers of their parents, the names of the children and the names and addresses of the places where the children hope to stay. Many families who leave take other people's children with them, helping to make sure that all the seats in their car are occupied. Every empty seat in a car travelling to the west represents a life that might have been saved.

Over the past three weeks, almost all the foreign students have escaped from Ukraine. They are no longer to be seen at the train stations or the border posts. I hope they have made it home by now, returning safely to Algeria, Cameroon, India or Jordan, or wherever their home is. Meanwhile, Ukrainian students have started to study online again, this time not because of the pandemic but because of the war. This is necessary because all the university campus dormitories in Lviv, Lutsk, Uzhhorod and Ivano-Frankivsk are now occupied by refugees rather than students. At the start of the war, the dormitories were used to house any refugee needing shelter. Later, when accommodation became very scarce, the men were evicted from the dormitories and only women and children were allowed to stay. Many men had to leave their families to find accommodation in other, less crowded places – mostly this has meant going east. This is also the direction others are taking. More than 400 thousand men have returned to Ukraine from abroad during the past three weeks. Mostly, they have come home to defend the country.

Those who do not care so much about the fate of Ukraine are still trying to leave. Among this number are members of the parliament from the pro-Russian parties. This includes the Surkis brothers, who are both oligarchs and owners of the famous Kyiv football club "Dynamo". They arrived at the border in expensive cars, along with their adult grandchildren and a Russian citizen who was accompanying them. At Ukrainian customs, they stated that they were not carrying anything of value. However, when they entered Hungary, they declared more than seventeen million dollars in cash. Now they will have no way back.

The Ukrainian relatives of the former Russian Prime

Minister and sort-of President, Dmitry Medvedev, also tried to leave Ukraine for Romania, but their two Rolls-Royces were stopped by Ukrainian border guards. They were also found to have huge sums of dollars in cash on them and so they were prevented from leaving Ukraine, at least with the dollars and Rolls-Royces.

The people who are fleeing the country are not indifferent to their own fate. That is why they leave. They are driven by fear for themselves or for their children. They leave behind all their real estate and the graves of their parents and relatives. Ordinary refugees I hope will return, but some, like the Surkis brothers and Viktor Medvedchuk, will have to keep running.

Medvechuk is another oligarch and friend of Putin who will no longer be able to live in his villas near Kyiv and Odesa. He and people like him will have to move to Russia or Israel. Since 2014, many "defectors" have already settled in these countries. Officially, there is an entire "government of Ukraine in exile" in Moscow. It is headed by former Prime Minister Mykola Azarov. Some members of this "government" have settled in the annexed Crimea, like former education minister Dmitry Tabachnik. All these people are long forgotten in Ukraine. I imagine them to be like dusty old statues. It is even strange to think that they are still alive. They simply belong to a past era, a very distant one.

Developments in Ukraine have been impossibly fast-paced. We seem to live at a speed three times that of the Germans or the French. During the thirty years since independence, our country has passed through several times more upheavals than any other European country.

"You're walking too fast!" says my wife, Elizabeth, when

we go for our daily walk. I don't think I have always walked like that. I call my friends and my brother. "You are short of breath," my brother says. "Walk slower! You can't speak properly when you walk like that." I promise to slow down. But I soon start walking quickly again, as if I were late for a meeting, which I am not, though I always try to be punctual.

I make a careful note of all the requests I receive for interviews and then get in touch with the journalists at the agreed time. From Monday to Friday, journalists from all over the world call me. I try not to let any interview last more than half an hour. Thirty minutes is easily enough time for me to explain the most important things that are happening in Ukraine. On Saturday and Sunday, I get very few calls. Journalists, it seems, take the weekend off. They are resting. At first, this surprised me. Now it does not. Let them rest; it allows me time to write down what I hear, see and learn.

Before too long, these weekday calls from journalists will probably grow less frequent as their interest wanes. The war nevertheless goes on without a break. The numbers of dead and wounded increase, the numbers of bombed villages, towns, and cities rise. Each day's news resembles that of the day before: the Russian army digs in, begins to defend the already captured territories, carries on bombing cities that have already been destroyed.

What will happen next? Putin hopes to defeat Ukraine and organise a parade of the Russian army in Kyiv. This is unlikely to happen. He continues to send reinforcements to Ukraine from all regions of Russia. He also promises to send sixteen thousand soldiers from Assad's Syria and has promised to pay them a good salary in dollars. So far, there are no Syrians on the territory of Ukraine. The Chechens sent by Ramzan

Kadyrov to seize Kyiv are almost all gone. Some were killed, others returned home with the body of the commander of the Chechens, General Magomed Taushev, who was killed near Kyiv.

In Russia, dead soldiers and officers have been buried in cities and villages in every region of the country. Yet the people still support Putin's war against Ukraine. Only the mothers of the dead cry. And though they cry for their lost sons, they do not protest against the war, as that would be unpatriotic. The dead are awarded medals posthumously. Their parents are told that they died heroes. No-one asks, why did they die?

During World War II, there was a slogan in the Soviet Union that said, "For the Motherland, for Stalin!" The soldiers who died did so for the U.S.S.R. and for Stalin. This was when the Soviet Union was defending itself against fascism. Now the Russians are dying, "For the Motherland, for Putin". Ukrainians die only for their Motherland, for Ukraine. Ukrainians do not have a tsar to die for. Nobody here thinks that he is fighting for Zelensky. We have never had and hopefully never will have a cult of personality, nor an authoritarian regime. Ukraine is a country of free people. These people will save Ukraine and defend Ukraine's freedom.

28.03.2022

Time to Sow Wheat

In Ukraine, the sowing campaign has begun. In villages where no explosions or gunfire can be heard, farmers go out to work the soil. Farmers near to battlefields can only watch nervously, their fields littered with burnt-out military hardware and unexploded shells. Yet they also want to get going with the spring routine. At great risk to themselves, some have even made a start. My friend Stas, who sells Dutch seeds to Ukrainian farmers, has returned to Kyiv having taken his wife and children to western Ukraine. He called to say he was working with farmers in the Kyiv region.

In Russia, the sowing season will also begin soon. It will, of course, be easier for Russian farmers to prepare their soil and to plant their crops. They will work in safe fields. For Ukrainian farmers, such work is now associated with a risk to life. Russian troops have long used up newly produced shells and missiles. Now they are firing shells and mines from old stocks, up to forty per cent. of which fail to explode. These dud missiles plough through the soft Ukrainian soil and lie buried a metre or much more beneath the surface, depending on the type of soil. The shells stay where they fell until someone accidentally disturbs them.

Some Ukrainian farmers have long been aware of these dangers. Since the start of the war in the Donbas in 2014, farmers there have had to bury colleagues who have been blown up in their own fields during the sowing season or harvest time.

Ukrainian farmers are gaining an interesting reputation. Recently, in the farmyards of one village in Zaporizhzhia region, the police found and confiscated eleven Russian tanks and a good many other enemy weapons. The police promised that after the war the farmers would be punished for driving off with the tanks while not informing the Ukrainian military about their finds. There is an ancient peasant proverb in Ukraine, "In a village farmyard, you can find a use for everything!" This is the attitude that probably inspired them to act as they did. The Russian soldiers had abandoned their tanks and weapons and fled into the forest when their column came under heavy shelling. They never went back for their tanks and most likely they have either now surrendered or made their way back to their own lines. I wonder what kind of reception they will have received?

Once the war is over, I can imagine that many farmers will try to keep the remaining tanks, cannons and other Russian weaponry – that is, if they have not already taken them apart and sold the metal for scrap.

Stories like these raise your spirits. It becomes possible to imagine an imminent victory. You begin to fantasise: what day will be celebrated as Victory Day in Ukraine? Ukraine has already abandoned the Soviet Victory Day of May 9, although a few Ukrainians, especially those of the older generation, continue to celebrate it. Others have switched to the European Day of Remembrance, May 8. But after this war, a new victory day or day of remembrance will definitely be instituted. World War II will cease to be the last important war for Ukraine.

Still, we have to admit that the news about the war is not always encouraging. Every day we learn about more soldiers and officers killed, about murdered refugee families, including those whose cars were shot at by Russian tanks. Every day someone on Facebook posts a photograph of their deceased relative, husband, brother. Every day there are new widows and orphans, for whom this war has completely crossed out not only their present life but also their future.

I still call my friends and acquaintances every morning. I also talk to our neighbours in the village of Lazarevka. They tell me that they can still hear explosions around the clock, though these sounds are now more distant than they once were. Ukrainian troops have pushed back the Russian invaders by some 30 to 50 kilometres from Kyiv. In some places, they have retreated as much as seventy kilometres. The region of fighting is now located between Kyiv and Zhytomyr, near to the town of Korosten.

"We've got some sunshine!" Nina tells me, as she stands in her front yard, watching her hens pecking at crushed corn. "It's warm during the day, fifteen degrees Celsius. I have already raked the leaves from the garden. The garlic I planted in the autumn is already sprouting. The cherry blossom is about to bloom. In a month, we will plant the potatoes." There is not so much fear in her voice now. The Russians did not enter the village; they drove past on their way to Kyiv. But they did bomb the village of Stavische, the turn-off point on the highway from Kyiv through which we all pass to reach our homes in the countryside.

Nor did Russian troops fire on or enter Brusyliv, six kilometres from Lazarivka and the nearest town. On the Brusyliv community Facebook page, residents ask where they can buy petrol and live chickens, or which shops have sugar. Refugees are looking for an inexpensive house to rent. One man offers his services to repair refrigerators.

Soon the locals will be completely absorbed with agricultural work. They will no longer pay attention to the distant sounds of explosions and artillery fire, unless the noises start to become louder yet again – or the Russian military go on the offensive said to be against Kyiv.

And this is quite possible. Russia is once again sending trains with military equipment and soldiers towards Ukraine and Belarus. It is pulling mothballed Soviet equipment out of army depots – old Soviet-made tanks and trucks, guns and personnel carriers. All these things are being sent towards Ukraine, together with more soldiers.

My hopes are placed on Russian military corruption. I have read that a great deal of equipment stored in the warehouses of the Russian army has been stolen and sold. Russian officers and soldiers know all about the price of precious metals and where to find them in military equipment. Any silver or other metals used in military radio and radar stations will have been pulled out long ago. They dismantled the engines of mothballed trucks and sold the bits as spare parts to the civilian owners of similar models of vehicle.

The other day I read in the news that the commander of a Russian tank unit committed suicide. At first, I assumed that he had shot himself because he did not want to kill Ukrainians. But the reason turned out to be quite different. Out of the eight tanks with which his unit was supposed to set out on a mission, only one was in a condition in which to leave the base. The rest were in disrepair. His suicide is most likely the outcome of his having to take responsibility for the state of his tanks.

We have a small garden and we hope that we can plant potatoes and carrots for ourselves. For us it is a hobby, but what kind of hobby can you have during a war? If the Ukrainian army manages to drive the Russian military away from our region, we will try to return to Lazarevka, to live a normal life again. Although the term "normal life" now seems but a myth, an illusion. In actuality, there can be no normal life for my generation now. Every war leaves a deep wound in the soul of a person. It remains a part of life even when the war itself has ended. I have the feeling that the war is now inside me. It is like knowing that you live with a tumour that cannot be removed. You cannot get away from the war. It has become a chronic, incurable disease. It can kill, or it can simply remain in the body and in the head, regularly reminding you of its presence, like a disease of the spine. I fear I will carry this war with me even if my wife and I some day go on holiday – to Montenegro or Turkey, as we once did.

This war has introduced me to other writers who carry war inside themselves. I now have many such friends, including the writer Ferida Durakevich from Sarajevo and the Armenian–Ukrainian artist Boris Yeghiazaryan, whose studio, along with all his early paintings, was burned down in Yerevan by supporters of the Soviet Union during the events of 1991. And all those Ukrainians, of course, known to me or as yet unknown, who are willing to share their war with both me and the world, even as I am sharing this war with you.

Will I ever be able not to write about the war? Maybe. I will definitely be able to write children's books in which there are no wars. But Ukrainian children will have their own war inside them. For small children, who do not yet understand what is happening, the war will be smaller and, I hope, for them it will be possible to recover from it. Older children will have a larger war and it will stay with them for life, especially if they witnessed destruction, if they lost friends or family, if they have had to run away from it. This is true also for all those who can look back and remember life as once being serene and happy, a life that has been left behind us.

30.03.2022

Bees and Books

I miss Kyiv, but I miss our village even more, especially now that the spring is coming. It is warmer there and in spite of the distant sounds of explosions, the birds will be singing. Soon there will be blossom on the trees. I follow the life of the village on Facebook, I read my neighbours' messages on Viber in the village group chat. I know their news.

A couple of days ago in Lazarivka, the Bucephalus food store received a delivery of beer and low-alcohol drinks. The shop owner proudly informed everybody about the delivery. Although wine and spirits are still prohibited, everyone knows who makes moonshine in the village. A month ago, when the wartime prohibition was introduced, police visited the houses of moonshiners and asked them to stop production. I do not think it can be stopped. If a person who lives in fear finds that a glass or two of homemade vodka calms him, then moonshine can be safely considered a medicinal tranquiliser.

My second journey out of warring Ukraine and into peaceful and happy Europe is coming to an end. Now it seems that I left Ukraine a very long time ago.

My first journey out of Ukraine since the start of the war was more difficult, both physically and psychologically due to several hours spent in a queue of cars at the border. I thought I had sufficient time and that I should wait in line like everyone else. After three hours of waiting without moving, I began to have my doubts. In the end, I pulled out a letter from the Ukrainian Embassy with a request to assist me and showed it to the border guards. It said that I was the president of P.E.N., a human rights organisation, and that my presence in the U.K. was required so that I could participate in conferences and radio programmes about the situation in Ukraine. The letter worked as it was meant to. I was fast-tracked into Slovakia and there were no further problems.

My second trip across the border was in contrast relatively stress-free. Now I feel like an experienced traveller who can solve complex logistical problems. I am pleased with my car, which is fifteen years old. Without it, I would not have made it to the airport in peaceful Europe on time.

My drive through Slovakia takes me along deserted roads. I notice churches that are quite unlike Ukrainian ones. I become the curious traveller, though my curiosity is a little feigned, not quite genuine. Somehow, I look at these churches and do not feel as if they add anything to my life, to my experience. In normal times, I like to observe new landscapes, someone else's history, someone else's architecture.

While it is also possible for me to get into Europe by car across the Ukrainian–Hungarian border and to then go to the nearest Hungarian airport, that would take a little longer, although not much. I will definitely go through Hungary on a future trip. This will offer a different landscape, a different language on billboards, different houses. I know Hungary a little better than Slovakia, so Slovakia is more interesting to me. At present, however, this interest does not make me think more deeply about Slovakia, its history or its traditions.

I drive with the radio on, listening to a music programme. I understand some of what they are saying. I hear Slovak rock and jazz and I like it. It is different from Ukrainian music, and different from English music too. It is unique, calmer and a bit more gentle – even the rock. It suits the tranquil and undramatic Slovak landscape.

Later, my journey is accelerated. I fly to Vienna, then to London, then to Oslo. In Norway, it is cool. Sometimes it snows. The capital has put up Ukrainian flags. They hang near the city hall, near the building of the Association of Norwegian Artists, in front of other beautiful buildings, all equally strict and severe, though in different styles.

On my first day in Oslo, I met Mikhail Shishkin, a Russian writer who has lived in Switzerland since 1995. We were to take part together in a public event about Ukraine. The organisers had cautiously asked me whether I would be O.K. with this "double act". I said I did not mind. I have known Mikhail for many years. I have visited him in his home. He has long been a critic of Putin and has refused to accept prizes and awards from the Russian government. He is a Swiss writer of Russian origin and he writes in both Russian and German. He has nothing to do with this war, but it is nonetheless very difficult for him to talk about Russia. He still feels guilty, as I do. I cannot help but feel guilty because my native language is Russian and Putin is destroying Ukraine in order to "save Russian speakers and Russians from Ukrainian nationalists". Every time Putin has tried to protect Russians and Russian speakers from Ukrainian nationalists in Ukraine, I have wanted to become a Ukrainian nationalist. Ukraine is full of Ukrainian Russian-speaking nationalists. But Putin does not understand this. He thinks that everyone who speaks Russian in the world should love Russia and Putin, or just Putin because Putin is Russia in today's Russia.

On stage, Mikhail Shishkin states confidently that Ukraine has a future but Russia does not, that Ukraine will win and rebuild itself, while Russia will remain in ruins. I have no illusions about an easy and quick victory, however. Or even about winning. But I have no thoughts of defeat either. Putin does not care about the citizens of Russia. He would send millions to their deaths to fulfil his final dream. He does not feel regret for the Russian economy, which is being destroyed by sanctions. He will go to the end in his war.

And the Ukrainians will go to the end in this war. They are already going to the end. The army command gave soldiers defending the destroyed city of Mariupol the option to leave the city and break through to their own forces, but they refused. They shoot at Russian soldiers and tanks from the ruins. They burn tanks and armoured personnel carriers. They die or get injured.

This has happened before, in 2014, at Donetsk Shostakov-ich Airport. All those who defended it perished in its ruins. They did not want to retreat to safer territory and continue the war from there. Why? After all, if they had moved away, they might have remained alive and could have continued to fight. At some point, apparently the mechanism of self-preservation in warriors is turned off. Instead, there is the confidence that sacrificing oneself for the Motherland is a necessity. Ukraine does not need their heroic deaths but their heroic lives. Especially now.

I fly from Oslo to Paris. There will be two dozen inter-views and one public speech about my novel *Grey Bees* and the war in Ukraine.

Yesterday, I did not after all talk about my novel, but at dinner the conversation turned to bees and the importance of beekeeping in Ukraine. It was surprisingly easy and pleasant to talk about Ukraine and honey, about the thousands of tons of Ukrainian honey which are exported to Europe and other continents. I said that collecting honey from the habitats of wild bees was one of the first crafts our ancestors learnt. They then became beekeepers, learning to make beehives from tree trunks, to which they moved families of wild bees, thereby domesticating them. Later, the ancient Slavs started to sow wheat, make flour and bake bread. As a child, I loved white bread with butter and honey. I still cannot imagine a time when there was already honey but no bread.

Russia continues to destroy food stores and fuel supplies. In Mariupol, among the ruins, more than 100 thousand people are hiding, with nothing to eat. No bread, let alone honey.

In the Ukrainian tradition, it is customary to consider everyone who is engaged in beekeeping as especially wise. Ukrainians also consider bees to be wise insects, the wisest and the most helpful. My novel is about a beekeeper who lives in the Donbas. At first, he protects only his bees during the war – all six hives – because he is himself a bee. He only knows how to work and live according to established rules. He does not know how to make decisions beyond those rules and he is afraid to do so. But the war forces him to make decisions. One of his most important decisions in this novel is to take the bees away from the territory of the war to a peaceful territory and to give them the opportunity to collect pollen in the fields where burnt gunpowder has not settled on everything, where there are no explosions or gunfire.

———

In Ukraine, the time of books has come to an end.

When we became refugees, we left all our books in Kyiv, all except a bible and my latest novel, grabbed by my wife at the last minute. I did not take any other book with me. Now, since my first wartime trip into Europe, I have some books again. I brought back five books in English from London, gifts from my British publisher.

I am now wondering when I will be able to take those books home and add them to my library. At home, my books are mostly sorted by language with separate shelves for English, French, German, Ukrainian. Every few years, I rearrange them to organise them in a different way. I also like to remove from the shelves those books that I will not read again. I give them to charity shops or libraries. I have to make room for new books. As long as you are alive, you cannot help but notice that new books are being written and that some of them are important or popular – and sometimes even both these things.

Nothing is being published in Ukraine right now and I cannot imagine much reading going on among Ukrainians either. I do not read, although I try to. War and books are incompatible. But, after the war, books will tell the story of the war. They will fix the memory of it, form opinions and stir emotions. I do not know if I will write a novel about this war. However, if I was told that the appearance of novels about this war would end it faster, then I would drop every-thing and start writing such a novel.

Among the books that I remember vividly is the novel *Doberdo* about World War I by the Hungarian communist writer Máté Zalka. I liked it very much. It explained a lot about World War I to me. Ever since, I have had the strange feeling that although World War I was over, that World War II was still going on. I think this is because I have not read a single novel about the World War II that shocked me in the way that *Doberdo* did.

I do not know when this war will end. I do not know whether or not it will become a third world war or remain a second or third Russian–Ukrainian one. But I do know that bees have also been its victims, along with books, as well as books about bees, such as my latest novel. You cannot buy it in Ukraine now for three reasons: it was sold out before the war, the publishers cannot reprint it and bookshops as such no longer exist. In Mariupol and cities in other cities in the south and east they were destroyed along with the books; in cities elsewhere in Ukraine, they simply shut down as a result of the war. When they open again, it will mean that peace has come to Ukraine.

When a bookshop opens again in Mariupol, it will mean much more.

06.04.2022

About the War and "Dead" Books

I just spoke on the telephone with friends in Kyiv. Those who left the capital and have since returned are meeting up and are exchanging experiences with those who stayed. Everyone who can, is now trying to return immediately so as to get back to business. The publisher Kravchenko, who never left Kyiv, continues to work on the manuscripts of young writers.

My brother Misha and his wife sit at home with Pepin their cat near the Antonov aircraft factory once more and listen to the silence. At least, this is how my brother explained what they are doing now. Previously, they heard explosions outside the windows of their apartment around the clock. After three weeks of this, they left the apartment for the village 150 kilometres from Kyiv. It was calmer there but also very disturbing. The explosions, while further away, sometimes seemed to be getting closer. So they came home.

More and more people are returning to the capital. Very few are now leaving. The trains run on schedule and there are empty seats even on the most popular routes – those going west. The city's mayor, Vitali Klitschko, has asked people not to be in a hurry to return. Time is needed to solve the problems with the food supply, transport and healthcare. I know that it is already possible to get to our village from Kyiv by bus, but the route is very difficult, along rural roads. Only the departure time is announced as no-one knows how long the journey will take.

Friends who have returned to Kyiv complain that as soon as the ban on strong alcohol was lifted conflicts broke out in the supermarkets. Apparently, no-one had changed the price tags in the vodka and whisky departments since the beginning of the war, when the prohibition on alcohol was first imposed. During this time, prices of all other products rose significantly and their price tags were updated, but the alcohol section had simply been cordoned off and their price tags forgotten about. The day before the lifting of the ban on the sale of alcohol, prices were raised but nobody had time to change the price tags. Accordingly, tired and stressed shoppers got some nasty shocks at the check-out.

There are still many fewer cars on the streets of Kyiv than before the war. This makes it less dangerous for inexperienced, young drivers to take lessons. Teenagers, who stayed in Kyiv, have earned themselves a bad reputation with soldiers at military checkpoints, where all cars must stop so that documents and car boots checked. These young drivers often stop their old cars clumsily, stalling the engine, especially if the car is old. The soldiers are then obliged to help push-start the vehicle to clear the way for others.

Large removal trucks are a more frequent sight on the streets of Kyiv than they have been for a very long time. They are there to clear out the contents of the apartments of people who have fled the city and who have no realistic plan of returning. They also pick up and evacuate the expensive cars that survived the beginning of the war in underground parking lots or garages. It seems to me that the richer the owners of apartments and cars are, the more they are afraid to return. Then again, they are more likely to have somewhere else comfortable to live.

The German embassy is among those paying for these "extreme" removal services in Ukraine. All the furniture has been taken out of their neat, grey building. It does not look as if they plan to come back anytime soon. The German Ministry of Foreign Affairs is also funding the removal of their diplomatic staff's furniture and property, while lease agreements on apartments rented by their diplomats are being terminated. Even as the Germany embassy is moving out, the Turkish embassy is returning in full force. I am unsure whether it is appropriate to talk about the real estate market in Kyiv while a war is going on. Real estate becomes something ephemeral at this time; it not only loses its value, it loses its form, volume, and meaning.

For Ukrainians, a strange connection to their homes often remains even among those whose house or apartment has been destroyed by the Russian army. The Ukrainian domestic gas service has continued to send out reminders about meter readings and payments. Confused people have been asking questions on utility service websites: "What if the apartment no longer exists? Do I still have to pay if the house is destroyed and the gas meter was damaged by the explosion?" The utility companies respond with an uncommon degree of flexibility: "Submit the last meter reading. Act according to the situation".

Giving the last meter reading of a house that no longer exists is like pronouncing the date the house died. Every house has a date of construction, a date of birth. For tens of thousands of houses and apartments, Russia has brought about the date of their death, the day when all the meters stopped: water, gas, and electricity. And all life stopped.

Kyiv has been relatively lucky so far. But nobody knows if this luck will last.

For two years, my brother Misha has been renting out the apartment of our late parents. The tenants, a young family with two small children, are very careful and always pay the rent on time. Before the war, the tenant's wife took the children to visit their grandparents in Donetsk region. Now she is in an occupied town, sitting in a basement, hiding. The husband has gone to the front as a volunteer and is now fighting. There is no-one in the apartment. But the husband continues to send the rent to my brother's bank account. My brother told him not to pay until the war is over, but the tenant insists. He says that he wants to come back to the apartment after the war and to continue to live in it.

God bless him. I very much hope that he will return and that his wife and children will return with him. Perhaps, she will move her parents into this apartment as well? It will be a squeeze, but as we have all recently learned, cramped conditions are not offensive conditions.

Meanwhile, Ukraine is going to confiscate the property of Russian citizens and collaborators. Two palaces belonging to Viktor Medvedchuk, the leading pro-Russian Ukrainian politician and friend of Putin, have already been shown on television. In the grounds of one palace, hidden behind three fences, they found railway tracks and on them his personal "presidential" passenger carriage – much more luxurious than one on the Orient Express. Twenty years ago, Medvedchuk dreamed of becoming president of Ukraine. He understood that he would never win a general election, so he tried to change the electoral system in such a way that the president was elected not by the people but by parliament. This did not work out as he intended.

In the carriage, which is now subject to confiscation, there is some very expensive furniture. Everything is gilded. In the cupboard there are crystal glasses in silver holders for drinking tea. The glass holders are adorned with a golden double-headed eagle, symbol of the Russian Empire. Television cameras have already looked into all the halls and rooms of Medvedchuk's palaces. I am struck by the complete absence of books: not a single bookshelf, not a single bookcase. But there is a separate large room for storing his wife's fur coats. Oksana Marchenko, a T.V. presenter and another friend of Putin, also had a collection of fur hats and caps all displayed on mannequin busts.

I have already seen on T.V. many such palaces, with similar expensive furniture and huge indoor pools and fences five metres high. That of the former prosecutor general Pshenka did have a bookcase in his office. In it, among other books, was one of mine. I felt a little scared to see my book there. I definitely did not sign it for him, I never met him and I cannot even understand where he got it from? Maybe my novel's presence on his bookshelves was for journalists, who were invited to his place, to show that the prosecutor general was aware of what was happening in modern Ukrainian literature. And what is happening in modern Ukrainian literature now? This is an interesting question that is not easy to answer.

Most Ukrainian writers have become refugees, certainly almost all those who lived in eastern and central Ukraine. Some have become refugees for the second time and have now gone abroad. Mykola Semena, a seventy-year-old journalist and writer, went to Poland after being taken from Crimea two years ago. The Russian authorities had wanted to imprison him for disagreeing with the annexation of Crimea. He is now in a country whose language he does not know. A poet from Luhansk, Iya Kiva, is in Poland too. She writes on Facebook that she feels like a homeless dog that no-one wants. Both are members of Ukrainian P.E.N. and receive financial support from P.E.N., but no amount of financial support can diminish the feelings of homelessness of those in exile. The homeless writer is the bearer of a trauma that is very difficult to cure.

Most writers, intellectuals, and artists have now gathered in Lviv, a city that has long been the cultural capital of Ukraine. Here the bookshops are open, although they have few customers. The war has pushed books and literature in general into the background. Writers now write newspaper columns, broadcast radio programmes and participate in informational projects. There are those who have stayed in Kyiv and write from there about life during the war. There are also those who have joined the armed forces. And then there are those who are no longer – those who have died at the front. Among them, is the poet and activist Yuri Ruf.

For the second time in a month, my publisher Alexander Krasovitsky came to visit me in Transcarpathia. We sat and talked about books and the war. His publishing house is in Kharkiv. All the windows in the building were smashed when three rockets exploded in the yard. There is no-one there now, but the computer system is working and his editors are still able to connect to it, working remotely. Alexander continues to prepare books for printing in the future so that his staff can work and be paid. At his printing house, there are about 60 thousand printed books, many still waiting to be bound. However, he has no access to the printing house. It is in the town of Derhachi, located between Kharkiv and the Russian border. The town is twenty-four hours a day under bombardment.

Among the books that he has already finished is one by a Russian historian, Mark Solonin, a political émigré living near Kyiv. The book is about the second Soviet–Finnish war, better known to historians as the Continuation War. I know nothing about this second war, although I do know quite a lot about the first Soviet–Finnish war of 1939 when Finland courageously defended its borders and did not allow itself to be occupied – although it did lose part of its territory, the bit that became Soviet Karelia. In some ways, the current war reminds me of the Soviet–Finnish war. Putin's plans to occupy Ukraine have failed, but the end of the war is far off and no-one will undertake to predict either the result of this war or the date of its end.

Solonin's book may perish under bombardment by the same army about which it was written. The first ten copies were sent to him, as per the contract, but the remaining copies of the book are out of reach and may find themselves in occupied territory. In which case, they will most likely be destroyed because the story that Solonin tells in his book does not coincide with the official history of the Soviet Union. Although Solonin spent years researching the book in the Russian military archives prior to writing it, everything that does not coincide with the official history in Russia is liable to be erased. The book will either be read by Ukrainian readers after the war or it will be destroyed by the enemy.

I cannot imagine life without books, but in Kyiv the book-shops are still closed. One of them, that on Lysenko Street and the one closest to my apartment, could have reopened by now. That it did not do so was for a rather an odd reason. It is located in the basement of a five-storey residential building just up the road from the Opera House. People who live in this house, remembering how Russians destroyed Mariupol Theatre, asked the store manager for permission to spend the night there safe from air raids. They say that the basement of this building was originally designated as a bomb shelter. It was only much later that it was allowed to be privatised and sold. Now the basement belongs to the bookshop and the director refused to let people shelter there. Was he afraid that the books would disappear? The decision is odd. I am friends with the former director and owner of the The Globe Book-shop in Paris, François Dever. Once he allowed emigrants who did not have money for a hotel or hostel to spend the night in his bookshop in Paris. They did not steal anything but they did remember his bookshop for life. Sleeping among books is a form of happiness. It would be an opportunity to escape from panic and fear for at least one night.

In the apartment where we now live there is not a single book by a living author. I think that in the future I will try to sort the books of my library in our village house into books by "living" and "dead" writers, just to see what happens. Doing so does not, of course, make much sense. If the book is read, the writer is alive. Even if he died two hundred years ago.

13.04.2022

Choosing a School for Your Child Has Just Got Harder

Almost half of the population of Ukraine are now refugees or I.D.P.s, that is, internally displaced persons. Many families are far from home. Hundreds of schools and colleges have been destroyed by Russian bombs and missiles. Universities have also been destroyed, although students continue to attend lectures online, just as they did during the pandemic. Sometimes they do not even know the location of their teacher – they could be speaking from Germany or Poland, or even from a bomb shelter in Kharkiv. This is the new reality and it is reflected in all spheres of life.

During wartime, it is much more difficult to get an education. It is much more difficult to focus on getting a place at university, on passing exams. During wartime, students have no idea what they will do after they graduate. Those who are in their first year of studies cannot be sure that they will be able to graduate. There are no guarantees for the future, not for the future of individual students nor for the future of the country as a whole. There is anger at the destruction of hopes and plans and there is hatred of those who have brought this destruction upon us. We can only imagine when this hatred will end, like the passing of a violent storm.

Nonetheless, the future academic life of Ukraine is being planned for. There is a calendar and, accordingly, the educational process continues, both in schools and universities. The calendar dictates that at this time of year, parents of future first-graders should be finalising their choice of elementary school, while schools should be drawing up lists of new entrants. The school year starts on September 1 and there is not much time left. This year, an awful lot could happen before the autumn.

Like parents all over Europe, Ukrainians put a great deal of nervous energy into choosing a school for their child. It is a stressful time. However, because of the war, only parents permanently resident in western Ukraine or in the southwest of the country have the luxury of this predictable and relatively straightforward concern. The number of Ukrainian citizens who have gone abroad is already higher than four million – mostly mothers with their children. Of the sixteen million internally displaced persons, over half are children. And now the parents have to decide to which school, in which village, which city, or even which country, they should send their children.

In Poland and the Czech Republic, schools are already accepting Ukrainian children in large numbers. This is a tall order, as children of all ages arrive in dribs and drabs and mostly speak no Czech or Polish. The schools are recruiting Ukrainian teachers to help with the new arrivals. It will be challenging for all involved.

I.D.P. families that have ended up in Lviv will have an even harder time. Although Lviv is a big city with many schools, there are simply not enough places for all these children. I imagine that places will somehow have to be found, but class sizes will be huge and it will be even more difficult than usual to cater to the needs of individual children, this at a time when their individual needs are likely to be unusually complex.

Meanwhile, the Zhytomyr city department of education has created an online application for first graders. Families from Zhytomyr who are currently scattered throughout western Ukraine and Europe can at least plan for September, but they face a dilemma. Should they stay where they are and send their child to first grade in, say, Hamburg, where no-one speaks Ukrainian? Or should they plan to return to Zhytomyr by the end of August? Although no-one knows how safe it will be to return to Ukraine, especially to the Zhytomyr region, which has already suffered greatly from Russian aggression. Predicting what the situation will be like in late August is impossible.

Despite the obvious danger of a new Russian offensive on Kyiv and other regions of central Ukraine, many people are returning home. Those who have already returned to Zhytomyr demand that the Russian language should no longer be taught in its schools. The Russian language is now associated only with the war and attitudes towards it have hardened, as the attitude of Soviet people hardened towards the German language after World War II. I learned German in 1997, when I was thirty-six, but I think my attitude to it had softened long before that. I am afraid that the hatred of the language and culture of our current aggressor might last even longer.

20.04.2022

The Tale of Rooster Tosha and the War

As soon as the Russian Foreign Minister Lavrov announced that the second phase of the Russian war in Ukraine had begun, several rockets fell on Mykolaiv zoo. Two of them hit the bison enclosure, but did not explode. We can only rejoice at the poor quality of Russian ammunition. It sometimes saves the lives of people and sometimes those of animals.

Ukrainian soil is already "sown" with shells and rockets, many planted deep in the ground. For a long time to come, they will explode periodically, reminding us of this war. In some ways, the Russian aggression against Ukraine is predictable, but in other ways it is strange, even bizarre. For example, during the battles for Mariupol, the well-known jazz pianist Nikolai Zvyagintsev died. He was a soloist with the Donetsk Philharmonic. He was killed by the Ukrainian defenders of the city because he was fighting with the Russian troops.

The personnel department of the Russian army is working hard. After heavy losses in the military units from Russia itself, the army is recruiting as many men as possible from the two "separatist republics" of Donetsk and Luhansk and also from countries where Russia is fighting on the side of local dictators, such as Syria and Mali. The Russian military recruitment office does not have to worry too much about the survival rate among these foreign and separatist soldiers.

Certainly, none of the relatives of killed separatist fighters will dare to complain about their deaths. Several hundred Syrian soldiers from the army of Caliph Haftar were recruited by the Russian "Wagner" mercenary group, flown to Russia, and then transported to Ukraine. They were promised a good salary, but they were not warned about the bad weather. Ukrainian soldiers have been surprised to find Syrian and U.S.A. currency in the pockets of dead soldiers and, sometimes, banknotes from the Republic of Mali.

In Ukraine, too, there are "recruitment surprises" but of a different sort – the entire Ivano-Frankivsk football team, Prikarpattia, along with their coach, signed up to serve in the Ukrainian army. They have been sent off for training. They will only go to the front once they have acquired the skills required for combat.

———

Kyiv is becoming more and more like an awakened beehive. Every day some 30 to 40 thousand people return to the city. Traffic jams on the approach roads to the city sometimes stretch for tens of kilometres. That from the western direction, the Zhytomyr highway, will also soon be open. They have nearly finished building a temporary bridge across the Irpin River. Car owners who have returned to the city very quickly realise that they need to switch to bicycles or electric scooters. There are many roadblocks in the city and a queue in front of each one. In order to drive from the south to the north of the city, you will need to stop several times, showing your documents and opening your car boot each time, as well as answering a few questions if required. Nobody stops cyclists or scooter riders.

I continue to telephone my friends regularly, especially my brother and my neighbours in the village. The villagers have already planted potatoes. Now they are planting onions. Soon they will sow carrots and beetroots. Where there is no war, the rumble of tractors is heard everywhere. There is now a frenzied sowing campaign. The government has asked people to plant vegetables and cereals on every bit of available land. This year a vast area of Ukraine will not be used for agriculture. In the east and south, instead of wheat, the Russian army is sowing death. For this reason, the government has announced its "Victory Gardens" campaign, calling on people to grow vegetables in their flowerbeds and on their balconies. I imagine that this call will be heard. I was planning to plant jalapeño and pasilla peppers this spring. It is good that I managed to give a portion of the seeds I had to friends. I know that they have already planted them in pots at home. I am now far from home, far from those seeds. But someday, I hope sometime soon, I will plant peppers myself in the garden around my village house.

Every time I speak to my neighbour Nina, she asks: "When will you be back? It's sad without you". "Not yet," I reply. I very much want to go back, to enjoy this sunny spring there. It is so beautiful in the village at this time of year. I still remember the wonderful pandemic spring and summer we spent in our village house during the pandemic of 2020.

Nina's seventy-year-old husband has decided not to shave until the war is over. Nina says that he now looks like an Afghan Mujahidin. "Please, send me pictures," I beg. "He doesn't allow himself to be photographed!" she answers. "Well, then, at least send photographs of your cats and dogs." Nina and Tolik still have three cats and three dogs. I miss the visual connection with our village. When before the war, we lived in the U.S.A. for nine months, we often spoke via video link. Nina would walk around the yard, showing me her chickens and roosters, dogs and cats, the lilacs that had just blossomed. Now she has turned off the Internet to save money. Food prices have risen, but her pension has remained the same, about $150 a month. Only the mobile telephone connection remains.

Sometimes it seems to me that Nina spends more on food for dogs, cats, hens and roosters than on food for herself and Tolik. At the same time, she frequently gets angry with the cats and dogs, although never with the chickens. She does not take offense, even if they refuse to lay eggs. It is true that Nina does sometimes shout at the two cockerels. They are very pugnacious and quite often pull out each other's feathers. Nina's cockerels are small, not like the powerful and eagle-like rooster from near Mariupol who has recently become famous on social networks. His name is Tosha and he was evacuated, along with his elderly owner, from a village near the now-destroyed Mariupol. The eighty-five-year-old grandmother had to leave her entire household behind, but Tosha she could not leave. "We survived under Russian bombs together. We both had nothing to eat for weeks! How could I leave him?" she asked. Along with other folk from the surrounding villages and towns, they were evacuated by bus to western Ukraine. The roads were terrible and the elderly woman had to hold on tight to Tosha the whole way to keep him from falling as the bus swerved to avoid potholes. At night, the refugees slept in school gyms, churches, or in local council buildings. And every morning the rooster woke everyone at 4.00 a.m. As some refugees left this group and others joined it, at least one hundred people considered themselves to be "victims" of this too vigorous rooster, Tosha. People did not get angry with him or the old lady, but they posted photographs and recordings of the rooster on Facebook and Instagram with unhappy, but not malicious, comments. Tosha's owner apologised to the worn-out refugees after each of his morning concerts. She could not live without him, she explained and had agreed to be evacuated only on the condition that Tosha could go with her. I do not know where the grandma and the rooster ended up, but I do not suppose they went abroad – it is unlikely that the rooster would have got through passport control or passed customs regulations. In any case, I hope they have found a friendly spot in some western Ukrainian village, where one additional noisy rooster will not be noticed. Meanwhile, the legend of the irksome rooster who took his grandma into evacuation will live on.

The other day I left Ukraine again for a few days. I hoped that I would cross the border easily and quickly but again I waited in a line of cars for four hours. This was not as long a time as previously, but lately I had been able to cross a completely deserted border checkpoint in just a few minutes. It seems that the new phase of the war has provoked another wave of refugees to flee abroad. On the Slovak and Hungarian sides of the border, volunteers are still at work. There are heated tents, where you can eat for free and everyone is presented with a free S.I.M. card for telephone and Internet access. The faces of the more recent refugees seem less frightened by the war than their predecessors of almost two months ago. After the horrors of Bucha and Hostomel, Irpin, and Borodianka, the new refugees think they are lucky – firstly, because they are alive, secondly, because they have made it to the border.

There is still a tent city for Ukrainians at the Bucharest railway station. This comprises several large, warm, orange tents with windows. Nearby there is a café with free food. I looked into one of the tents. There were about fifteen people lying on folding beds. Some were sleeping, some were reading books and some were talking on their mobile telephones. My Romanian friends said that the first refugees from Ukraine did not want to be called refugees and said they did not need to sleep in tents. They arrived with suitcases and went to look for hotel accommodation. They were interested only in how to move on further – to Italy, Croatia, Austria. The next and much larger wave of refugees was very different. They were happy to receive any help and constantly thanked the volunteers. They tried to eat less free food, fearing that others might not have enough. What really struck my Romanian friends was that these refugees did not have suitcases. Many arrived with large plastic bags full of clothes and shoes. It was fairly obvious that they had never needed to think about luggage before. Some had holdalls, but very few had suitcases.

I immediately assumed that these refugees must have been from the Donbas. Residents of the small towns and villages in the Donbas region rarely travel, certainly not as tourists. When there is an economic crisis, they go to the nearest big cities to buy food or clothes. When they do travel, they always carried large, chequered oilcloth bags that are closed with zippers. These bags, which could hold a small diesel generator, are popular not only in the Donbas. Residents of western Ukraine also use them when they go to Poland to sell power tools and to buy clothes and cosmetics for sale in Ukraine.

Once upon a time, such tourist-traders were called "sackers", then "shuttles" and, later, "business-tourists". I remember how my own parents made one such brave but unprofitable "business trip" to Poland in the late 1980s, hoping to sell electric irons and to buy crystal wine glasses. Some glasses remained still in their boxes when we came to clear out their flat after they had passed away. This fairly recent period of Ukrainian history now seems so distant.

In the forced displacement of millions of people, I sense something medieval. This has happened before, when the Tatar-Mongol hordes of Genghis Khan attacked the territory of today's Ukraine. People then had also to drop everything and flee as far as possible towards the west. The west has always been the place of safety for those fleeing from the east. Now the invasion of the Russian hordes is once again pushing Ukrainians to the west. But the refugees keep looking back, both physically or emotionally. They want to go home, even if their homes are no more.

At the beginning of the war, the Russian army managed to capture several towns in the south without bombing or destroying houses. There are still a good many civilians in these cities. Only those who could not agree to live under occupation fled. The rest stayed on. Some take part in pro-Ukrainian demonstrations. The Russian military scares them with machine gun fire aimed above their heads. F.S.B. officers photograph and film them. Local collaborators help the F.S.B. to find out the names and addresses of the activists. Then the activists are taken away for interrogation. Some of them do not come back.

Russian flags hang above all the administration buildings in these towns. The occupiers have introduced Russian rubles and are forcing local businessmen to re-register their businesses in line with Russian laws. Farmers are forced to send their early vegetables to Crimea. In Crimea, Russian T.V. crews film a market and claim that Kherson farmers are bringing their produce to the annexed Crimea. In Crimea itself, they joke that in the near future the occupied Ukrainian region of Kherson will be officially annexed to Crimea.

One of the first towns captured by the Russian army was Henichesk, in the Kherson oblast. There, in front of the city hall, the Russian military has erected a monument to Lenin – not the one that stood there before the Ukrainian policy of decommunisation but another one. They must have brought it with them on the train from Russia, along with the tanks. I am trying to find a logical explanation for the appearance of a monument to Lenin in Henichesk. Maybe the idea is to make the residents think that they are back in the U.S.S.R. Or is this some kind of joke by Putin, who has said that Ukraine was invented by Lenin? As in the Soviet Union, monuments to the "founder of the state" should stand in front of all state institutions. But then why is there no monument to the Tatar–Mongolian Genghis Khan in Moscow in front of the Kremlin or even inside the Kremlin? After all, it was he who practically organised the tax system for his Moscow principality and other Russian principalities. It was Genghis Khan who appointed the local elite as his representatives. It was he who programmed the Russian brain with the belief that the people should be kept in fear and, at the slightest sign of disobedience or disagreement, be severely punished or killed.

Someday Kyiv will present Moscow with a monument to Genghis Khan. The culture of monuments both in Russia and in Ukraine is purely oriental. They serve to mark a geographical or spiritual territory. Ukrainians are proud of the unverified statistic that says there are more monuments to Ukraine's national poet, Taras Shevchenko, than to anyone else in the world. I think that there are many more monuments to Lenin in Russia than to Shevchenko in Ukraine. There are also monuments to Ataturk in every Turkish village.

I do not believe that the monument to Lenin will survive in Henichesk for long, although it is clear that the Russian army will protect it to the last. After all, it was not for nothing that the Russian court sentenced Oleg Sentsov to twenty years in prison for talking about the need to blow up the monument to Lenin in Simferopol. And this despite the fact that, according to the testimony of witnesses, no such conversation took place.

Almost every day, I find more and more parallels between the events of the civil war in Ukraine during 1918–21 and current events. At that time, the Bolsheviks destroyed everything Ukrainian in order to make Ukraine Soviet. Today, the new Bolsheviks bring with them a monument to Lenin and destroy everything Ukrainian in order to make Ukraine Russian. Ukraine has its own history and culture for which it has always paid dearly. Ukraine will resist to the end. Ukrainian hopes and pleas to the West for help to supply weapons is a repetition of what happened in 1918. Then it was Germany which helped Ukraine to remain an independent state for several months. This time Germany is in no hurry to help, but there are other, more reliable partners. So, I do not lose hope that Ukraine will win and that I will be able, albeit not this year but hopefully next, to plant peppers again. And, of course, I will plant pumpkins too. You cannot do without pumpkins in Ukraine. Come the autumn, we will also be able to celebrate Halloween, my sons' favourite festival. This is not the kind of Halloween that Russia has arranged for us now but the more usual one, more fun than anything scary, with monster pumpkins, in the middle of which candles will burn at night.

21.04.2022

Two Months of War
Looking back and Thinking Ahead

In the mornings, I check the weather forecast. I am glad whenever I see that it is raining or snowing in the war zone. This means that the Russian army cannot move quickly and that the mercenaries from Syria and Lebanon, who were brought to Ukraine on Putin's orders, are feeling cold and uncomfortable.

This war gets weirder by the day. The root cause of its weirdness is the Russian military leadership. Putin promised twenty thousand Libyan and Syrian soldiers for the fight in the Donbas, but no more than five hundred have arrived so far. Russian contract soldiers increasingly often refuse to go to war. You might expect them to be obliged to go if they receive orders. But in Russia, this aggression is officially not a "war". Officially, Russia is conducting a "special operation" in Ukraine. As it turns out, Russian soldiers have the right to refuse to participate in "special operations". They are, of course, decommissioned immediately and their military I.D. books are stamped with the words "prone to lies and betrayal".

This stamp will remain in their record for life and will prevent them from returning to military service in the future. But this is hardly a disadvantage! Maybe they will find a peaceful profession.

Russia says it has captured more than seven hundred Ukrainian military personnel and civilians. However, according to Ukrainian official information, more than one thousand civilians have been detained – or rather kidnapped – by Russian forces. The Ukrainian side claims to have captured more than six hundred Russian soldiers, among them many senior officers. The exchange of prisoners is going very slowly. It seems that Russia is not really interested in the return of its captured soldiers. Either that, or Russia simply does not want to part with Ukrainian prisoners of war. For some time now, I have been wondering why this could be. But the other day, in the Russian State Duma, deputy Sergei Leonov, from the Liberal Democratic Party (do not pay too much attention to the name, it has nothing to do with ideology) announced the need to pass a law allowing blood to be taken from Ukrainian prisoners of war for use in the treatment of Russian wounded soldiers and officers. Could this be the reason for keeping hold of Ukrainian prisoners? The practice was employed by Hitler during the Second World War, when blood for German soldiers and officers was taken from concentration camp prisoners.

Even without a war, Russia does not have enough blood for transfusions. The practice of donating blood is unfamiliar and undesirable to most people. Their main problem, however, is a lack of people in general. Since 2014, Russia has been luring residents of the "separatist republics" – as well as refugees from Ukraine – to Siberia and the Far East.

Now tens of thousands of refugees from Mariupol and even entire orphanages from Ukrainian territory occupied by the Russian army are being taken there. No matter how Russia tries to hide its demographic problems, they remain visible. It seems to me that these problems are also one of the main reasons for the Russian aggression. Russia lacks population, just as the Russian army lacks soldiers. Russian military units sometimes capture towns and villages, but then leave them and move on. According to the usual "rules of war", they should have left a garrison and a military commandant's office in each location. They probably expected more support from sympathetic Ukrainians. Collaborators are few and far between and the Russians simply do not have the manpower to maintain control of the territories that they have "taken". Then there is also the Ukrainian partisan movement which, in occupied Melitopol alone, has killed around one hundred Russian soldiers.

Lately, I am beginning to worry a lot about Ukraine's future demographic problems, ones now being created by Russia. How many Ukrainians will return from Europe after the war? What about those whose houses and apartments have been destroyed? Will they stay abroad forever, or will they risk returning? Among the five million Ukrainian refugees who have found shelter in Europe, there are very many families with small children. I cannot see families with children returning if their homes have disappeared. The Ukrainian government must be thinking about this already, but it is clear that the scale of the problem is such that a vast amount of international assistance will be required.

Before the war, the average age of a resident of Russia was a little over forty-two, whereas the average age of a resident of Ukraine was a little under forty-one. After the war, given the loss of Russian troops, the average age of the Russian population is likely to increase a little, but the average age of the Ukrainian population will increase much more because of the number of children who have gone abroad as refugees.

A worsening demographic situation will not be the only negative effect on both countries of Russia's aggression against Ukraine. It will also impact hugely on the economy and on agriculture, on freedom of speech and culture, as well as the provision of medical services and education.

It is possible to say that this aggression has fortified the Ukrainian national spirit. This should benefit the country in the hard years to come and may encourage people to return from emigration. Perhaps it is still too early to consider solutions to all the problems that Russian aggression has created. But the fact that these problems are now being discussed in Ukraine means that Ukrainians believe in their victory. They believe that Ukraine will be able to defend its pro-European course and that Ukraine will remain an independent and democratic state, despite all the efforts of Putin's Russia.

25.04.2022

Culture Goes Underground

In the Uzhhorod Drama Theatre, the play "Agreement with an Angel", based on the work by the Kyiv playwright Neda Nezhdana, had just started when an air raid siren began to howl. The actors froze. The theatre's manager hurried onto the stage and asked everyone to go down to the bomb shelter below the theatre in an organised manner. He added that if the all-clear sounded within the hour, the performance would recommence – if not, a new date for the performance would be announced. Luckily for the audience, the all-clear came forty-five minutes later. They took their places once more in the auditorium and the play was performed, starting from the beginning.

Uzhhorod, the capital of the Zakarpattia Region, is a picturesque town on the western side of the Carpathian mountains. They love coffee and *bograch* here. The latter is a key dish in Hungarian cuisine – a soup comprised of meat, potatoes, carrots and hot peppers. Situated right on the border with Slovakia, the city is within easy reach of border crossings into Hungary and Romania. Together with neigh- bouring Bukovina, on the border with Romania, it is the safest place to be in Ukraine right now. That could change in an instant, of course, but so far not a single rocket has been aimed at the Transcarpathian region. There are proba- bly several reasons for this. The region is small and not very densely populated, although for the present, due to the influx of refugees the population has doubled. There are practically no large cities or military facilities here either. The most likely reason for this "non-aggression" is the high number of ethnic Hungarians who have lived in Transcarpathia for the past several centuries. Hungarian Prime Minister Orbán is Putin's only friend among the European Union leaders. Many Ukrainian Hungarians have both Ukrainian and Hungarian passports. They also have their own "Hungarian" political party, for which they always vote. Having said that, there has never been much of an active political life in the territory. Hungarians are calm, hard-working people who preserve not only their language but also their culture and traditions and, especially, their cuisine. Until 2017, Ukrainian politicians paid little attention to culture in general and made no attempt to integrate the cultures of its national minorities, including Hungarian culture, into the national culture of Ukraine. It is no surprise, therefore, that out of the several dozen Ukrainian authors who write in Hungarian, none of their books have been translated into Ukrainian. As a result, they have remained unknown in Ukraine, except among residents of Ukrainian-Hungarian towns and villages, such as Berehove, Vinogradov, Bono, and Peterfölvo.

In the 2019 presidential election, many Ukrainian Hungarians voted for Volodymyr Zelensky. They could not accept Petro Poroshenko's policies and especially his slogan "army, language, faith", which was aimed at patriotic Orthodox Ukrainians. Hungarians are Catholics. Their native language is Hungarian. Poroshenko had also brought in the law on the state language, which put a stop to the practice of teaching children in the languages of the national minorities. Ukrainian became the only language of instruction in schools and universities. In fact, the Law on the State Language was adopted in order to remove Russian as the language of instruction, the Hungarian language becoming an unintended victim. From that moment on, relations between Ukraine and Hungary deteriorated, while relations between Orbán and Putin improved. The Russian secret services seized on the opportunity to help "improve" these relations still further by organising the arson of the Hungarian Cultural Centre in Uzhhorod. They wanted to blame Ukrainian nationalists for this, but video cameras installed on buildings near the cultural centre interfered with their plans. These video recordings led to the arrest of two Polish citizens who had arrived from Poland to carry out the attack. They had received money for their arson from their Russian minders.

Fortunately, there have been no further provocations. Today, many Ukrainian Hungarians are fighting for Ukraine's independence in the Ukrainian army. There are, of course, those who do not want to fight and who are trying to leave Ukraine on Hungarian passports, but the border guards in Transcarpathia easily distinguish the Hungarian Hungarians from the Ukrainian ones. Ukrainian Hungarian men are not allowed to go abroad until they reach the age of sixty-one according to the law on general mobilisation. The border guards look at the birthplace of the owner of the Hungarian passport. If the place of birth is in Ukraine, then the border guards know that this person is, first of all, a citizen of Ukraine. Dual citizenship is still prohibited in Ukraine.

On the same evening that the theatre performance in Uzhhorod was interrupted, the presentation of a "children's book for adults" by the American writer Adam Mansbach: *Go The F…. .To Sleep* was successfully held in Kharkiv in an underground bomb shelter. The book was presented by its translator, the cult Ukrainian poet, writer and musician, Sergiy Zhadan. While working on the translation, Zhadan was inspired to write a song, which he performed at the presentation together with the Kharkiv rock band "The Village and People". The book has not actually been released yet. Publication has had to be postponed due to the war and is now scheduled for June 13. But those who came to the presentation already know its content: the book is a poem on behalf of an irritated father, whose little daughter cannot sleep.

The war has changed the plans of many publishers.

Flexibility is now essential and they try not to cancel what is planned so that literary and cultural life in Ukraine can continue even during the hostilities. This year Ukraine participated in the work of the Salon du Livre in Paris. The Ukrainian stand presented books by Ukrainian authors translated into French and published there. It was not possible to organise the delivery of books in Ukrainian from Ukraine to France. However, as France accepts more and more refugees – the majority of whom are mothers with children – there will be ever more need for children's books in Ukrainian. The French Ministry of Culture is already considering the possibility of purchasing such books for both children and teenagers for France's libraries. Soon Ukrainian cultural life will be encouraged in France, as well as in many other European countries.

It is almost impossible to preserve one's identity without contact with one's native culture, but Ukrainian refugees in France have an equally important task – to get to know and understand the country that hosts them, to try to learn their language and, of course, to get acquainted with the riches and diversity of French culture. There is much work to be done to facilitate this, but at least the Ukrainians who have made it to France can now begin their orientation in French language and culture – and can do so above ground without fear of interruption from air raid sirens.

26.04.2022

Choosing the Lesser Evil?

When war approaches your home, you are left with a choice – to evacuate or accept occupation. A person starts thinking about this choice well before the first explosions are heard on the outskirts of their city or village. War is like a tornado. You can see it from afar, but you cannot easily predict where it is going next. You cannot be sure whether it will blow your house away or only pass nearby, whether it will uproot a few trees in your garden, or blow the roof off your house. And you can never be sure that you will remain alive, even if the house itself is only slightly damaged.

Several days ago, in a village near Zaporizhzhia, a rocket exploded in a vegetable garden. The house remained intact but the owners, a family of three, died. They were planting something in their allotment, thinking about the future harvest, thinking about what they would eat next winter. There will be no next winter for them nor a next summer. For them, everything ended on April 25.

In Ukraine, it is a common belief that the most delicious apricots grow in the Donbas and that the best cherries grow in Melitopol. Melitopol was called "the cherry capital of Ukraine". But on March 1, the city was captured by Russian army units which invaded Ukraine from annexed Crimea. No-one greeted the Russian military with traditional welcoming gifts of bread, salt and flowers. On the contrary, from the very beginning of the occupation, there were mass protests against the Russian occupation in the city centre. Residents of Melitopol shouted "Go home!"

at the soldiers. They replied, "We are home! This is Russia!"

After a month of daily protests, some residents began to consider evacuating. Many of the protesters had been arrested, beaten up and seen their Ukrainian documents taken away and destroyed by the Russian military, who told them that they no longer meant anything. The most ardent protesters were first taken in cars some 50 kilometres outside the city and put out into the fields there. Stubbornly, they walked back to the city and went on to protest once more. In the end, many realised that it had become too dangerous for them to stay. One activist, after several days in detention by the Russian military, announced on camera that he had been "misled" and that the Ukrainians were to blame for the war. Others, especially those with families and children, began to think about leaving for Ukrainian-controlled territory.

Leaving your home is invariably very difficult and painful, but evacuating from an occupied city is much more difficult than leaving an as yet free one. Almost every day some people have managed to leave. There are already "professional guides" who know the safer roads and who can negotiate with the Russian military at checkpoints so that the cars are allowed through. These "evacuation convoys" are small, five or six cars at most. Before leaving, the "guide" gives instructions on what to take with you, what to say at checkpoints and how to behave in general. The vital rule is to keep up with the other cars on the road. If you lag behind, nobody will wait for you. If you fail to keep up, there is no guarantee that you will reach the territory controlled by the Ukrainian government at all. You must also take with you at least twenty packets of cigarettes, even if no-one you know smokes. Russian soldiers at checkpoints willingly take cigarettes and then treat the travellers a little better. The average journey for evacuees from Melitopol to Ukrainian Zaporizhzhia costs sixteen packets of cigarettes per car.

Another important thing for evacuees to remember is that the Russian soldiers often undress men who are leaving the zone of occupation. They are looking for patriotic tattoos and traces of the long-term effects of carrying a machine gun on their shoulders. Evacuees must also take into account that the Russian soldiers are very nervous and can start shooting at any moment and at the least suspicion. They are right to be nervous, during the period of occupation, more than a hundred of them have been killed by the partisans while out on night patrol.

Of course, not everyone can leave. There are those, now hiding with friends, who, if they tried to leave, would definitely be detained by the Russian military. And there are those who disappeared during the first days of the occupation. It is not clear whether they are still alive. One such missing person is Irina Shcherbak, the head of the city's Department of Education, who was taken away by the Russian military to an unknown location after she refused to order the city's schools to switch to teaching in Russian using the Russian curriculum. There has been no news of her since. The same goes for a number of other kidnapped Melitopol residents.

On October 6, 1941, Melitopol was captured by the Nazis. That day some citizens really did greet the invading soldiers with flowers, hoping that the German army would help them retrieve some of the property expropriated by the Bolsheviks after the 1917 revolution. In 2022, although no-one met the Russian soldiers with flowers, a certain percentage of the population did perk up at their presence and some were positively enthusiastic. For example, former activists of the banned communist party and others who were nostalgic for the former Soviet Union. They felt that their time had come and went to the invaders to offer help. One of the best-known of such people among the Melitopol collaborators is Taras Genov, a former city council member from the "For the Future" party. As soon as the city passed into the hands of the Russian army, he started making a show of hanging up red Soviet flags around the city, while recording his activities on video. Then he went further, asking all the townspeople who still had Soviet flags at home to bring them to him so that he could decorate the city. Having hung out every available flag, he then staged a flash mob event on camera that involved tearing down Ukrainian street names. Again, he called on the townspeople to join him in cleansing the city of Ukrainian names and asked the representatives of Russian occupation forces to make new signs with "correct" Soviet street names.

At first the invaders did not much appreciate the pro-Russian activism of Taras Genov and even confiscated his Grand Cherokee jeep for the needs of the Russian army. Later the jeep was returned to him. This vehicle has Polish license plates. Like many other cunning Ukrainians, Genov had imported it illegally, bringing it into Ukraine from Poland without paying the required customs duty.

Today Genov is busy with a new public project. It turns out that he owns a small statue of Lenin. He brought this to the city centre on a trailer attached to his jeep. He then placed the statue on the corner of Hrushevsky and Getmanskaya streets. The same evening, just before midnight, he took it away because he was afraid that it might be stolen or destroyed during the night. Now he is looking for a better site for the monument, a safer one, preferably guarded by Russian soldiers. I assume the Russians are in no hurry to help him.

Taras is a traditional Ukrainian name. The national poet Taras Shevchenko is the most famous Taras in Ukraine. Taras Genov also wants to become famous in Russia, but the invaders do not seem to be paying much attention to his efforts as yet. He is too small a collaborator for them to be bothered with and perhaps a bit too comical. They need V.I.P. collaborators whose actions are less likely to make people laugh. They need collaborators who command respect and who are willing to appear on Russian television and thank the Russian army for "liberating the city from Ukrainian fascists". It is not easy to find such people, but great efforts are being made – not so much by the army as by the Russian secret services. They have succeeded in finding some help in fulfilling this objective from the head of the Melitopol Pedagogical University, Lyudmila Moskaleva. She remained in Melitopol but has failed to re-register the university, following the occupation, at a location in territory controlled by the Ukrainian government, as is required by Ukrainian law. As a result, the university's teachers have been left without salaries and their students without scholarships. The students may also be left without diplomas if the university is not re-registered soon. In contrast, the Melitopol State Agrotechnological University has been re-registered in Zaporizhzhia and now conducts its classes on the premises of Zaporizhzhia State University. All its teachers receive a salary and its students receive their scholarship grants.

The Russian army is trying to advance on Zaporizhzhia and perhaps the Agrotechnological University will have to travel further, together with Zaporizhzhia State University, towards the west of Ukraine.

No-one knows what awaits the teachers and students of the non-re-registered Pedagogical University. But Moskaleva herself regularly visits the occupier's administrative headquarters. It is assumed that she is preparing to register the university under Russian law.

The "occupation administration" consists both of collaborators and Russian citizens. The Russians fire or replace collaborators every now and then. At the moment, several are sitting in a Melitopol prison, including the former local deputies from the party of the pro-Russian opposition bloc. Apparently, they were found to have misappropriated the occupiers' funds. It really does not matter why they were put in jail. It is clear that the Russian military does not have much confidence in them. However, without collaborators, the occupying forces cannot function. They need local people to work in the "local authorities".

The head of the pro-Russian "local government", Galina Danilchenko, was featured on Russian television news the other day. She was filmed gifting a newly-built apartment to a young family from the Ukrainian city of Vuhledar, where fighting is still going on. Accompanied by Russian T.V. journalists, the family was taken to Melitopol in a Russian military helicopter. The representative of the invaders presented them with the keys to an apartment in a building constructed by Germany for refugees from the Donetsk and Luhansk regions. The building should have been opened in a ceremony at the end of February in the presence of representatives from the German embassy in Ukraine. The young family who received the keys to this apartment told Russian viewers about the horrors of "Ukrainian fascism" on camera. An apartment in exchange for a few public lies – it is a dubious deal, but there will always be those who are prepared to do such things.

To date, thirty per cent. of the population has left Melitopol. The Russian occupation authorities have brought in people from Crimea and Donetsk to the city to try and revive some city life. Children's attractions and play areas are already operating in the Melitopol parks. Ice-cream is on sale. Prices for everything are still indicated in hryvnia, and sometimes you can withdraw hryvnia in cash from the city's A.T.M.s. Residents can even get transfers of money from Kyiv or Lviv to their bank cards. How this is possible and how long it will last, I do not know. In the occupied villages and towns of Kharkiv region, the invaders are already introducing Russian rubles and demanding that businessmen should set prices in rubles.

"Ukrainians will no longer be able to enjoy Melitopol cherries," Russians write gloatingly on their social networks. Stealing a city and stealing cherries are different crimes. But in this case, they are two parts of one and the same war crime committed on behalf of the Russian people by the Russian army. It is not only Putin that will have to answer for this and the many other crimes.

29.04.2022

Whose Side are the Black Sea Dolphins on?

Online publications write that Russia has put "combat dolphins" on duty in the Sevastopol Bay, where several warships of the Black Sea Fleet are located. Ukrainian missiles cannot reach the bay, so the ships are safe on that score. Apparently, the dolphins have been trained to attack scuba divers and enemy submarines. I do not know how dolphins are able to distinguish their submarines from enemy ones. I only know that the Ukrainian Navy does not have a single submarine. Actually, it is difficult to call it a "navy" at all. It is mostly a "mosquito" fleet, consisting of small speedboats. But since Russia's flagship, *Moskva*, was destroyed by Ukraine from the mainland, I have come to think that Ukraine does not need a bigger navy. Most definitely, Ukraine does not need militarily trained dolphins. The phrase "Russian military dolphins" sounds like something out of an ironic science fiction novel. But it is reality.

Ukrainian dolphins have also recently been in the news when evacuated from Kharkiv to Odesa, a location which must seem much more like home for them. These are dolphins that were specially trained to treat children with learning issues such as Asperger syndrome or autism. The evacuation of the dolphins, with all its complexity and danger, was not very different to a full military operation. Special trucks with indoor swimming pools left from Odesa to Kharkiv, travelling via Kyiv. They had to take a detour for security reasons, as the front-line creeps south and further areas come under more frequent shelling attack.

It proved possible to rescue not only the dolphins from Kharkiv using these mobile aquariums but sea-lions and seals too. The sea animals were accompanied by dolphin trainers and veterinary doctors on their journey to Odesa. It is always possible that one day the dolphins could be released back into the sea in Odesa and that they could then swim across the Black Sea, perhaps even accidentally ending up in Sevastopol Bay. How would the "Russian combat dolphins" then greet them, I wonder? Like Ukrainian saboteurs?

There are still two young white whales left in the Nemo aquarium in Kharkiv. It is not yet clear whether it will be possible to take them to Odesa. At a time like this, it is difficult to make whales a priority. Nonetheless they are still living creatures and should be cared for.

During war, even a large country can seem too small and too cramped. The thousand kilometres that separate Kharkiv from Odesa does not mean that Odesa is much safer than Kharkiv, even if it might be for the dolphins. What is crucial is that Odesa is on the sea, unlike Kharkiv. In the event of the bombing of the huge oceanarium in Kharkiv, there is no possibility for saving the fish and sea mammals there by releasing them into the sea, unlike in Odesa.

Odesa is also being shelled, however. So far, the attacks come from the sea and from Russian-held territory. To the west of Odesa lies the "separatist republic" of Transnistria, annexed from Moldova back in the 1990s. On its territory, are located some of the largest warehouses of old Soviet-made weapons. Russia also keeps three thousand "peacekeepers" there and employs men who carry Kalashnikovs to control the "republic" . Although Russia could at any moment give an order to these "peacekeepers" to start shelling Odesa from the rear, the people of Odesa do not panic. They live almost normal lives. They are preparing, like all Ukrainians, for *Grobki* ("little graves days"). This is what we call the special days around Eastertime each year when we honour the memory of deceased relatives and friends. At this time, all of Ukraine dedicates itself to the care of the graves in its cemeteries. This year, some of the residents of Odesa will not only have to remove the old scrub and weeds from the graves but will also need to repair the monuments and fences destroyed or damaged by Russian missiles.

Many cemeteries in Ukraine have been damaged or destroyed by Russian troops, including Kyiv's Berkovtsi cemetery located near to Tupoleva, the street where I grew up. Some cemeteries have been bombed, others have been crushed by Russian tanks and personnel carriers. Russian sappers have also left booby traps in many cemeteries. As a result, the authorities are trying to persuade Ukrainians not to go the cemeteries this year, especially to those that were or remain under the occupation of the Russian army. But Ukrainians are used to not doing what they are told. They do what they consider necessary. They will still go to tidy up the graves of their relatives.

The church has often asked Ukrainians not to bring plastic flowers to the graves but to bring live ones instead, but still many Ukrainians bring plastic ones because they do not fade. Some Ukrainian families will also try to go where they were only allowed to go only once a year, even before the war – to the cemeteries in the closed Chernobyl zone. There are dozens of cemeteries in the villages and towns that were evacuated after the disaster of 1986. Previously, former residents of these areas and their relatives went there from all over Ukraine to mark the anniversary of the Chernobyl disaster on the "little graves days". But this year, visiting the Chernobyl zone is strictly prohibited. After the Russian army captured the Chernobyl nuclear power station and the entire zone around it, the level of radiation there has risen sharply and had become very dangerous once again.

The Russian army controlled the zone for more than a month. During that time, they paved a road to Kyiv through the radioactive territory. About ten thousand tanks, armoured personnel carriers and other military vehicles travelled along it, carrying thousands of soldiers towards what they hoped would be their triumphal entry into Kyiv. Prior to this, Russian soldiers had dug tens of kilometres of trenches throughout the dead zone and had then sat in the trenches for an entire month. The headquarters of the Russian army which was supposed to capture Kyiv was also located there. Now the Russians are gone and only the radiation is left.

Some of the Russian soldiers who had been stationed in Chernobyl later returned with their surviving military equipment along this same road to Belarus, together with the things they had stolen from Ukrainian homes – washing machines, computers, scooters, even children's toys. The soldiers who returned through Belarus shipped home their booty to towns and villages all over Russia. Many of these postal transactions were filmed on the courier services' video cameras and all the addresses and names of the recipients of the stolen goods remain in the system. Perhaps this would have been forgotten by now, if it were not for Chernobyl and its radiation.

Shortly after the Russian military left the Chernobyl zone for Belarus, courier service employees began to feel ill.

Several went to their doctor. The doctors soon identified that they were suffering from radiation sickness due to exposure to radiation. After this discovery, the Belarusian K.G.B. launched its own investigation, which, no doubt, will lead nowhere. After all, Belarus is already *de facto* a territory under the control of Russia. From the Russia point of view, it is not important how much radiation Russian soldiers brought into Belarus or how much they shipped home in parcels to their relatives. For Russia, it is also not important that military equipment, which twice passed through the Chernobyl zone, has became itself a source of radiation that is affecting Russian soldiers who use it when in action. For Russia, the lives of these soldiers are not important either. Most likely, they will die on the battlefield and not in hospital from radiation sickness.

Another problem, one facing Ukraine, is that the Russian military equipment destroyed in Chernobyl remains on Ukrainian territory. It has become a source of dangerous radiation for Ukrainians and Ukrainians may become the next victims of Chernobyl's radiation problem. Once again, if we are not careful, the number of fresh graves will increase in Chernobyl's cemeteries and even more people will then come to the cemeteries in late April and the beginning of May to remember their dead on the "little graves days".

On these days, Ukrainians visit the cemeteries with picnic baskets and bags, sit on the ground near the graves or at special tables dug into the ground next to the fences around the graves. There they commemorate the dead, toasting them with a drink. These traditions are stronger than the shelling and the occupation. War or no war, they will go on. The war might even strengthen these traditions because there are now so many new graves in the cemeteries of Ukraine – those of the Ukrainian military and of the civilian population killed by the Russian military.

Putin would like to kill all Ukrainian traditions. Then it would be easier for him to say that Ukrainians do not exist, that they are just Russians who were deceived, a people who were told that they were not Russians but Ukrainians. But war kills only people. Traditions remain and they cement national identity – and Ukrainians have a lot of traditions. Many of these traditions are related to agriculture because Ukrainian farmers are used to being independent. Even now, even in the occupied territories, they cultivate their land and sow wheat and rapeseed, buckwheat, and rye. And they continue to do so even under shelling and threats from the Russian military. Although the Russian military promises to confiscate up to seventy per cent. of the future harvest from these farmers, the farmers continue to sow their crops in the hope that by the time the harvest comes there will be no Russians in Kherson region. Whilst sowing, the farmers sometimes wear body armour including, if they can find them, steel helmets. This results in another danger in addition to the threat of shelling. Russian soldiers tend to react aggressively when they see the farmers wearing body armour. This means the farmers need to wear something over the top of their bulletproof vests to hide them, otherwise they might be shot at.

It is not only in the occupied areas where farmers are in danger. Tractors too can be blown up by landmines. Recently, a farmer in the Kyiv region was seriously injured when his tractor was so destroyed. He was not wearing body armour or a helmet.

In Soviet times, any agricultural work was described in

newspapers as "a battle for the harvest". Thanks to Russia and Putin this phrase has now acquired a different, quite literal meaning. Ukraine is already paying for its future bread with blood. With the blood of soldiers and with the blood of farmers.

01.05.2022

Ukrainian Culture at War

On February 24, 2022, all citizens of Ukraine found that their lifetime had been cut brutally in two, into the period "before the war" and that "during the war". Of course, we all hope that there will be a period "after the war" as well. Tragically, for many, that possibility has already been lost. For the rest of us, the end of the war remains far off.

Many Ukrainians believe that the current war began in 2014 with the annexation of Crimea and the appearance on maps of Ukrainian territory of the so-called "separatist republics". Russia had declared that it was not participating in the war but was only supporting the separatists and "restoring historical justice" in Crimea. But it was also the moment when Russia participated directly in the hostilities in the Donbas and entered the territory of Ukraine with entire artillery brigades in order to shell the city of Ilovaisk and try and capture the city of Debaltseve.

In fact, Russia started its war for cultural dominance over Ukraine and other ex-Soviet countries much earlier than this. Tens of millions of dollars every year have been spent by the Kremlin since the early years of this century to prove to the whole world that Russian culture dominates not only in the former Soviet Union but is dominant even outside Eastern Europe. The Kremlin has paid for Russia to be the guest of honour at all international book fairs. And when Russia has already been an honoured guest as, for example, at the Paris Salon du Livre in 2005, then the next move was for St Petersburg to become the honoured guest a couple of years later, and then Moscow and so on.

Constant broadcasts about how great Russian culture is on Russia Today could not but convince the foreign viewers of this channel that there is no more powerful or more important culture in the world than Russian culture. For Russian-speaking viewers around the world, the satellite T.V. channels of Kultura, Nostalgia and many others have worked – and are continued to work – to underline the exaggerated pride in the achievements of Russian art that flourishes among the former residents of the U.S.S.R., regardless of their country of residence.

Hundreds of artists, musicians and writers from Russia travel to visit the Russian-speaking and Russophile audiences around the world so that this "cultural" connection is not lost. If you examine this more closely, you can see that what we are talking about is the cultural component of the political project of the Kremlin, the dominance of the "The Russian world".

This project is designed to create powerful support groups for Russian international policies and for Russian influence. The constant tours of the Mariinsky Theatre ballet from St Petersburg and the tours of the Red Army Choir, now more usually called the Russian Army Choir, also work towards this goal. Yes, the historical achievements of the Russian theatre in the twentieth century really were great, but after a Russian bomber very precisely dropped its half-ton bomb on the city theatre in Mariupol, I no longer feel like discussing Russian theatrical art and Russian culture in general. I am more concerned about how Russia has tried and is trying to destroy Ukrainian culture and to erase the history of Ukraine. During this war, these attempts are especially noticeable. In the occupied cities, Russian soldiers use hammers to smash the commemorative plaques placed on the houses where Ukrainian writers and poets, philosophers and scientists once lived. In Chernihiv, the Russian military burned the archives of the N.K.V.D. and K.G.B. This was done to prevent Ukraine from citing the specific dossiers that show how the Soviet government cracked down on Ukrainian cultural figures. Countless Ukrainian writers and poets of the 1930s were arrested; many were sent to the prison camp on Solovki in the White Sea and later shot at Sandarmokh (in north Karelia) – nearly three hundred of them, known as the "Executed Renaissance".

Two months of Russian aggression are behind us. During this time, tens of thousands of houses, hundreds of schools, libraries, museums, and cultural institutions have been destroyed. A third of the country is in ruins and almost half of the population of Ukraine has become refugees or I.D.P.s. Plants and factories have stopped working. Many of them no longer exist. Hundreds of thousands of Ukrainians are left without work and therefore without means of subsistence. They are saved from starvation by European and world solidarity. They are rescued from deprivation with the support of many countries. Millions of citizens of the world have come together to participate in charity events in aid of Ukraine and Ukrainians, but many Ukrainians no longer have homes, businesses, careers, vegetable patches or even flower gardens.

On the very first day of the war, the work of Ukraine's theatres and publishing houses, film studios, and philharmonic societies stopped. The cultural life of this large country of 40 million people was put on hold. Ukrainian writers, like all Ukrainians, immediately felt the burden of Russian aggression. Many moved to western Ukraine. Writers who lived in western Ukraine busied themselves with caring for their fellow writers and their families who had moved there from further east. Some writers and artists went to Europe with their children. Others remained in the cities occupied by the Russian army. One writer of children's stories is now in Kherson. He remains holed up in his apartment. There is almost no reliable information about the situation in the occupied city. Another writer remains in occupied Melitopol, where local collaborators and Russian intelligence officers roam the city with lists of journalists and pro-Ukrainian activists. Many have already been taken away to who knows where.

Before the start of the war, I began work on a novel about events in Kyiv in the spring of 1919 during the civil war that began after the Russian Revolution of 1917. The present war crossed out all my plans for that novel. I spent the first few days moving my family away from Kyiv. Like hundreds of my colleagues, we are now refugees. In our new shelter in western Ukraine, as I soon as I had a table top to work at, I sat down at my computer again, but I could no longer think about fiction. I began to write articles and essays about Russian–Ukrainian relations, about Ukraine and about this war. I began to publish my texts in the U.K. and the U.S.A., in France and Germany, in Norway and Denmark. The rhythm of my life has not altered for two months. That novel will be completed at some point in the future. For now, every writer, every artist, or representative of any creative profession, must work for their country and for victory in this war.

Ukraine has given me thirty years of life without censorship, without dictatorship, without control over what I wrote and what I said. For this, I am infinitely grateful to my country. I now understand very well that if Russia succeeds in seizing Ukraine, all the freedoms that the citizens of Ukraine are so used to will be lost, together with the independence of our state. While soldiers are fighting with weapons in their hands in the east and south of Ukraine, writers are fighting on the information front against fake news and false narratives by which Russia is trying to justify its aggression to the residents of other countries and continents.

In Europe, Russia is losing this war. Europe has recovered from its naivety and now understands perfectly well what is happening in Ukraine. But in Latin America, Russia is winning the information war. Wherever there is anti-American sentiment, there is always more sympathy for Putin and the Russian Federation. Ukraine is very far from Latin America and few people there know where Ukraine is on the map of the world. It is easy for them to believe that fascists are sitting in the Ukrainian government and that Ukraine as such is an anti-Semitic and Russo-phobic state where Jews and Russians living in Ukraine are afraid to go out on the streets. I have already received numerous requests from Latin American journalists to confirm or deny these Russian narratives. Even though a search on Google is enough to refute easily all of these stories, journalists and readers want to hear the voice of a Ukrainian person answering their questions. So

I explain that an "anti-Semitic and Russophobic" state is hardly likely to elect a Russian-speaking Jew as its president, especially not with seventy-three per cent. of the vote, as was the case for Volodymyr Zelensky. As for the "fascists" in the government, I tell them that there is not even a single nationalist party member represented currently in the Ukrainian parliament. Can they say the same of their own country? Not to mention the absence of both the radical left and the radical right. Ukrainians traditionally do not vote for radicals, although for a brief moment following the Orange Revolution, a number of right-wing radicals did become politically active.

Ukrainian culture, both contemporary and classical, has been a victim of the war. While many museums were able to evacuate their most valuable exhibits to the west of the country, many others did not have time to do this. Among the museums that have since been destroyed, I feel most sorry about the loss of the house museum of Ukraine's best-known primitive artist, Maria Pryimachenko. Her house was near Kyiv, where she lived all her life. It no longer exists. It was blown up by the Russians and its contents burned. This happened at the very beginning of the war when Russian troops were trying to capture Kyiv. At the time, a lot was said about how most of the original works by the artist had been destroyed in the fire. Now there is information that as many as ten of her paintings were saved by people living in the neighbourhood. They ran into the museum when the fire was raging around them and carried out everything that could still be saved. The rescuers are said to have taken the paintings to their own homes, awaiting the end of the war, when they plan to return the rescued works of art to another, new museum, which they hope will be built "after the war".

Today, this abstract concept of a future "after the war" or "after victory", as we prefer to say, inspires not only cultural figures, writers, and musicians but makes all Ukrainians speak about their plans. Ukrainian politicians are talking now about projects to restore the country destroyed by Russia. They can already state the specific amounts of money that will be needed for building materials. They are already counting on volunteers from many countries who may want to come and work on the reconstruction of Ukraine. Some European architects have suggested creating projects for the renewal of destroyed cities, such as Mariupol or Chernihiv.

It is strange to peer into this post-war future while sitting in the middle of the war. The future looks Technicolor-bright. It seems to me that examples of such heightened optimism during a bloody war have rarely if ever been observed. But in Ukraine, this optimism is very much present. This is in part because cultural figures have, each in her or his way, stood up to the war. Almost every one of them has found a use for their abilities and talents on one front or another. They are united by a common goal, to protect the independence of their native state.

In the cities of western Ukraine, now crowded with refugees, theatres are open again and literary evenings are being held. Even in Kharkiv, recent weeks have seen presentations of new books and rock concerts – though it is true that some took place in bomb shelters. What is more, you cannot buy any books at these book presentations as there is still no publishing or printing going on in Ukraine at the moment. But these future books can be heard as they are read by the authors or translators.

People cannot live without water, without air, or without culture. Culture gives meaning to a person's life. It thus becomes especially important in times of catastrophe and war. Culture becomes something that cannot be abandoned. It explains to a person who he or she is and where he or she belongs. Whereas Putin has placed Russian culture at the service of his dictatorial regime, Ukrainian culture remains independent of the authorities and politics. It serves to protect the dignity of each Ukrainian, regardless of their ethnic origin or mother tongue. It is the invisible armour of the human soul. For Ukrainians, it protects their way of life and their way of thinking.

I had coffee yesterday with Andriy Lyubka, a popular young writer from Transcarpathia. We talked about life. "In a month I will invite you to a picnic. I'll cook *bograch* on the fire!" he promised. Will the time of "after the war" come in a month? I do not know the answer to this, but you have to make plans.

Andriy also said that in only a few days he had collected enough money on Facebook to buy two pickup trucks for the Ukrainian army. This is another role of cultural figures and writers – raising money for the army, for refugees, and for humanitarian needs. Traditionally, Ukrainians are far more likely to trust a cultural figure than a politician. It is no surprise then that of the most successful fundraisers the majority are musicians, writers, theatre actors and rock singers. After all, what is happening now is not just an attempt by one army to destroy another. It is an attempt to destroy Ukraine. It is an attempt to destroy Ukrainian culture and replace it with Russian culture. If Ukrainian culture is destroyed, there will be no more Ukraine. Everyone understands this. It is understood best of all by Ukrainian cultural figures themselves. That is why they are not giving up. That is why they are fighting back – just like Ukrainian soldiers on the Eastern Front.

Tattoo
Life in Someone Else's City and in Someone Else's Apartment

Soon it will be two months since we started living in someone else's apartment. The place has become almost like home to us. I know where to find a medium-sized pot or pilaf spices in the kitchen. I know where the iron is and where the ironing board is hidden. I know where the owner keeps clean bath towels. I am also already on nodding terms with several vendors at the local market and I know a man who sells bad potatoes. I asked him twice, "Are your potatoes O.K.?" And he assured me both times that his potatoes were excellent. Half of them had to be thrown away; inside they were black, rotten. He sells them already packaged in two-kilogram bags. That is what all the merchants do. You buy potatoes like a pig in a poke. I do not buy potatoes from him anymore, but I greet him when I walk through the bazaar.

During this time, I have discovered fifteen acquaintances temporarily settled near us. "Near" does not mean next door. Here in Transcarpathia, on the western side of the Ukrainian Carpathian mountains, if someone lives 50 kilometres away from you, then that is nearby. For two months now, close

Kyiv friends have been living 60 kilometres from us, in a spacious apartment on the ground floor of a two-storey house in the town of Berehove. This is the family of the widow of my first publisher, Irina, and includes her daughter Alena, grandson Artem and three other acquaintances. They do not pay rent. They live according to the official rules for refugees and I.D.P.s. They have registered as "displaced persons" and have received certificates to prove their status as such. With these certificates, you can receive humanitarian assistance. There are several humanitarian hubs in Berehove. Each hub has its own schedule, but no-one knows what kind of help will be made available or exactly where and when it will be. I.D.P.s make regular circuits of the town centre, walking from one hub to another. If they see a queue of people, they immediately join it – most likely this means that food has been delivered. Food aid now appears irregularly. Irina, my publisher's widow, refuses to stand in the queues. "I don't look like someone who should be taking handouts!" she said. "I am ashamed to do it." But she does ask her daughter Alena to go and get whatever is on offer. This is usually sunflower oil, canned fish, buckwheat and other cereals.

Alena is happy to go to the distribution points for her mother. She enjoys interacting with the other folk in the queue. Last time she stood in line for an hour for a box of hygiene products. She brought home twelve rolls of toilet paper, ten bars of soap, three kilograms of laundry detergent, five tooth-brushes, three tubes of toothpaste and five disposable razors. All this was packed in a cardboard box with the inscription "hygiene kit for a family of five for one month". It was also indicated that this set was from the Austrian Red Cross. To get it, Alena had to show her I.D.P. registration certificate.

Not far from the hygiene kit distribution point there is a kiosk where you can always get free, warm, fresh bread without a certificate. A little further along there is a disused shop with two rooms full of free clothes collected by the residents of the town and nearby villages. In its make-shift changing rooms, you can get changed into the outfit you have selected and off you go! The only problem is that there are no "humanitarian shoes", but fortunately refugees did not come here barefoot.

Very often it is the elderly women who stand in line for humanitarian aid. They also like to talk to each other to find out who fled from where and what they left behind. Generally, these are urban grandmothers. They are well-dressed and have professional haircuts. Rural grandmothers are easy to recognise by their clothes and their gait. All their lives, in addition to their main work, they have worked in their gardens. They are bent over and almost always have back problems.

Yesterday, after reading the latest news, I had a strong desire to introduce two elderly Ukrainian women to each other. It is not possible for me to do this, of course, as I do not know either of them personally, but I can imagine the conversation they would have if I did so. The two grandmothers have surprised me greatly. One of them, an eighty-five-year-old villager from Horenka, a village that can be reached by tram from the centre of Kyiv, made *paskas* – a special sweet bread eaten at Easter. She cooks this in a badly damaged stove which, until recently, she used both to cook her food and to heat her house. The house was destroyed by Russian artillery, but the stove, built into the inner wall of the building, survived almost intact. You can still cook food in it, but there are no walls or windows around it and no roof above. This grandmother, who now lives in the ruins of her home, has baked almost a dozen Easter *paskas* in this oven. No doubt, once they were done, she then took them along to her church so they could be blessed for Easter. That is, if the church itself survived the Russian bombing.

The second grandmother, Nadezhda Radionova, an eighty-year-old pensioner from Vinnytsia, has been more fortunate. Her apartment has not been damaged by bombs. Influenced perhaps by her granddaughter, who is a professional tattoo artist, she decided to get a patriotic tattoo on her leg, that of the coat of arms of Ukraine, the trident, along with the accompanying symbol of ears of wheat. For an adult, choosing to have a tattoo is a matter of some responsibility, especially if the tattoo is in a conspicuous place. During the Russian aggression, having a patriotic tattoo can even cost you your life. Wherever they can, especially at checkpoints, the Russian military undress men to check for patriotic tattoos. If they find any, the Ukrainian is at once recorded as a "Nazi" or "fascist" and taken away for interrogation. The Russians have forced Ukrainian military prisoners to "erase" patriotic tattoos, along with their skin, by rubbing them with stones. Among the bodies of murdered Ukrainians, there were many whose tattoos had been cut away from their arms, shoulders, and legs, along with skin and flesh. If grandmother Nadezhda Radionova fell into the hands of the Russian military with her new tattoo, would she be shown any mercy? Russians do not understand or accept anyone else's patriotism. For them, tattoos of Stalin and Putin are still in fashion, along with a whole set of tattoos based on the prison stories of criminals, about which entire encyclopaedias have been written.

In the circumstances, it would seem logical for the grand-mother with the tattoo, Nadezhda Radionova, to invite the grandmother who has been left with what is now her outdoor stove, to her residence for a while. But I understand what attachment to one's home is, even when the house is badly damaged. The stove is the heart of a traditional Ukrainian home. In winter, children would have slept on the stove in which the grandmother from Horenka baked her Easter bread. This is the warmest place in the house. I can imagine the thoughts of this grandmother. She most likely thinks that the main thing is that the stove survived only a little damaged. The house around it and the roof above it can be rebuilt.

In the Ukrainian language and in Ukrainian tradition the word *toloka* means "community work done for the common good", including for the benefit of a particular person or a particular family. In this tradition neighbours and fellow villagers will help to build a new house for those whose house has burned down, or help lonely, elderly folk to harvest crops from their allotments. I imagine that after the war there will be a lot of community work parties like this, organised to help those who were left without anywhere to live. Not so long ago, another word with a large number of meanings was added to the concept of *toloka*. It is the word "volunteer". This concept, which involves helping people who you do not know, is relatively new to Ukraine. The family of my cousin Kostya went as volunteers to clean up the ruins of Bucha after the withdrawal of the Russian army. They drove there, cleaned the streets from morning till night, sorted through the rubble of destroyed houses and informed the military when they found unexploded bombs or grenades. The huge amount of work done in Bucha could not have been possible without volunteers. The army is fighting at the front, and the military units that defend Kyiv and other cities cannot be expected to be engaged in the restoration of destroyed villages or roads. This work is being done by volunteers.

Volunteers also bring humanitarian aid to residents of front line villages and cities left without supplies. Volunteers are even trying to evacuate residents from the occupied territories. This activity is always associated with a risk to their life. Several volunteers have been killed by the Russian military or have died under shellfire from artillery or tanks. And, of course, the Russian military has no respect for them. But volunteers nevertheless continue to offer their services, believing that without their help victory will not be achieved, that those who might be saved could be lost.

By chance, or rather because of a photograph taken by Christopher Okkichene for the *Wall Street Journal*, a young resident of Irpin became one of the most famous of the Ukrainian volunteers. Her name is Nastya and she managed to evacuate some eighteen disabled dogs from Irpin during the Russian occupation. By the way, Nastya did not want to become a star either. She did not even give her last name to journalists and did not say where she was taking the disabled dogs. Of the many thousands of volunteers helping refugees and the military, most prefer to remain anonymous.

In western Ukraine, where my family and I now live, albeit temporarily, the volunteer movement is also very active. Interestingly, as well as seeking to relieve basic needs, volunteer organisations here also aim to support I.D.P.s emotionally and psychologically. There are a lot of refugees from other regions, including many women with children. Some live for free in schools and hostels, others rent rooms and apartments.

Those of working age would like to be able to work, but there are few jobs in Transcarpathia, Bukovina, or the Lviv region. It is good that there are free canteens and cafés, as well as humanitarian aid centres in every larger settlement, but it is psychologically hard to live in an unfamiliar region without work.

To keep both adult refugees and their children busy, volunteers have organised a variety of courses, from sewing and dressmaking to acting and animation. In many cities and towns, there are free foreign language courses. In Berehove on the Hungarian border, Alena, and her new refugee friends attend Hungarian language courses. Each lesson lasts three hours and those who have signed up for the course take it as seriously as if they were preparing for an exam.

"What is the teacher's name?" I asked her when she left the university building at 8 p.m. I expected to hear a Hungarian name in response because there are a lot of ethnic Hungarians in this city. "Angelica," Alena said. "How does she teach? Is she cheerful?" I asked. "She doesn't have the strength to smile. She holds three classes a day for three groups, each of three hours. But she tries very hard."

Alena has a favourite phrase in Hungarian: *Jó reggelt kivanok!* – "Good morning!" This sounds a little funny to Ukrainians because it reminds us of the Ukrainian words for "hedgehog under the sofa".

The Hungarian language teacher Angelica is not exactly a volunteer. She is paid for her work, but she works a lot more than she needs to teaching Hungarian to refugees, some nine hours a day. This is her contribution to the life of Ukrainian society, to its psychological stability.

Can war be a time for self-improvement, for self-education? Of course it can. At any age and in any situation, even in wartime, you can discover new aspects of life, new knowledge and new opportunities. You can learn to bake *paskas* in a damaged stove. You can get a tattoo for the first time in your life at the age of eighty. You can start learning Hungarian or Polish. You can even start learning Ukrainian if you did not know it previously. Now free Ukrainian language courses are on offer in western Ukraine and refugees from the eastern, mostly Russian-speaking part of Ukraine are willingly starting to study Ukrainian. They understand that knowing only Russian is dangerous. After all, Putin might decide that you need "protection" as a Russian speaker. He might order the Russian army not only to "protect" you but also to "liberate" you from your house or apartment, from your former happy life. Language matters, especially if your life suddenly depends on what language you speak.

18.05.2022

Will Zelensky Become a True Best-Selling Author?

May weather indulges Ukraine with both warm sunshine and violent thunderstorms. Nature has come to life, the trees are green and the very pace of life in the country has increased.

Once again, for the third time this century, Ukraine has won The Eurovision Song Contest. Each of the country's victories in this competition has come in the wake of historical upheaval. I want to believe that this year's victory will be the last for many years. I do not usually watch "the Eurovision" and I missed this one too, but I have listened to the winning song and I like it. Most of all, I like the solidarity shown by the Europeans who voted for Ukraine – of course, not for the song itself but for the fact that Ukraine shows amazing courage in successfully resisting the Russian army, which is many times larger than its own.

For days now, Ukrainian Facebook pages have been boiling over with the joy arising from this victory. Ukrainians joke that Putin woke up last Sunday morning and was horrified to hear that Ukraine had won. It took him a while to realise that Ukraine had won the Eurovision, not the war. Not yet.

The war goes on, as does life in Ukraine and some people, as usual, die from natural causes. On Tuesday, Ukraine's first president, Leonid Kravchuk, was buried in Kyiv. Opinions about his significance for independent Ukraine are divided, just as opinions are always divided in Ukraine. I was not one of his supporters and still believe that it was because of him that Ukraine did not follow the path of Lithuania, Estonia and Latvia in implementing effective reforms of the country's obsolete Soviet economic management structures. In Soviet times, Leonid Kravchuk was responsible for ideology in the Politburo of the Communist Party of Ukraine. It was said about him that he could walk in the rain without an umbrella and remain completely dry – he knew how to dodge the drops! His political stratagem was famous, but his leadership did not bring any genuinely positive change to Ukraine. If he is remembered at all, it will be for the *Kravchuchka*, the shopping bag on wheels which Ukrainians used to take their belongings to the flea markets in order to sell them. They needed to do so to raise sufficient funds to buy food during the severe economic crisis of the early 1990s.

That crisis now feels like ancient history. Since then,

Ukraine, despite its many problems, has become an independent country with a fairly prosperous population. From the intercepted telephone conversations between Russian soldiers and their relatives in Russia, it is clear that the invading soldiers were surprised at how well Ukrainians lived. Perhaps this is what irritates the Russian military most and stirs their hatred and their desire to destroy Ukrainian homes and property or to expropriate it wherever possible – just as happened after the 1917 revolution, when the Bolsheviks took clothes, furniture, factories, shops and horses from wealthy citizens.

Russian officers have taken many vehicles with them back to Russia, including stolen tractors, John Deere combines and a good many cars. Unless these officers live in Chechnya, they will now have the bother of needing to register their stolen vehicles according to Russian laws. After all, even a stolen car must be registered with the police and will require a Russian number plate. The Russian police are still unsure what to do in this situation. The State Duma has not yet prepared a law on the legalisation of property stolen from Ukrainian citizens and foreign states. Such a law will almost certainly appear in the near future. For every Russian crime, a new law to justify it is soon adopted. Things are simpler in Chechnya – whatever you bring into the country is yours. As long as you are loyal to Kadyrov, you can drive cars with Ukrainian license plates on Chechen roads.

Just as Ukrainian opinions are split over its first president, Leonid Kravchuk, Ukrainians are divided over the surrender of the defenders of Mariupol, the several hundred soldiers who held out in the dungeons of the besieged Azovstal plant. Most Ukrainians are afraid that they will be killed by the Russians. Others are unhappy because they feel that the Ukrainian military should not have surrendered. Personally, I am glad that the soldiers are still alive and I hope that sooner or later they will be repatriated.

A level of cautious optimism among Ukrainians is also evident in the recent revival of their interest in books. It makes no sense to talk about any special successes for the Ukrainian book trade. In the whole country there are only two or three dozen bookshops still operating. Nevertheless, we already have the first wartime bestseller, although the name of the author of the book could sell almost anything, not only a book. Right now, his surname is the most expensive in the world – the U.S.A. has paid out forty billion dollars for it. We are of course talking about President Zelensky and his book, which is entitled *Speeches*. Naturally, Zelensky continues to speak and there are already speeches that are not included in this book, but in due course a sequel can be published.

The Kharkiv publishing house Folio is searching for paper in order to reprint the first volume of Zelensky's *Speeches*. We are not talking about reprinting a best-seller of the type you might get in Europe or in America. Not surprisingly, the first print run, of one thousand, two hundred copies in Ukrainian and eight hundred copies in English, sold out in a week. The publisher has managed to find paper for another one and a half thousand copies of the Ukrainian edition and they will soon be on sale.

Paper in Ukraine is so hard to come by at present that people can get killed for it, not by competitors but by the Russian army. Folio's Kharkiv printing house in the town of Derhachi, near the border with Russia, has been standing without windows for more than two months after coming under bombardment from Russian artillery. During all this time, twenty-four tonnes of paper, about sixty large rolls, have been sitting in the warehouse. Although the roof of the printing house was pierced by shells and the torrential rain and thunderstorms of the past month have damaged some part of this paper, it remains invaluable as there is no other paper in Ukraine!

Alexander Krasovitskiy, the C.E.O. of Folio, has already managed to transfer more than twenty rolls to Kharkiv. This at a time when there is neither petrol nor diesel fuel in the country, when desperate drivers stick advertisements on lampposts, saying, "I will buy ten litres of 95 petrol" and giving their mobile telephone numbers. Even before Russia used dozens of missiles to destroy virtually all of Ukraine's fuel reserves, there were no stocks of paper anywhere else in Ukraine, the global paper crisis saw to that.

In the story of the success of *Speeches,* I am less interested in the content of the already well-known texts than in the names of the speechwriters. Their names are not given and remain secret. As I see it, it is they who should be declared heroes! Such powerful examples of rhetoric have never before been written in Ukrainian. I can even imagine Russian intelligence seeking information about these speechwriters so as to deprive President Zelensky of his ability to so effectively influence foreign audiences. One more question occurs to me, but it concerns Ukraine's future after the war, will President Zelensky arrange autograph sessions? Will he take part in future book exhibitions and festivals? After his term as president, he should be able to write a book about the war, his actions and experiences. In the meantime, he has other things to think about, including preparations for further public performances in front of more foreign audiences.

Ukrainian refugees living temporarily in Bulgaria in the ancient town of Pomorie, built by Greek colonists in the fourth century B.C., have very different concerns. Before the war, the population of Pomorie was about fifteen thousand people. Pomorie is a popular Black Sea resort, where in summer there are more vacationers than locals. There are hotels, apartments, and houses for rent. After the start of the Russian aggression, up to five thousand citizens of Ukraine moved there. They were given temporary protection status by the Bulgarian authorities. They explored the town, began to get to know each other, and, by and by, realised that there were many Russian citizens also living there. Now they get to know each other more cautiously. Some Ukrainians communicate with the Russians they meet, but most try to stay away from them.

Ukrainian mothers who came to Pomorie with their children made friends fastest. Courses and special interest groups for children have sprung up – drawing classes and Bulgarian language classes. Adult refugees without children are often bored and regularly call relatives who are still in Ukraine to ask when they should return.

Svetlana, an old friend, a professor of philosophy, is there. She writes regularly to me asking if I think it is safe to return home. A couple of days ago, I wrote back for the fourth time discouraging her from returning. I dare not risk giving her any other advice. The war could return to Kyiv at any moment – once again a Russian missile could hit a residential building and more people will die. Or the war might return in the form of an attack by the Russian army, or even in the form of an invasion by the army by Belarus, which is now conducting large-scale manoeuvres on the border with Ukraine. The end of the war is as yet far away. And although many Kyiv residents have returned home, more stay away from Kyiv and only occasionally come to check on their apartments and houses or to pick up some necessary things. My wife Elizabeth also went recently to Kyiv, visited our apartment and met up with friends. She took back our winter clothes and collected some summer ones. Our apartment has become a place to keep our belongings and our material memory, including the family archives.

My friend Svetlana has been lucky, she met a Ukrainian woman in Pomorie who has been living there for several years and who has books in Russian. The woman is a psychologist and her library consists mainly of books on psychology. Svetlana is now studying the human mind and during her breaks she paints watercolours, trying to capture landscapes. Most of all she likes the sunsets in Pomorie. She tries not to miss a single one, taking countless photographs, which she sends to friends, including me. She hopes to perfect the art of watercolour sunsets.

Svetlana has also discovered the Lebanese-American essayist Nassim Taleb, and fallen in love with his book *Black Swan: The Impact of The Highly Improbable*. I can only envy her. Taleb writes about the human habit of finding the simplest explanations for complex and tragic events and circumstances. Svetlana's elderly parents died before the war. On February 23, the day before the start of the invasion, she added an urn containing her father's ashes to her mother's grave. It was as if she were saying a final goodbye to her former life – ten years of caring for her elderly parents. The very next day, February 24, the invasion began. She is still trying to find a connection between their deaths and the start of Russia's deadly war against Ukraine. I think Taleb will help her create such a connection. At the very least, his book will help to take her mind off the Internet news and her longing for home in Kyiv.

23.05.2022

Russian Shamans against Ukrainian Amulets

In Kharkiv region, Ukrainian troops have pushed the Russian army back almost to the border with Russia. Russian artillery can no longer bombard central Kharkiv, a city of a million people, but it can still bomb the suburbs and most northern districts. Residents of Kharkiv have begun to go out more often, although what they see when they do – destroyed houses and burned-out cars – must be hard to bear. They are trying to restore city services and have even promised to get the metro, which has been immobilised since the start of the war, running again in the coming days. True, thousands of people still live on the metro platforms where, all this time, they have been sheltering from the Russian bombs and missiles. They have now been offered free accommodation in hostels equipped with all the amenities, but, so far, Kharkiv residents have proved to be in no hurry to return to the surface. Some people now appear terrified of open spaces. During the first days of the campaign to convince the metro dwellers to move into the hostels, only thirty-three have agreed to do so.

Before allowing the trains to run again through the underground tunnels, dozens of volunteers with flashlights have been sent into them to check for stray animals. During the war, many cats and several dogs, which had been living with their owners on the platforms, have gone missing, this despite many having kept their cats on leashes so that they could not run away and get lost in the tunnels. All of these missing animals must be accounted for before the trains start to run again.

On the streets of Kharkiv, the sound of trams can once more be heard. When air-raid sirens, explosions and gunshots are all you have heard for so long, the gentle ringing of a tram's bell against a background of general silence must sound like paradise.

Heaven and Hell have taken concrete form in the minds of Ukrainians over the past three months. Hell is Mariupol, Bucha, Hostomel, Vorzel – and the many other destroyed cities, towns, and villages. Paradise is these same cities and villages as they were before the start of the war. Hell is now a specific place on the map with its own capital – Moscow. It is the greatest misfortune for any state to have a common border with Hell. While many think this way, notions of this sort are strongest among believers.

In Ukraine, petrol has finally become like a narcotic. It is not sniffed or injected into veins but, like narcotics, is sold anonymously in the underground "hoarding system". To buy petrol, you first need to contact an anonymous seller through a secret messenger. He will send you an address for a money transfer. Once completed, he then tells you where you can find the hidden can of petrol. By agreement, its location will be no more than one kilometre from where you are. Half of these sellers are scammers who do not supply what they claim to sell, but car owners have no choice but to engage with their services – they will do whatever it takes to fill up their cars.

The system of selling drugs through such messengers surfaced a long time ago. This practice continues, but the demand for drugs has fallen off. Drug users, like many others, have also become refugees and are now no doubt looking for drugs in other countries.

Recently, the police reported the arrest of several scammers who had been supposedly collecting money for the army and for refugees. Such scams are not so common, but their activity makes those who are real activists and volunteers, of which there are tens of thousands now, very nervous. Those who try to be of genuine help to the army and support to refugees involve their friends and acquaintances in their activities and post activity reports and cash receipts on Facebook to show how they have spent the money they have raised. Trustworthy activists can achieve a great deal. Andriy Lyubka, a writer from Uzhhorod, collects money on Facebook to buy old pick-up trucks, for instance. Such vehicles are very much needed on the front line. Andriy is very popular in Ukraine, so when he asked on Facebook for money for a vehicle, he was able to raise enough money within a couple of days to buy two.

Having bought the vehicles, Andriy and a friend drove them to the eastern front line. It is almost fourteen hundred kilometres one way from Uzhhorod to the Donbas. On the way, he learned a great deal. He then hitchhiked back from the Donbas in cars going west. Since that first trip, he now makes sure the vehicles are in good condition before taking them to the military, sometimes even changing their tyres. There are many checkpoints along the route where the Ukrainian military carefully inspect everyone leaving the war zone to ensure that they are not carrying grenades or weapons as dangerous souvenirs.

Andriy has already become a professional in moving the vehicles. He now travels in a convoy of four carefully-repaired and checked pick-up trucks, together with a minibus filled with humanitarian aid and medicines. Each vehicle has two drivers, so that they can travel non-stop. "Don't ask me where I get petrol and diesel!" Andriy says, smiling. I remember as he says this that his most popular book is the crime novel *Carbide* about life among smugglers in the Ukrainian border region. Once the vehicles and humanitarian aid have been handed over to the military, Andriy and his fellow volunteers all get into the now empty minibus and return home to Uzhhorod.

The flow of cars with humanitarian and other aid towards the front is regular and intense. Everyone tries to drive non-stop and not to leave the road for a rest. It is dangerous to pull over as there may be mines on the verges. Hand-knitted socks and other comforts for Ukrainian soldiers are among their cargoes, as well as various amulets – most often these are the soft, handmade doll talisman known as *Oberig* or "Protectors". Irina Ryadchuk, a schoolteacher from Zhytomyr, makes rabbit-soldiers from rags. They are small and weigh almost nothing. Irina sincerely believes that her rabbit dolls will help soldiers stay alive.

When I travelled to the war zone in the Donbas in 2015

and later, I often saw the heads of small dolls peeking out of soldiers' pockets. Most often, these were gifts from their children. The soldiers always carry them. Now, when I see a doll peeking out of a soldier's backpack or from the pocket, I will no longer be so sure about where it came from. Maybe it was indeed given to the soldier by his daughter so that he would always remember his family. Or maybe he received it from an unknown woman, someone who has chosen to do what she can to protect Ukraine's soldiers.

The fact is that paganism did not vanish after the adoption of Christianity. It has remained in the forms of white witches and the all-knowing wizards, called *molfars* in Ukrainian Transcarpathia. It is usually simple, not very educated people, who turn to these *molfars* for help. This means the *molfars* do not have to answer very difficult questions. What is more, no-one asks them about politics and the authorities do not turn to them for help. In Russia, it is very different. There are no *molfars*, but there are many shamans who not only make predictions and come up with answers to difficult questions but who also engage in both political and medical activities. The most famous Russian shaman, Alexander Gabyshev, is now in the Novosibirsk Psychiatric Hospital. In 2019, he started organising hiking trips from Yakutia to Moscow with the aim of driving Putin out of the Kremlin.

According to Gabyshev, Putin is a demon that Nature does not like. Where he appears, cataclysms are bound to occur. Only a shaman can cope with a demon. Gabyshev calls himself a shaman-warrior; he considers it his mission to restore democracy and harmony in the country, if possible by peaceful means but, if necessary by force.

He had twice started this campaign, both times gathering

like-minded folk around him. In Buryatia, residents who liked his ideas gave him a red Zhiguli car, but it was soon taken away by the police. He was of course not allowed to reach Moscow. After facing several arrests and medical examinations, he was declared dangerously mentally ill and shut away in a closed psychiatric hospital. Thus, punitive psychiatry, which was so widespread in the U.S.S.R. in the 1970s, has reappeared in Russia.

The role of shamans in Russia has grown significantly in recent years. In 2019, a story was heard throughout Russia that Irkutsk shamans, under the leadership of the deputy chief shaman of Russia, Artur Tsybikov, had performed a "rite for strengthening Russia and its peoples". During this ceremony, they burned five camels as a sacrifice. The previous time such a ceremony was performed was four hundred years ago. The shamans were accused of cruelty to animals and people expected them to face criminal charges but the shamans got off with a minimal fine, one for violating sanitary standards rather than cruelty to animals. The charge stated that the camels had been brought from another region without the appropriate veterinary inspection.

The biography of the Russian defence Minister, Sergei Shoigu, connects to both Siberian shamanism and to Ukraine. He was born in the Republic of Tuva on the border with Mongolia. His mother was of Ukrainian origin and, in 1960, Shoigu was baptised into the Orthodox Church of Ukraine in Luhansk. It is, perhaps, not surprising that since 2009 Shoigu has been the president of the Russian Geographical Society. It was he who instilled in Vladimir Putin a love for Siberia. In the past ten years, Shoigu and Putin have flown regularly to Siberia, to Baikal and other regions where shamanism is practised very commonly. It is not known whether rituals were held there to strengthen the Russian army in the war against Ukraine. It is nevertheless a fact that the majority of shamans, including the supreme shaman of Russia, Kara-Ool Dupchun-Ool, support President Putin. The supreme shaman of Russia also lives in the Republic of Tuva. By the way, there is a street in Shoigu's hometown of Chadan which is named after him. What is more, General Shoigu Avenue is a central street in the city of Shagonar in Tuva.

Among the Russian soldiers who have died in Ukraine, there are many from Buryatia, a region neighbouring Tuva, as well as the other Siberian autonomous republics. Did the local shamans encourage them to go to war, promising them protection with a blessing, or did they join the army because of poverty? These questions are still difficult to answer, but Shamans probably do perform rituals to "strengthen the military victory". So far, these rituals do not seem to have been of much help.

I do not believe that the Ukrainian amulet dolls have any magical qualities, but I do believe they are made with love. As such, they warm the souls of Ukrainian soldiers. Nor do I know how many rabbits the teacher from Zhytomyr has already sent or plans to send to Ukrainian soldiers on the front line, but the outcome of this war will not depend on rabbits or shamans. The outcome of the war depends on what assistance from that promised by Ukraine's allies is actually provided. Judging by the fact that Ukrainian troops are not able to launch a counter-offensive to liberate the territory occupied by Russia, this assistance is as yet insufficient.

Who is Afraid of Ukraine's Victory?

I do not know what will happen tomorrow. To be honest, I find this lack of certainty about the future almost unbearable. I do know, however, upon what and upon whom the future of my family, of that of all Ukrainians and Ukraine itself, depends. At the same time, I understand that those upon whom our future depends, upon whom the outcome of this war depends largely, may not be interested sufficiently in Ukraine's victory. They may not be committed to returning the occupied territories to Ukraine to thereby ensure the country's further independence. Yet, in doing so, they would also ensure their own safety and prosperity.

For three months now, every day, indeed almost every hour, I have been reading and re-reading the Ukrainian news feed. I read C.N.N. or Reuters as well, but a lot less often. I want positive news. I need news that gives me strength and hope. My biggest fear is losing my sense of optimism. The Ukrainian news feed provides much more positive reports from the front line than you see in the headlines of the international news agencies. Almost a quarter of Ukrainian news is devoted to reports of military assistance provided by our allies

For three months now, I have been reading every day of news that this or that country has handed over modern weapons to us, or that they are about to hand them over. Several times Ukraine has been promised deliveries of military aircraft – not modern ones, of course, but old Soviet era planes that are still lying around on the airfields and airbases of former socialist countries – aircraft that have been promised but not delivered. Something was handed over once but this turned out to be a supply of spare parts for Ukrainian aircraft.

My publisher, Alexander Krasovitsky, lives in Kharkiv. Every day he hears Russian missiles and shells exploding around his city. He also reads the news feed and gets increasingly angry seeing items concerning Hungary's latest *démarche* – Hungary does not support sanctions against Russia and also prohibits the transport of military aid to Ukraine through its territory. "Until European weapons get here, they will continue to bomb us every day," he says. "Getting the right supplies through Hungary could have let us push the Russian artillery away from Kharkiv!" Although Alexander's house is still intact, a few days ago a Russian rocket exploded just two hundred metres away from it.

Today, I read in the news feed that the negotiations with Poland about the transfer of old M.I.G.s to Ukraine have not been stopped. They have been rumbling on for three months. I imagine many dozens of similar negotiations on the delivery of weapons to Ukraine from abroad continuing, with no end in sight.

On the other hand, Lithuania has again sent armoured infantry vehicles and trucks to Ukraine. Lithuania sends weapons to Ukraine almost every day, Estonia too. Help also comes from Poland and Slovakia. Of course, most help comes from the U.K. and the U.S.A. But I am unsure what kind of military assistance comes from Germany, France and the other European countries? Are these countries supplying us with weapons covertly, and unreported in the press? In wartime, anything is possible. I understand that much of what is happening is shrouded in "military secrecy".

At the start of this war, Germany provoked a surge of anti-German sentiment in Ukraine with its promise of five thousand helmets for Ukrainian soldiers instead of weapons. As far as I remember, a month on from the date of that promise, the helmets had still not been delivered. At the same time, Germany declared that it would not supply weapons to Ukraine so as not to provoke Russia. Now, almost every day, sharp, anti-Putin statements are being made in the press either by German Defence Minister, Christine Lambrecht, or by Chancellor Olaf Scholz. As yet, I have not read of any specific reports about military equipment being delivered to Ukraine. I did see an article saying that the German government had allowed Ukraine to order weapons from a German manufacturer, weapons that can be produced and delivered by the end of summer.

On April 23, the German company Rheinmetall requested permission from the government to repair Marder armoured vehicles for supply to Ukraine. The first hundred vehicles could be repaired within six weeks, the rest would take fifteen months to repair. Permission has not yet been granted to carry out the repairs. This means that not even the first one hundred vehicles have been sent to Ukraine. They are not being used to defend Ukrainian territories on the eastern front. Even if they are eventually delivered, there remains the problem of supplying ammunition for these vehicles. Switzerland produces shells for the Marder, but Switzerland does not allow Germany to transfer shells to Ukraine in view of Switzerland's neutral status. Likewise, Israel has banned Germany from giving or selling to Ukraine the Spike missiles produced at a factory in Germany. Israel is afraid that Russia may take revenge on Israel in Syria.

Anti-war sentiment in Germany may end up being anti-Ukrainian sentiment. The German press has already published at least two open letters from "German intellectuals" demanding that Ukraine not be provided with heavy weapons. These letters appeared after the publication in Russia of open letters in support of the "special operation of the Russian army in Ukraine", signed by hundreds of Russian writers and cultural figures. A separate letter of support for Putin's policy in Ukraine was published by professors and students of St Petersburg University. Some Ukrainian intellectuals have seen a connection between the German and Russian open letters and have even decided that Russia is behind the letters from the German intellectuals. This is a typical Russian tactic and Russia is certainly interested in preventing any German military assistance to Ukraine. On Twitter, the Ukrainian ambassador in Berlin depicted German military assistance as a snail with a single rifle bullet attached with sticky tape to its shell. Loud anti-Putin speeches by German politicians do not compensate for the lack of concrete military support. They seem purely decorative: "We are with you in spirit. We know that you are right, but we need to think about ourselves and we do not want to anger Russia".

Germany was obviously thinking only of itself when it continued to cooperate with Russia on the Nord Stream 2 gas pipeline project after the annexation of Crimea and the start of the war in the Donbas. Now Germany and other European countries are prepared to buy Russian rubles so as to buy Russian gas, thereby strengthening the ruble inside Russia and thereby supporting the Russian economy and partially offsetting the damage caused to it by international sanctions.

Ultimately, this is helping Russia to continue financing its aggression in Ukraine. What further concessions will Europe make to Russia? I do not know this either, but most likely Europe will at some point demand concessions to Russia from Ukraine.

In Europe and even in the U.S.A., voices are heard increasingly often calling for Ukraine to accept the losses of its territory and to sit down at the table to negotiate with Putin. At first, the voices were those of largely unknown political scientists and self-appointed "experts". Now we hear former politicians such as Silvio Berlusconi and Henry Kissinger issuing the same message. When similar words proceed from the mouths of the current European heads of state, it will be safe to say that pragmatic calculation has won the day and that the democratic world has betrayed Ukraine. "These statements by Henry Kissinger and Silvio Berlusconi are interconnected," says Stanislav Varenko, a Ukrainian businessman. "They are part of the plan of the pro-Russian lobby in the U.S.A. and Europe. European politicians are secretly pro-Russian because they are afraid of changes in the world order in the event of Ukraine's victory over the Russian Federation". This opinion is shared by the well-known Ukrainian historian and journalist Danylo Yanevsky: "This is an obvious attempt to break the unity of the collective West in relation to Ukraine. The collective West is already divided into two coalitions. One is fighting to 'save Putin's face' – that of Paris-Berlin-Rome-Budapest-Nicosia. The second is completely on the side of Ukraine – that of Washington-Ottawa-London-Warsaw-Vilnius".

The latter coalition, now at the Ramstein airbase in Germany, is working to bring about decisions that will be positive for Ukraine and its army. "Some European politicians are chained to Russia by sentimental and corrupt ties. They will delay, as long as possible, any decision that is harmful to Russia," says Gennady Chizhikov, President of the Ukrainian National Chamber of Commerce. "Others are *a priori* afraid of the Russian Federation because of its size. They are still convinced that it is invincible and that it is better not to provoke Putin. If Ukraine were afraid of the size of the Russian Federation, it would already be occupied!"

I have tried hard to find a person here who would approve of a deal with Putin for the sake of an end to this war, but I have failed. Nina Yanchuk, the retired neighbour at our summer home in rural Zhitomir Region, was typically defiant when I asked her if it would not be better to come to some agreement with Putin. "No, there can be no negotiations with Putin! Only war to the bitter end! How can you talk about anything with him after such atrocities? What's more, he's a cheat! How many times has he deceived everyone!" The voices of such Ukrainians are in stark contrast to those of Berlusconi or Kissinger!

If by the time you read this the Luhansk region has been taken over in its entirety by Russia, along with the city of Sievierodonetsk, it will mean that Germany has in effect helped Russia to capture that territory. The same thing could happen to the last Ukrainian-controlled territories of the Donetsk region.

In Crimea, in Kherson and its surrounding region, Russia is already distributing its passports to residents. Reinforcements are arriving to bolster the Russian army for a further offensive from Crimea against Odesa and Mykolaiv. New Russian tactical battalions are forming on the Ukrainian border near Chernihiv, which may indicate preparations for a new campaign against Kyiv. All this is happening because the Ukrainian army does not have sufficient weapons. This situation gives the Russian army the time and opportunity to prepare for new attacks. As a result, there will be further destroyed cities and villages and there will be new victims among the Ukrainian military and the civilian population.

When reading the Ukrainian news feed last night and this morning, I noticed for the first time a more cautious tone and the admission of bad news in the pronouncements of the "official blogger" of President Zelensky's office, Aleksey Arestovich. For three months, he has been telling Ukrainians several times each day how well all is going at the front and how we will defeat the Russian army with the weapons that the allies give us. He now seems to have lost some of this optimism. He now says that a month of heavy fighting awaits us, with possible further loss of territory. Of course, he goes on to assure us that, later, when our allies supply us with weapons, we will recapture all the territories and even get Crimea back. Knowing that the N.A.T.O. countries have agreed not to anger Putin and not to supply aircraft and tanks to Ukraine, I cannot be sure that Arestovich's promises will come true.

I cannot be sure about Ukraine's future because, when making decisions about the supply of arms to Ukraine, its future is balanced with that of European countries' own political and economic interests. Even countries such as Greece, which managed to provide symbolic help in the form of supplying Ukraine with a planeload of Kalashnikov assault rifles and another flight of portable, hand-held missile systems, are in danger of equivocation. A sociological study shows that 62 per cent. of Greeks are against the supply of arms to Ukraine. I fear that soon Greek politicians will also start saying that Ukraine needs to stop resisting and accept further annexation of its territories, as if this is something that cannot be avoided.

At the same time, Ukrainian sociological analysis reports that more than 80 per cent. of Ukrainians are determined not to accept any loss of their territories and are absolutely not prepared for a peace treaty on Putin's terms. Although Greeks and Ukrainians have very different histories, I had hoped that after the mass killing of Ukrainian ethnic Greeks in Mariupol, Greece might have been firmer in its opposition. That has not happened.

In the meantime, the Ukrainians are still determined to win this war. Near Kharkiv, they have been able to push back the Russian army using old Soviet guns that have long passed their use-by date.

28.05.2022

Gin without Tonic

Since the Soviet era, every queue has served as a people's news agency. While standing in line for meat or cheap potatoes, people exchange news, rumours and thoughts. In the village of Lazarivka, which I already miss a lot, there are rarely queues. A small line might form along the road when the mobile shop arrives selling products that are slightly cheaper than otherwise available. In the past two weeks, however, a new queue has appeared there every Friday, in front of a Lada pulling a trailer that comes from the neighbouring village of Yastrubenka. The residents of Yastrubenka keep a lot of pigs and, once a week, they bring fresh meat and lard to Lazarivka.

My village neighbour, Nina, was standing in that queue when I called today. There were nine people in front of her. I did not ask how many there were behind. "The nights are cold," she complained. "The garden is not growing. Only arugula, radish and dill have come up. And there's no salt in the shops!" I suggested to Nina that she should go to our house and take our salt. We definitely have a kilo pack in the kitchen. "No, we have enough salt in the cellar," she said.

It is true that it is almost impossible to catch Ukrainian peasants unprepared for shortages of basic foodstuffs. In every house, there will be a supply of salt, sugar and flour. Now, during wartime, these stocks have become much larger than in peacetime.

Life in Lazarivka has become a little calmer. Almost all the refugees from the east of Ukraine have left. This even includes the people from Kharkiv, who have gone home despite the ongoing shelling of their city. The remaining residents in the Donbas region have all started to move slowly west, following in the footsteps of the almost 6 million Ukrainians who have already left for Europe.

Thanks to online communication, I often feel like I am living in the village of Lazarivka and the small town of Brusilov nearby. I am subscribed to several groups on Facebook focused on life in Brusilov. On Viber, I participate in the village chat and in the chat of one of the village shops, which is called Bucephalus. The shop owner regularly posts photographs of fresh deliveries of sausages and yogurt. Someone posts the question, "Are there any cigarettes? Is there fresh bread?" The manager answers right away. I feed on this news from the community and our neighbours and feel very close to them, even though we are eight hundred kilometres apart.

I am not too worried about the lack of salt. The front line of fighting is approaching the largest salt producer in Europe, the Artemovsk salt plant in the Donbas. The plant is being shelled by Russian artillery and it has now stopped production, but Turkey and Poland are rushing to our aid by supplying salt. I have a feeling that they will deliver this well before Germany delivers any of the heavy weapons it has promised to Ukraine.

It is hard to predict what will stay in short supply and what will not. When I returned to Ukraine by car a few days ago, I assumed that there would still be no petrol on sale in Ukraine following the destruction of all our fuel depots by Russian missile attacks, so I filled up my tank before crossing the border. I was pleasantly surprised, however, to see that there were no queues at the petrol stations in Uzhhorod. Apparently, petrol and diesel have been brought in from neighbouring countries. In Kyiv too, the queues for petrol have become shorter, although you can only purchase twenty litres at a time.

Shortages remain, however. The first thing I wanted to do after returning was to have a gin and tonic and relax. Here I was dealt a severe blow. Between the border and my current place of residence, I stopped at several supermarkets but could not find tonic water in any of them. I feared that this deficit could be country-wide, so I called a publisher friend in Kyiv and asked him to check in stores near him. Sure enough, there was no tonic there either. The open bottle of gin that stands in the apartment where we now live has lost all meaning.

To sit down with a drink and a book in the evening has always been a summer tradition for me. In the last three months, I have forgotten how to read. I hope this is only temporary. I do continue to follow developments in Ukraine's book industry. It too is struggling to keep its head above water. Russian artillery and rockets have destroyed dozens of libraries, bookshops and printing factories. Even the homes of dead writers have been targeted. The museum of the home of my favourite Ukrainian writer and philosopher, Hryhoriy Skovoroda (1722–1794), was destroyed by a single missile. This could not have been a mistake given Russia's high-precision missile system. A nonconformist who wrote poetry and essays in five languages, Skovoroda spent most of his life walking through Ukraine, writing and teaching. He refused Catherine the Great's offer to serve as a court philosopher. To paraphrase one of his most quoted utterances, "The world tried to catch me but failed".

In classical military tradition, artillery attacks are usually followed by an infantry offensive. A similar two-phased strategy is employed in the Russian offensive against Ukrainian books and literature in general. In the occupied territory of Ukraine, where the Russians now wield power, many libraries have not been destroyed by shelling. Now, "librarians" from the Donetsk library, recently renamed as Nadezhda Krupskaya after Vladimir Lenin's wife, have been sent out to check all the books in the libraries surviving in the newly occupied areas and to select so-called "extremist" literature to pulp.

In practice, this means that any literature published in independent Ukraine since 1991 can be seized and destroyed, including books by the Ukrainian poet Vasyl Stus, who was born in Donetsk and died in a Soviet prison during the Gorbachev era. Soviet books, of which there is also a huge number in Ukrainian libraries, will remain. No doubt these libraries will be "replenished" with books published in Russia, often full of anti-Ukrainian messages like Eduard Limonov's, *Kyiv Kaput*, Anatoly Wasserman's, *Ukraine and the Rest of Russia*, and even Marine Le Pen's, *Looking up to Putin*.

The Ukrainian Ministry of Culture, together with the Ukrainian Book Institute, is working on a counteroffensive. The director of this national institute, Oleksandra Koval, has already issued a statement about the estimated 100 million Soviet books in the libraries in unoccupied areas of Ukraine, saying these should be removed from the libraries' collections and sent for recycling. Given the serious shortage of paper in Ukraine, which currently prevents the publication of new books, the recycling of one hundred million Soviet books could, theoretically, facilitate the printing of a few million new Ukrainian editions. But this will only be once the war is over and once other more urgent problems have been resolved. Oleksandra Koval also said that works by Dostoevsky and Pushkin should be available only in university libraries, so that students could study the influence of classical writers on the emergence of the Russian superiority complex and their messianic ideology. I have, more than once, heard the idea that Russia is a collective Raskolnikov, the character from *Crime and Punishment*. Much more often I hear it said that today's Russia is a collective Putin.

Ukrainians do not argue about how to characterise the people who have scattered booby-traps throughout the Sumy and Chernihiv regions, as a result of which adults and children have been killed. One might say that these mines were planted by the collective Putin, but one could also easily imagine the collective Raskolnikov, or even the collective Dostoevsky, doing this. Sowing landmines on foreign territory is the same thing as sowing suffering, sowing evil. The cult of suffering has always been present in Russian literature, only now Russia wants Ukraine and its people to suffer.

These booby-trap "petal mine"s are popularly called "moth mines". They come in different colours and look like butterflies. Any child would want to pick up such a "toy" from the ground. Moth mines have already left many children without arms and legs and killed many others. Soviet troops used these mines against the civilian population of Afghanistan. Now they are a huge problem for residents of the regions of Ukraine bordering Russia. This explains the urgent push for additional enrolment on sapper courses, where the recruits are taught how to disarm these moth mines and other explosive "gifts" from the Russian aggressors. Volunteers from a variety of professions are joining these courses. In the town of Romney, near to the city of Sumy in northern Ukraine, for example, many farmers and agricultural workers are among these future sappers. For them, the ability to make safe Russian landmines and shells is important. Their lives depend on it.

According to military experts' most conservative estimates, it will take at least five to seven years to clear Ukraine of landmines and unexploded shells following the end of the war. From my understanding of the consequences of World War I, I imagine that it will actually take much longer. I know a place in northern France, near the village of Vimy, where unexploded mines and shells are still occasionally unearthed which have been lying unseen in the ground for more than a hundred years. Given the scale of the current offensive, it is simply not realistic to believe that everything could be cleared in a few years.

Thoughts about landmines and books lead me to think that a book can become a mine. It can explode, blowing up all harmony to become the cause of murder and hatred. Some books have become mines accidentally, while others were written as weapons. Many such literary mines have been written against Ukraine. A separate classification of anti-Ukrainian literary novels and their authors has already been created, that of "the anti-Ukrainian military science-fiction writer". The most prominent representative of this genre is Fedor Berezin, a retired officer from Donetsk, who even served as the Minister of Defence in the so-called "Donetsk People's Republic". Other science fiction writers, like Sergey Lukyanenko, Viktor Poberezhnykh and Artem Rybakov have also been engaged in this "literary" war against Ukraine for more than twenty years.

Now that the war with Ukraine and N.A.T.O. countries has moved from the pages of their books into reality, I imagine that these books will have lost some of their popularity. After all, you can now see something of their imagined world on YouTube. Their fantasies have materialised, at least in part. I say "in part" because in all these novels, Russia wins and the defeat of Ukraine is swift and decisive. The reality has turned out to be somewhat different.

12.06.2022

A Ukrainian Princess and "Good Russians"

A couple of days ago, I finally decided to register on TikTok, partly because materials on the platform are becoming a frequent topic of discussion among my friends on Facebook, but mostly because of one young woman by the name of Tetyana Chubar. Tetyana is 23 years old, blonde and 160 cms tall. She is divorced, with two small children. None of this would matter if it were not for one more fact: she is the commander of a self-propelled cannon – an armoured vehicle something like a tank – and she has four men under her command. She also manages to paint her nails yellow and blue and maintains her TikTok account under the nickname "Princeska - 13".

She used TikTok to publicise the difference between a tank and a self-propelled cannon and to announce her dream of painting her combat vehicle in "pink camouflage". I can imagine only one situation when pink camouflage might work, if the vehicle ever stopped in a field of pink roses. Nonetheless, her command allowed her partially to fulfil her dream. She has been given permission to paint the interior of the combat vehicle pink. Tetyana has already bought paint for the job. I wonder how the four men under her command will take this? I do hope they do not object. It is both an honour and a responsibility to have a clockwork commander whose TikTok site is followed by hundreds of thousands of people.

Tetyana has admitted to reporters receiving many messages from men who say they are in love with her. I wonder if those men are now at home or at the front? In any case, they probably understand that were they to win her hand, they would always be out-ranked by Princeska-13.

A key protagonist of Russian TikTok, the master of Chechnya, Ramzan Kadyrov, has millions of followers. His posts invariably threaten Ukraine and Putin's enemies. His videos get millions of likes. Apparently, Russians admire people who try to scare others.

Social networks around the world have long been a battlefield. The battle on Ukrainian and Russian social media complements the battles going on in the real world in the east and south of Ukraine, where the hottest battles are now taking place in the city of Sievierodonetsk. For the second week running, the Russian army has been trying to capture the city but has not succeeded. Nothing is known for sure about the losses on either side but, as in the case of Mariupol, the city of Sievierodonetsk – now destroyed but refusing to surrender – has become another symbol of the courage of Ukrainian soldiers. Official Ukrainian media outlets have reported that Ukrainian troops recaptured half of the city from the Russians and that they are about to recapture the entire city. However, one of the best known, and probably most independent Ukrainian journalists, Yuriy Butusov, who regularly goes to the front line and spends time with Ukrainian soldiers, has asked the authorities to stop lying. He reports that the Ukrainian troops have been pushed back into the industrial area of the city from where they are continuing to defend themselves. "The situation has in no way changed in favour of the Ukrainian troops," he said.

This is not the first time that Butusov has come into conflict with the official authorities. Before the war, in November 2021, during a press conference, he entered into an open skirmish with President Zelensky, accusing officials from the President's entourage of deliberately disrupting several Ukrainian special services operations. This time around, after the journalist's statement about the lack of honesty in official reports on the fighting, a member of Zelensky's Servant of the People party, deputy Maryana Bezugla, berated Butusov and publicly called on the secret service of Ukraine, the S.B.U., to "deal with this journalist". She accused him of giving away Ukrainian positions to its enemies. Civil society came out sharply in defence of Butusov. As a result, Bezugla decided to go to the front line herself and to visit one of the command posts there. Usually, politicians post their photographs from the front line on Facebook or Instagram, but on this occasion a photograph of Deputy Bezugla in a camouflage suit was sent to journalists by outraged officers who accused her of trying to interfere in military affairs about which she understood nothing.

Early last Saturday morning, my wife and I were awoken by the sound of the telephone. Our daughter, who is visiting Kyiv from London, said that she had for the first time heard missiles exploding. Five Russian rockets had hit the left bank of the Dnipro river, reminding the capital's inhabitants of the fragility of their world. These explosions may encourage some Kyivites to think about leaving the city, although the number of people returning to the capital continues to grow. Theatres and cinemas are already operating once more. Even gyms and swimming pools have reopened. Restaurants and cafés are once again full of people. Bathers have reappeared on the beaches of Kyiv's Hydropark, a resort island located in the middle of the Dnipro river. This is one of the capital's favourite destinations for a day out. It is nicknamed "Kebab

Island" because during summer the dominant fragrance here is that of the grill. This year the island is less crowded than usual but it nonetheless remains a popular place for picnics and celebrations, which sometimes include firework displays.

During wartime, fireworks are more likely to frighten than to please and a petition has already appeared on President Zelensky's desk asking him to ban fireworks until the end of the war. Recently, a wide variety of petitions have been registered on the Presidential official website. The President is obliged to respond to any petition that is signed by 25 thousand citizens, although most of the recent petitions have very few signatories. Ukrainians take more interest in news from the front than in the President's website. At the moment, among the least popular petitions are the "Petition for the transition from the Cyrillic to the Latin Alphabet" and a "Petition for the replacement of the national anthem". A petition demanding a complete ban on the entry of Russian citizens into the territory of Ukraine has more signatories, but not many more. There are also not so many signatures for the petition to break off diplomatic relations with the Republic of Belarus. Nonetheless, these topics and those like them occasionally cause heated discussion on Facebook. An impassioned debate is currently taking place there on the topic of "good Russians".

A "good Russian", in the understanding of more tolerant Ukrainians, is one who does not support Putin and opposes the war in Ukraine. Using this definition, it is not easy to identify many well-known "good Russians". Even so, some Ukrainians refuse to acknowledge even those who seem to fit this definition of a good Russian. In recent days, two such "good Russians" have brought attention to themselves by coming to Ukraine. One of them is the well-known Russian T.V. journalist, Alexander Nevzorov, who supported Russian imperialist policies for many years and once even made a documentary film supporting the actions of the Soviet police who killed civilian protesters in Vilnius near the T.V. tower in 1990. More recently, he started to criticise Putin and the war against Ukraine. Nevzorov recently left Russia and has asked for Ukrainian citizenship. There were early reports suggesting that had already been given a Ukrainian passport, but after a wave of protests, government representatives said that the procedure for obtaining citizenship had not yet been completed. The loudest protests against the granting of a passport to Nevzorov came from Russian citizens who had moved to Ukraine to defend the Donbas region during the Russian-backed breakaway movement in 2014. Many later applied for Ukrainian citizenship but few of them have yet to receive Ukrainian passports.

The second "good Russian" is also a journalist, Marina Ovsyannikova. From 2000, she worked as an editor for a state-owned Russian T.V. channel until at the beginning of the war when, famously, she appeared on air with an anti-war poster. She then left Russia and got a job in Germany. In Ukraine, she tried to hold a press conference and a meeting with students from Kyiv State University. Both events were cancelled after protests by outraged Ukrainians. Protesters pointed out that, in a recent interview in Europe, Ovsyannikova had argued for the lifting of sanctions against Russia because, she said, they were making life difficult for ordinary people in that country.

The topic of sanctions harming ordinary Russians was also raised recently at a press conference at the Cannes Film

Festival by the "good Russian" film director Kirill Serebryan-nikov. True, he later went further and asked for the lifting of sanctions against the oligarchs Roman Abramovich and Vladislav Surkov. The latter, until a few years ago, had worked in President Putin's administration and is held to be respon-sible for much of the ideology behind the Russian president's anti-Ukrainian policy.

Defending her pro-Ukrainian position, Ovsyannikova calls herself Ukrainian and has promised to change her surname to Tkachuk, which is her Ukrainian mother's sur-name. I imagine she will soon turn to President Zelensky for Ukrainian citizenship. In any case, on Facebook, she thanked President Zelensky for "helping her to leave Russia". To date, Ukrainians have not been told how this escape operation was achieved. I would love to know more. In the West, President Zelensky already has the image of a James Bond character. After the war, it will be possible to make a nail-biting action movie about the daring rescue of the journalist who spoke out in Moscow against the war in Ukraine.

The topic of "good Russians" is complex and ambiguous. Among the genuinely good Russians one can find such significant writers and moral authorities as Mikhail Shishkin, who lives in Switzerland, and Vladimir Sorokin, who lives in Berlin. Sorokin well remembers how followers of Putin's youth movement, "Nashi", burned his books in Red Square. For some reason, the two writers are rarely mentioned in the context of "good Russians", but perhaps that is just as well. Today, many Ukrainians believe that there is no such thing as a good Russian. Even those who oppose Putin often continue to support Russian imperialism by refusing to recognise Crimea as part of Ukraine. It does seem that many Russian liberals could only be considered liberals in Russia. They would never be described as such in Europe.

Ukrainians will soon face a new controversy: "good Belarusians". Recently, a number of reports have appeared in the Ukrainian press concerning Ukraine's aggressive northern neighbour. These items have been about Belarusian officers fighting in the Russian army, the missiles launched from Belarusian territory that have hit Ukrainian cities, the Belarusian airfields being used by Russian bomber squadrons and, of course, the suggestion that ex-Soviet military equipment, previously stored in Belarussian hangers, has been handed over to the Russian army. So far, however, a petition to break off diplomatic relations with Belarus has only 1,085 signatures, although there are more than 80 days left until the deadline for signature collection. During war, eighty days is a long time, especially when each day brings new worries.

Having registered on TikTok to follow the account of artillery officer Tetyana Chubar, I have started worrying about her too. I am willing her to emerge victorious from each new artillery duel and I would gladly support her quest to paint the self-propelled cannon pink all over — albeit after the war, of course. I think this will not only be her biggest reward but will be the icing on the cake for all her TikTok followers.

Selling a War

The war in Ukraine has entered a protracted, slower-paced phase. Europe has now become accustomed to it, although the U.S.A. has not. In the U.S.A., they understand that getting used to war is extremely dangerous. Together with the U.K., Norway, Lithuania and Poland, they are actively helping Ukraine with weapons. They see this as the way to get Russia to agree to negotiate sooner rather than later. Germany, France and Italy, on the other hand, are afraid to strengthen Ukraine in this war. They calculate that by slowing down the supply of weapons or even refusing to help Ukraine with heavy weapons, they will hasten the end of the war. They seem to think that when Russia has occupied all the territories it planned to take over, then it will cease aggression and call Ukraine to the negotiating table, putting a *fait accompli* before the Ukrainian leadership. In such a situation, the message from Russia would be "recognize the annexation of the occupied territories, or we will annex more".

Russia has its own plan. This includes the destruction of the entire state of Ukraine. Its plan was announced in an article titled, "What Russia Should Do with Ukraine" by Russian political strategist Timofey Sergeytsev and published by the state-controlled Russian news agency R.I.A. Novosti on April 3 this year, five weeks after the new Russian aggression began.

Meanwhile, in Transcarpathia, an area that has been little affected by the war so far, except for the huge inflow of I.D.P.s, an active programme of "street enlistment" has begun.

Ukrainian military recruitment officers have started visiting hotels, hostels and any places where I.D.P.s are living. The military officials write out on the spot enlistment summonses to men of military age and demand that they go to the nearest enlistment office and register for military service. Being registered in this way does not mean necessarily that you will be taken immediately into the army and sent to the front line, but you are very definitely one step closer to that happening.

This enlistment process intensified after the Ukrainian authorities for the first time announced approximate figures for the losses in the Ukrainian army of about ten thousand dead. In an interview, President Zelensky also admitted recently that Ukraine loses up to one hundred fighters every day, and up to 500 are wounded. Probably it is not surprising that many male I.D.P.s try to hide from the military enlistment officers so as not to be registered.

In the fourth month of the war, maintaining a fighting spirit in Ukrainian society is not as easy as at the beginning of hostilities. The pressure from the Russian forces at the front is relentless. They have fifteen to twenty times more artillery than the Ukrainian side and more soldiers too. Despite this, there have been no drastic changes to the shape of the front line in the south or east.

On the "Western Front", that is, in the war of narratives within Europe, Ukraine has already defeated Russia. Ukrainian flags hang in the centres of almost every European city or town. Sometimes the Ukrainian flag flies among the flags of the member states of the European Union. This especially pleases and inspires most Ukrainians, as it pleases me too. But I do see another meaning in this which, perhaps, is not yet so obvious. There will come a moment when European leaders will say to Ukraine, "That's it, we can no longer help you! Agree to the Russian annexation of the south and east of the country and, in return, we will accept what remains of Ukraine into the European Union". In foreseeing this eventuality, the important question for Ukrainians is what will be left of Ukraine at this moment? Will Odesa remain? Will Kharkiv remain? European geopolitics is the art of elegant cynicism, although many will not see anything cynical in such a formulation. On the contrary, they will say, "You see, the European Union did save you from Russia!"

It is probably too early to think about such a scenario, especially if the U.S.A. and the U.K. are still not tired of helping Ukraine. After three months of war, however, even President Biden could not restrain himself from recalling publicly how he had warned President Zelensky about the certainty of Russia's attack and how the Ukrainian president had not wanted to listen to him. Nonetheless, according to *Time* magazine, Zelensky is now one of the most influential people in the world together, of course, with President Biden. Ukraine is now also much more than just a well-known country. There can be few adults in the world who do not now know where Ukraine is located and with whom it is at war.

Ukraine is still being talked about a great deal in world media. Ukrainian refugees are still being helped by Europeans. Ukraine's sympathisers see Ukraine as a child lost in a very dangerous forest. Some Ukrainian modern art fortifies this image. At the international competition in chainsaw carving in the U.K. this year, the sculptor from Transcarpathia, Mykola Gleba, won the main prize. His wood carving depicts the figure of a crying, five-year-old Ukrainian refugee boy lost on the Ukrainian–Polish border. The photograph of this boy appeared in many newspapers all over the world. Now his image has been captured in sculpture.

This war, like any successful blockbuster, has merchandising potential. Of course, it is disturbing to compare the merchandising around the "Shrek" movie with that around a war. Nevertheless, the same economic and commercial rules apply. Ukraine became popular thanks to this war, thanks to its courageous resistance against a bigger and better-equipped aggressor. Ukraine has become a symbol of resistance against the forces of evil, a symbol of the struggle for truth and justice. That is why thousands of cities around the world have raised Ukrainian flags in their central squares. That is why ordinary citizens of many countries began to buy Ukrainian flags and hang them on their balconies or windows. The production of such flags must be very intensive. After all, demand has risen extremely steeply. Are they being produced and sewn in China? Certainly, China is very good at reacting to sudden changes in demand. Even so, it seems that flag manufacturers are not able to keep up with the demand from stores and online shops. A month ago, some residents of Detroit and Washington complained to me that in the U.S.A., in order to buy a Ukrainian flag, once you have placed an order, you still had to wait two weeks.

In France, from where I have just returned to Ukraine, another problem has arisen. This is connected with the lack of guidebooks about Ukraine. No, the flow of tourists to Ukraine has not increased. I am sure that there are no tourists from France in Ukraine right now. But after the start of the war, French people rushed to the bookshops and bought up all the guidebooks about Ukraine because they wanted to know more about the country and no other books about it were available in French. There were not many guidebooks either. So as not to deal with the thorny issues of Crimea and the partially captured region of the Donbas, French publishers have not produced any new guidebooks about Ukraine since 2014. Just now, not a single publishing house in the world would consider such a publication. Once all the old guidebooks had been bought up, interested French people then bought up all the maps of Ukraine. Now there are no maps or guidebooks. And publishers are unlikely to make any effort to deal with their total deficit until they receive guarantees that Ukraine's borders will not change for a good while. And who knows when they will get that kind of guarantee, given that Ukraine's neighbour has promised to destroy Ukraine and rename all the territory it occupies, so that the very name of Ukraine disappears from geography?

But Ukraine will not disappear, not from history textbooks, nor from maps, nor from European and world geopolitics. Ukraine will survive because, among other things, hundreds of thousands of Ukrainians are fighting for it, because hundreds of millions of people around the world are rooting for it and worrying about it.

A few days ago, in the western Ukrainian city of Rivne, several hundred citizens were on their knees in the central square. This is the way they say goodbye to soldiers killed in the war. This time, Rivne buried the deputy commander of the Rivne Territorial Defence Battalion, Captain Mykola Savchuk. He became the first victim among the soldiers and officers of his battalion. At the same time, an excavator was working in the central park of Rivne without spectators. There, the pedestal of a monument was demolished and the bones of the legendary Red Army soldier Aleko Dundich, who died in battle in Rivne in 1920 at the age of 23, were dug up and removed from the grave. His bones were uncovered at a depth of two metres, removed and placed into a black plastic bag. The bag was placed in a cheap wooden coffin and then taken to the city cemetery, where the bones were reinterred.

This is the Bolshevik Aleko Dundich's fourth reburial. His first burial took place five days after his death in the battle with the Polish army on July 5, 1920. Soon afterwards, the Polish army recaptured Rivne. The Poles disinterred the coffin with Aleko Dundich's remains in 1927 and reburied them in the city cemetery. The city remained part of Poland until 1939. When the Soviets came to Rivne again, after World War II, the remains of the legendary Bolshevik cavalryman were once again reburied in the central park and a new monument erected to mark the spot. Now, some one hundred and two years after his death, Aleko Dundich's remains have been moved yet again.

Aleko Dundich became the hero of stories by Isaac Babel, as well as in a novel by Alexei Tolstoy. Films were made about him, plays were written. He called himself a Serb, although his parents were Catholic Croats. After he was captured by Russian soldiers during the World War I, he escaped and joined the Bolshevik detachment in Odesa. Although unable to read and write, he was to become one of the most legendary of all the commanders of the Bolshevik cavalry, famous for his ability to cut down his enemies with a sabre when in the saddle. If Russian soldiers were ever to return to the city of Rivne, then you can be sure that Aleko Dundich would be due for a fifth such reburial and that he would then be likely to make a return to the central park. I hope and believe this will never happen.

The most recent reburial of the Bolshevik Dundich took place at the request of the inhabitants of the city, who have been more actively involved in the process of decommunisation than the inhabitants of many other Ukrainian cities. This activism could be explained by the city's unusually turbulent past, or perhaps it reflects the fact that many of Rivne's men and women have been fighting on the new front line since the first days of the current Russian aggression.

There was a time when the image of Aleko Dundich was used in Soviet propaganda merchandising. Collectors bought postage stamps with his image, there were postcards with his portrait and even small plaster busts were sold of the famous cavalryman. All of this is now in the deep past, although I imagine Dundich memorabilia has maintained its value, especially among collectors of Soviet memorabilia.

In Ukraine, the most successful example of war merchandising in the current conflict has to date been a postage stamp commemorating the sinking of the Russian cruiser, *Moskva*. The Ukrainian Post Office was able to sell one million of these commemorative stamps and sent part of the money it received from sales to help the Ukrainian army. There are no stamps dedicated to Ukraine's dead soldiers as yet. But in toy stores, a children's soft toy dog called Cartridge has become a big hit. A real dog, named Patron, is the most famous animal in Ukraine at the moment. He helps Ukrainian sappers find Russian landmines and unexploded shells. Someday a movie might be made about Patron and, no doubt, a book will be written. Even today, Ukrainian children all know his story, love him and want to have their own fluffy version of this canine hero. Children also follow Patron on Instagram (at ua.patron), where he teaches children how to take care of themselves should they chance upon any explosive objects.

28.06.2022

Everyone is Looking for Blood

The city of Kremenchuk is looking for blood. In this once cosy little town, a Russian rocket with a ton of explosives blew apart a large shopping and entertainment centre where about a thousand people were spending the afternoon. The exact number of those killed is still not known, but hundreds of people were at the epicentre of the explosion. For some, nothing is left of them. Police have taken dozens of statements about missing persons, about those who did not return home that evening. The number of wounded is known. They all need blood. The survivors were left without arms, without legs.

Kremenchuk will not forget about this Russian war crime for a very long time. Most likely it will never be forgotten and a monument to the victims of this terror attack will be erected. Cities remember their tragedies and they place memorial days in their calendars. June 27 will become a day of mourning for Kremenchuk. Citizens will come to the site of the destroyed shopping centre and they will remember what happened and think about that Russian rocket. This tragedy has given a new impetus to blood donation efforts. Blood is needed everywhere in Ukraine right now, wherever Russian missiles and shells explode, wherever wounded soldiers are brought from the front lines.

In Lviv, they are waiting for blood at the military hospital which is located on the street named after the Russian writer Anton Chekhov, as well as in the regional hospital on the street named after the Russian writer Leo Tolstoy. While the search for blood goes on all over Ukraine, the scientific council of the Pyotr Tchaikovsky Conservatoire in Kyiv has met to discuss whether to rename the conservatoire after the Ukrainian composer, Mykola Lysenko, who, by the way, was friends with Tchaikovsky. The scientific council decided not to rename it. The conservatoire will remain named after Pyotr Tchaikovsky.

Despite the dynamism of young Ukrainians and Ukraine's official demand that other countries boycott Russian culture, many older Ukrainians remain more conservative and do not wish to go that far and quietly oppose the total boycott of Russian culture. An opera-loving friend of ours shed tears at the thought of not being able ever again to hear "Eugene Onegin" at the Kyiv Opera House.

A well-known poet from Odesa, Boris Khersonsky, recently spoke at a literary evening with Sergey Gandlevsky, the Russian poet, human rights activist and a well-known critic of Putin. This little-noticed event infuriated some Ukrainian intellectuals and provoked a wave of hatred against Khersonsky, who now writes poetry in both Russian and in Ukrainian. Until recently, he wrote only in Russian.

Waves of hatred are sweeping Ukraine and pushing Ukrainians to look for internal enemies. Plenty of real internal enemies exist. Someone shared the coordinates of Ukrainian military training centres with the Russian military and the barracks were destroyed by missiles launched from Belarus or Russian territory. Others are spreading pro-Russian propaganda on the Internet. At the same time, this creates more and more distrust and sometimes even hatred. All too often this is being directed towards Russian-speaking authors and intellectuals, who must now show themselves to be three times more patriotic than their Ukrainian-speaking counterparts. Even if they achieve this, it does not save them from accusations that it is they who are to blame for the war because they speak, think and write in Russian. Russian-speaking Ukrainians are all-too used to such constant accusations, just as the country has almost become used to war. Not that this means that people are now accustomed to rocket explosions, although we have all become used to the idea that this war is very likely to last a long time. "Experts" constantly name the date for the end of the war. Some of them say September. President Zelensky says that the war will end before the frosts set in, before winter. Other politicians think spring of 2023 is more likely.

People are now so used to sirens that they react only after a Russian missile explodes somewhere nearby and kills several people who did not or who were unable to run to a bomb shelter. I myself wonder what words would make people take the sirens more seriously. I worry about this, as I also worry about evidence that the criminal world has adapted to the presence of war. There has been an increase in cases of attempts to sell stolen humanitarian aid and even protective equipment that was supposed to be destined for the military. As a result, volunteers who buy bulletproof vests or helmets to give to our soldiers run the risk of buying what has been stolen from others.

A few days back, on the street named after the Soviet and Russian aircraft designer Tupolev, where I spent fifteen years of my life and where my older brother and his wife still live, a drone fell unexpectedly from the sky. Passers-by saw a package attached to the drone and found that it contained 50 thousand dollars! They called the police. It turned out that several hundred metres from this place, two criminals had opened an illegal currency exchange office. As soon as a client handed packs of dollars to them through an open window, the fraudsters put the money into a bag and sent it by drone to their accomplices. Meanwhile, they escaped through the backdoor without giving the client anything in return for their dollars. In this case, it proved beneficial that the weight of the dollars was too much for the drone.

The criminals were arrested. The client, an unsuspecting I.D.P., will get his dollars back. The threat of many further scams remains, however. In Ukraine, after the series of economic crises and bank failures, people keep cash at home. Hundreds of thousands of refugees have lost their homes. Many of them managed to take their savings with them and now carry these around with them wherever they travel to. Sometimes it becomes necessary to change a large sum of dollars into hryvnia, maybe to buy a car or to move further on, or for some other purpose. Ukrainians usually keep much of their money in dollars or euros, the currencies they trust. Then comes the dangerous part: they look for the best exchange rate. The illegal currency exchange dealers always offer the best rates. These places work just like real currency exchanges if you wish to change a small amount, say twenty dollars or ten euros. But as soon as a person appears with a large sum, the criminals take their money and disappear quickly through the back door. Or they use a drone to remove the money before they disappear, so that no evidence of the crime can be found on them if they are caught.

Another criminal industry that has arisen serves men of military age who want to go abroad at any cost. They are afraid of being drafted and so therefore try to either get false medical documents, stating that they are too sick to join the army, or false student documents from foreign universities that entitle them to return abroad to continue their studies. Another way to go abroad illegally is to go to the border and find a guide who is an experienced people smuggler. Here, of course, there is the danger of falling into the hands of scammers who take your money in advance. They charge from five to twenty thousand dollars per person. Once you give them the money, they then disappear. There are also "honest" guides who really do take people to the other side of the border. True, sometimes they and their clients are caught by the border guards. From all angles, this is a dangerous venture. Travelling with false documents is always a lottery. According to unofficial estimates, up to half a million men of enlistment age have found ways to leave Ukraine over the last four months. These are the men who do not want to fight. Members of Parliament proposed a bill that would give such men a month to return to the country and, if they fail to return, it was proposed that they would then be deprived of Ukrainian citizenship. The proposed bill received more criticism than approval and was safely thrown out.

Ukrainians who do not want to fight and are afraid of mobilisation continue to try to go abroad, often unsuccessfully. The other day, on the Polish–Ukrainian border, border guards removed six young men from a train. They had fake documents from foreign universities. Then and there, they were given summons to report for the military registration at the enlistment office. They are now registered as liable for military service.

Delivery of subpoenas from the military registration and enlistment offices has become something of a traditional punishment for violators of various laws and wartime rules. Recently, the police raided a nightclub in Kyiv which had been working despite the curfew. The detained men were all handed summons to attend the military registration office. True, I doubt that all of these nightclub lovers will have then rushed to the military registration office the next day. Some of them will have sought out manufacturers of fake documentation or found guides to help them cross the border. This is the reality of today's Ukraine. I imagine that things would be much the same in any democratic country during wartime.

While the relatives of Ukrainian prisoners of war loudly and very publicly demand the earliest possible exchange of prisoners between Russia and Ukraine, another process is going on quietly and out of the public eye: the exchange of the dead.

I do not know where these exchanges take place, although I believe it to be somewhere near the front line. Wherever it might be, a refrigerator truck with the number two hundred on its windscreen arrives regularly at the regional morgue on Oranzhereinaya Street, nearby the botanical gardens in Kyiv. This number signifies how the dead are designated in military terminology. Accompanying soldiers, who bring back black body bags with the remains of the war dead, then place these in the morgue. Pathologist-anatomists work with these remains. Their main task is to try to identify the soldier so that their remains can be transferred to relatives for burial. If the deceased has tattoos, this is a much easier thing to do. The black bags do not always contain the body of a soldier, however. Often there are only a few bones or a skull, sometimes just parts or fragments of bone. Relatives of soldiers known to be missing in the war hand in their D.N.A. in order to make it easier for the authorities to find and identify their deceased loved ones.

Bodies are exchanged on a one-for-one basis – one dead Ukrainian soldier for one dead Russian soldier. In an attempt to obtain as many bodies as possible, the Russians resort to tricks. They put the corpses of killed civilians in black bags. As a result, the work with bags begins with a general sorting process. "Civilian" remains are also processed. This is a longer and more complicated matter because it is not known from where the Russians have brought these remains. The remains are kept for some time in the refrigerator of the morgue and are then transferred to other regional morgues for further identification in the ongoing search for missing relatives. In many cases, this task is impossible. Especially when it comes to identifying dead civilians from the Donbas or the Zaporozhzhia regions.

The database of the D.N.A. of relatives of Ukrainians whose have gone missing in the war is constantly growing. Anybody at the epicentre of a Russian missile explosion at the shopping and entertainment centre in Kremenchuk last Monday disappeared completely, nothing remains of them – not even traces or fragments. He or she has gone missing forever. We do not know exactly how many such people there were. In their case, D.N.A. will not be of any help.

While residents of the city donated blood for the wounded,

local authorities declared three days of mourning. Usually at such times of mourning, entertainment events, concerts and circus performances are at once cancelled. However, I cannot imagine the inhabitants of Kremenchuk were in any case planning to have fun during these three days, nor for a long time afterwards.

While periods of mourning could quite legitimately be declared in dozens of cities and towns in Ukraine following the shelling and massacres of Ukrainian citizens by the Russian army, it nonetheless seems strange to go into mourning in the middle of a war. After all, after the end of the mourning period, life usually returns to normal – comedies are again shown on T.V. and theatres and circuses once again open their doors. Since the start of the war, there has been only one T.V. channel in Ukraine – a news channel that replaces all the previous T.V. channels. And while it is still possible to go to the theatre in some cities, there is no guarantee that sirens warning of an air raid will not interrupt the performance.

It would, of course, be better if some strong, dramatic theatrical performance could interrupt this war, or even stop it altogether. Alas, the real drama of war remains unstoppable. Its director and producer, Putin, wants to shed as much Ukrainian blood as possible. Individual Ukrainians still do have a choice of sorts – to go to war or to try and avoid mobilisation, to flee to a bomb shelter when an air raid warning sounds or to ignore the sirens. But the dead in Kremenchuk and those in hundreds of other cities, towns and villages, no longer have a choice.

05.07.2022

The Power of Thought

Fighting in summer is a very hot thing to do. There is the dust to contend with, the body armour, helmets, heavy weapons. The fiery barrage of artillery shelling further raises the air temperature and adds scorching dust to the atmosphere – together with the dust and smoke from burning houses, trees and other vegetation. Along the entire length of the front line, there is now very little close combat, except for street battles in a few cities. Having fought intense battles for Sievierodonetsk and Lysychansk, Ukrainian troops have retreated. Now that the Luhansk region has been almost entirely captured by the Russian army, the fighting will shift to the western area of the Donetsk region, which is still under Ukrainian control. The Ukrainian military command says that the troops have been pulled out to save the lives of soldiers and that the intention is to return and liberate the occupied territories as soon as possible. Watching the process from afar can sometimes feel depressing. Fortunately, Ukrainian depression is not usually very deep. When spirits sink, Ukrainians simply look more carefully to find some positive news. And they always find it.

A few days ago, Ukrainian artillery knocked the Russian military off Snake Island in the Black Sea. The remnants of the island's Russian garrison fled on two or three boats, leaving all their weapons behind. The Russian leadership announced that the troops had left the island to show that they were not threatening Ukrainian ships taking wheat out of the ports of the Odesa region. After the announcement, two Russian bombers destroyed all the military equipment left there, so that it could not be captured by the Ukrainian army. Now the island is back under Ukrainian control or, to be more precise, it is no longer under Russian control. This is significant because, while the Russians were there, their missiles could threaten a very large area of the Black Sea and Ukraine. However, since the island is very exposed, it will probably remain deserted for the remainder of the war. It is too easy a target for Russian ballistic missiles and military aircraft.

The second piece of good news came from the cultural front, where the fighting is also very active. The director of St Petersburg's famous Hermitage Museum, Mikhail Piotrovsky, in a long interview with *Rossiyskaya Gazeta*, said that the promotion of Russian culture is the same sort of "special operation" as the invasion of Ukraine. This is not exactly good news, but it is another piece of evidence for the case being made in The Hague of Russia's crimes against humanity. Then Piotrovsky's "special operation" appeared to be slapped down by the announcement that U.N.E.S.C.O. had registered the "culture of Ukrainian borscht" as part of Ukraine's intangible cultural heritage. The delight which greeted this news was much more satisfying than the outrage caused by Mikhail Piotrovsky's interview and resonated throughout Ukrainian media: "Borscht is ours!" Ukrainians declared this to the world with the same level of enthusiasm as the Russians had shouted, "Crimea is ours!" in 2014. The fact that the text of the U.N.E.S.C.O. pronouncement does not actually say "borscht" but "the culture of cooking Ukrainian borscht" does not seem to matter! The war over borscht, between Ukraine and Russia, has been going on a long time. It is surprising that Poland has never become involved. Borscht also occupies an important place in the Polish epicurean tradition, although Polish Borscht is different to the Ukrainian one. In fact, it is not "Polish Bortsch" but "Polish Bartsch". Poles use apple cider and vinegar in their recipe, a thing which would outrage most Ukrainians. In any case, there are not any conflicts over borscht between Ukraine and Poland, only between Ukraine and Russia.

The spokesperson for the Russian Foreign Ministry, the infamous Maria Zakharova, has made public statements repeatedly defending Russian borscht from the "encroachment of Ukrainian nationalists". The U.N.E.S.C.O. decision certainly made my day. I am very happy that the words "Ukraine" and "borscht" are now combined in an official statement of this kind. I know that Ukrainian front-line soldiers eat borscht with great pleasure and that Ukrainian volunteers, from all regions of the country, bottle and send the main ingredients (beetroot, herbs and spices) to the front so that the soup can be prepared more quickly in the military kitchens.

Verified data shows that Ukrainians make borscht according to at least 300 different recipes. In my experience, each family has their own recipe. I also have my own recipe for borscht. Actually, I have several. Our old friend Tatiana has thirteen borscht recipes. Her favourite is made with the addition of some sour "Antonovka" apples. Both she and her husband, Valentin Suslov, the ninety-two-year-old professor of medicine, are now in Mainz in Germany. The other day, I was able to visit them there as I happened to be nearby in Frankfurt at an event about the situation in Ukraine.

Valentin and Tatiana now live on a quiet street nearby to

a park, almost in the very centre of Mainz, at the home of Valentin's former colleague, Almut. Almut, herself eighty-seven years old, still drives a car and helps her refugee guests in many ways. She has given over the entire ground floor of her two-storey house for them to use. Almut still has the energy to go up and down the wooden stairs and has moved to the first floor. When Valentine first arrived in Mainz, he returned to hospital, where he was subjected to further amputation because his wounds, disturbed by the long and painful journey, had failed to heal properly. Thanks to the German surgeons, he is now better and can get around in a wheelchair on the ground floor. Every day, with help from Tatiana and a social assistant called Raia, who is from Moldova, he is taken over the high threshold of the French windows out into the garden where, in the shade of the trees and with bird-song in the background, he reads in German a multi-volume illustrated encyclopaedia on the ancient civilisations. On the day that I arrived in Mainz, he was studying the Etruscans.

To celebrate our unexpected get-together, Tatiana quickly prepared lunch. There was no borscht because in the "culture of cooking Ukrainian borscht" this requires two to three hour's preparation. We started our conversation not with the news about the status of borscht but with the culture of the Etruscans. However, the conversation very quickly turned to the subject of Ukraine. Valentin admitted that he had first resigned himself to the idea of dying in Germany but that recently he and Tatiana had started thinking about returning to Kyiv. They have acquaintances who have already returned. One of them visited Tatiana's and Valentin's apartment and even packed a suitcase with their summer clothes to send to them in Germany. Not everything in the case was what

Tatiana had asked for but she says it is the thought that counts. Right now, your thoughts sometimes appear to be the strongest things you have – you think about others and help them if you can. In any case, you hold them in your thoughts.

The social payments that Tatiana and Valentin receive from the German state really only cover the cost of food. They are glad that their host, Almut, also receives compensation from the German government for taking in Ukrainian refugees. Valentin and Tatiana can also access their Ukrainian pensions using their bank cards. They are O.K. for now.

Hundreds of thousands of German households are in a similar situation. I am sure it is not always easy, but it seems to me that Almut, who lost her husband a few years ago, is glad that she has someone to talk to, to drink tea with. The war in Ukraine has filled her quiet house with people, as it has filled all of Europe with Ukrainians – Ukrainian women and their children and pensioners, many of whom are not sure in which country they will die. Many of the husbands of the refugee women are either fighting in the summer heat, or working, or possibly even relaxing in the Ukrainian countryside. Men under sixty still cannot travel abroad, unless they are state employees and have to go to Lugano for the international conference dedicated to the future rebuilding of Ukraine, that is.

There are quite a lot of doctors among the refugees. In 2020, 95 per cent. of Ukrainian medical personnel were female, so you might expect there to be problems with medical care in Ukraine now that so many women have left the country. Apparently, the situation is nonetheless reasonably good. The problems with medical care in the occupied territories are much more serious, however. Indeed, the situation there is tragic. There are no doctors in Mariupol at all. After the capture of what was left of the city, medical care was provided by the Russian military alone. Then the occupation administration asked for doctors to be sent from Russia. Immediately, in mid-May, seventeen doctors arrived from Moscow, with a few coming from annexed Crimea. The State Duma deputy from Putin's United Russia party, Dmitri Hubezov, arrived in Mariupol with television journalists, medicines and some medical equipment. A report about his humanitarian mission was shown on the Russian Federation's main television channels. A few days ago, all the Moscow doctors left. It turns out that they had taken unpaid leave from their work in Moscow hospitals to help out in Mariupol. No new volunteer doctors have since arrived to replace them. And there are no more medicines in the city either.

Former doctors from Mariupol have already taken up posts in territory controlled by the Ukrainian government. One of them, the surgeon Oleg Shevchenko, moved to Andrushivka, a town in Zhytomyr region not far from Lazarivka, where our house is located. Like many provincial hospitals, Andrushivka hospital had long suffered from a lack of doctors. Now almost all the vacancies have been filled by doctors from the I.D.P. community. Shevchenko still lives right in the hospital, sleeping in his office, although he is looking for accommodation in Andrushivka. He managed to leave Mariupol at the last moment and is extremely grateful to the Ukrainian military, who shared their petrol with him.

While it is quite easy for internally displaced surgeons and other doctors to find work, dentists have a harder time. There has always been a lot of competition in the dental services market in Ukraine. Now the competition is even more fierce. At the same time, there are practically no dentists left in the newly occupied territories. Residents who have remained there have to travel to the so-called "Donetsk People's Republic" or "Luhansk People's Republic" or even to Russia, if they need dental care. Only those who have transport and money can afford to do this. In addition, numerous Russian checkpoints can prevent residents of the occupied territories from reaching the border with Russia or with one of the "separatist republics". Soldiers at the checkpoints are suspicious about whether or not the car occupants are really looking for dental treatment. Maybe they are "Ukrainian commandos" pretending to be going to the dentist and are in fact are trying to get closer to the Kremlin. God forbid that you find yourself alone with a toothache in the newly occupied territories during this war.

Interestingly, some dramatic events in the field of dentistry have also been taking place in Russia. Recently, the Chechnyan overlord, Ramzan Kadyrov, received the "Order of Merit for Dentistry" from the Russian association of dentists. The award ceremony took place in Grozny, the capital of Chechnya, during the opening of a new building for "Grozny Dental Clinic No.1". The most up-to-date dentistry equipment was brought into the clinic's new wing. During the same ceremony, the Head of Chechnya presented the country's highest award, the "Order of Kadyrov", to the chief doctor of the dental clinic, Yunus Umarov. This all looks logical, the Russian dentists and Ramzan Kadyrov are now united by friendship and cooperation. Kadyrov no longer has to fly to Moscow or Krasnodar for dental treatment. However, Russian dentists, including those who live and work in Chechnya, are not so optimistic. The supply of some key consumables for dental treatment, the dental equipment itself, along with its spare parts, are now all subject to sanctions because of the Russian aggression. Russia's pre-war stock of imported materials for fillings and prosthetics has already run out. The quality of Russian-made materials is very poor and only suitable for temporary fillings. In general, dentists do not want to risk their reputations and so avoid purchasing Russian-made supplies. According to Russian media, China and South Korea are trying to enter the Russian market for dental materials. In the meantime, buyers for Russian dental companies have started flying to Israel to bring back the materials necessary for implantation and fillings in their suitcases. As a result, prices for dental services have risen sharply and continue to rise. Many Russians can no longer afford dental treatment. So, what hope is there for Ukrainians seeking dental care in the occupied territories? In a move to try and ameliorate this situation, the Russian government has adopted another resolution on "import substitution" – in other words, piracy.

In the end, these shortages will also affect the condition of Russian soldiers' teeth. After all, they will be treated with domestic Russian materials. However, for a Russian soldier, a filling that flies out of a tooth after only two weeks is not such a big problem. Their main challenge is to survive the war until the day their filling falls out. If they survive, they can always put in another one.

In Ukraine, everything is fine on the "dental front". There are Swiss and German materials available for fillings and the treatment itself is not as expensive as in Europe or Russia. The Ukrainian soldiers and civilians can afford to smile and show their teeth. They believe in victory. They believe in their doctors. They believe that everything will be fine on all fronts of this war: military, cultural, epicurean and medical.

11.07.2022

War, Cars and the Summer

The most popular governor of Ukraine – the head of front-line Mykolaiv region – wears brightly coloured socks, speaks Russian, Ukrainian, French and Korean and, in his video messages, he regularly tells jokes in an attempt to cheer up the residents of Mykolaiv region, which is bombarded almost every night by Russian artillery and ballistic missiles.

The governor's name is Vitaly Kim. He is a Ukrainian of Korean origin. A successful businessman who entered politics at the same time as Volodymyr Zelensky, he is a member of Zelensky's "Servant of the People" party.

One of the first Russian missiles fired at Mykolaiv destroyed the building of the regional administration, including the governor's office. The governor was not there at the time, but the collapse of the building killed more than thirty employees of the regional administration, including the governor's press secretary. Vitaly Kim has found new premises for his office and continues to lead the region – to the increasingly loud accompaniment of military operations.

Recently, in addition to organising restoration work on damaged residential buildings and regional infrastructure, Governor Kim has had to "fight" with the Ukrainian military. There are a great many soldiers in Mykolaiv region and Kim has no problem with most of them. He is concerned about the military drivers who regularly violate traffic rules and cause accidents on the region's roads.

Clearly, military personnel do not usually obey civilians, but Vitaly Kim has taken on a firm military manner in stating that if army drivers violate traffic rules unnecessarily, he will confiscate their vehicles. It is not tanks or personnel carriers that are causing the problem, but high-speed pickup trucks that volunteers from all over Ukraine and abroad have donated to increase the army's mobility and make operations more effective.

Things would be better if all drivers, both military and civilian, were trained to drive cars under wartime conditions. The usual rules of the road still apply, but you could be forgiven for thinking they had been cancelled as military drivers hurtle about, often without license plates and with lights flashing, as if warning that anything may be expected of them.

No doubt as a result of the increased number of road accidents involving military vehicles, the government recently decided that military drivers must be trained to drive in difficult and extreme conditions by professional racing drivers.

In fact, many military drivers are already highly skilled, especially if they have experience of driving on the front line, where the life of the entire crew depends on the speed of the vehicle and the ability of the driver abruptly to change direction.

In this war, most of the hostilities take place by night. One of the mandatory safety rules for military drivers at the front is that headlights must be switched off. That is, the drivers must not only be able to drive fast on the roads, across fields and over rough terrain, but they must also be able to drive blind. That might be easier on a moon-lit night when you can at least make out the shape of obstacles in your path. But if the night sky is overcast, you can go only on intuition and your ability to discern the noise of the motor of another car over the noise of your own engine.

Along the front line, night traffic across the fields is so intense that accidents are quite common. But even during daylight hours the roads to and from the front remain dangerous, not only because of the shelling by Russian artillery but also because of the nervousness of drivers and the poor technical condition of the old military equipment and trucks which were produced back in Soviet times.

One of the most tragic vehicle accidents of recent weeks occurred when a volunteer ambulance-bus collided with a military truck, which had suffered a blown tyre. The bus, which had been converted into a mobile unit for tending the wounded during their evacuation from the war zone, was a write-off. Unfortunately, there were casualties – a female accident-and-emergency doctor from Austria died and three volunteer paramedics and the driver were seriously injured.

Cars that have been wrecked in accidents are usually left on the side of roads or in fields, causing problems for other drivers. In Mykolaiv region, the debris from car accidents is removed rather quickly. Most of the region is under the control of Ukraine and under the close supervision of Governor Kim.

There are no foreign pickup trucks on the other side of the front line. Could it be that sanctions make it impossible for Russian volunteers to procure them? I think not. Russia can still buy cars from India and China. It simply doesn't have to. The Soviet Union left the Russian Federation tens of thousands of units of military vehicles. From all over that vast country, these vehicles are regularly loaded onto trains and transported towards Ukraine. The roads on the Russian side of the front, which is now more than 2000 kms long, are teeming with old Soviet military vehicles brought out of long-term storage, hundreds of Soviet military U.A.Z. jeeps along with many more modern all-terrain jeeps. There is one more type of vehicle used by the Russian army – one for which the Ukrainian army has no match – the mobile crematorium. These very special vehicles may not be a hazard on the road, but they do help to conceal the true number of victims of the Russian aggression.

The Russian car market seems to be facing some problems at the moment. The imposition of sanctions means that Russians have nothing to buy at car dealerships. So, Vladimir Putin has ordered that production be resumed of the Soviet car brand "Moskvich". To make production easier, the Russian government has relaxed the safety requirements for its cars. Now the presence of an airbag for the passenger seat is optional. Airbag systems are not produced in Russia, so reducing the number required is a big help. But for Russians, safety is not the main thing. The main thing is that there are wheels and a working engine. The most popular models of Soviet/Russian cars like the Lada, Moskvich and Volga never had airbags and, for people who could not afford an imported car, an icon glued to the dashboard did just as well. The Russian army still has enough wheels and engines, and the supply of icons is endless.

While the best-known Ukrainian governor is "fighting" with military drivers, a pizza-truck from the Scottish charity Siobhan's Trust has arrived in the area. An international team of volunteers arranges pizza parties near the front line for residents who have decided not to evacuate, but to stay at home. Last week this mobile operation fed thousands of residents in Mykolaiv region with freshly baked pizza.

There are now five pizza-trucks in Ukraine, each with a team of volunteers. Siobhan's Trust has also sent a refrigerator truck to support them. It distributes ingredients to the pizza-trucks from a warehouse specially set up in the Polish town of Medyka, near the Ukrainian border. The plan is to keep the pizza-trucks serving Ukraine until the end of the war.

For Ukrainians on the edge of the fighting, as well as for I.D.P.s, freshly made pizza brought to your door is something very special – something to make the summertime more cheerful.

Residents of Mykolaiv have always thought that they were very lucky. After all, they have the Black Sea nearby with its well-known resorts and sandy beaches, but they also have the broad Southern Bug River, the banks of which are another popular holiday destination.

The sun is hot these days – along the front lines in the Donbas, on the borders of Mykolaiv and Kherson regions, where the southern front line now passes, as well as in Odesa region, and in Kyiv. It's hot everywhere. Summer is in full swing, but this year nobody is jealous of those who live near the sea.

In Odesa region visiting the beach is officially prohibited. All beaches are closed and, in many places, they are shut off by barbed-wire fences. At least two Russian naval mines have exploded near the beaches of Odesa, killing or injuring holidaymakers with shrapnel. The same kind of incidents have happened in the territories occupied by Russian forces, only the occupying authorities have not banned swimming in those areas. People still go for a dip in the sea off the beaches of the now destroyed Mariupol even though some bathers have died there because of naval mines and shelling.

Along the beaches of Mariupol, Russian military boats constantly patrol the coastline. Russian armed patrols walk along the beaches with machine guns in their hands, checking the documents of those who, despite the war, are trying to get a tan in the southern Ukrainian sun.

Recently, a boat slowly and solemnly passed along the Mariupol coast, accompanied by a warship from Novorossiysk. Both vessels were carrying Russian Orthodox priests. This maritime "procession", together with the display of icons and the recitation of prayers, was arranged for the Moscow military T.V. channel "Zvezda" (The Star). They probably wanted to show Russian believers that God is helping the Russian army. The channel's T.V. journalists included footage of a few people enjoying a sunbathe on the beach. Indeed, the sight of people resting near the sea is always calming and tends to inspire thoughts of stability and peace.

In Mykolaiv, the majority of townspeople can now rest safely on the banks of the Southern Bug. It is quieter there and there is little danger of stepping on an explosive device.

The beaches of Kyiv are also full of people. Sappers have checked everything thoroughly – there are no mines. The city's sanitation services have also announced that all of Kyiv's beaches have been treated with anti-tick substances. So, now you need to worry only about Russian missiles.

Despite the war, many Ukrainian families still want to

relax at the seaside. If not on the Black Sea, then on the Mediterranean or the Aegean Sea. Travel agencies are working, and foreign holidays have not become more expensive because of the war. In fact, if anything, they are now a little cheaper, especially if the holidaymakers are prepared to travel by bus. For a week at a Black Sea resort on the Bulgarian coast, prices start at two hundred dollars per person, including bus transportation. If you want to go to Egypt, Turkey, or Italy, you will probably have to fly out of Chisinau, Moldova. Moldova's main airport is now doing a great deal more business than before the war, having become one of the base airports for Ukraine, which has had no air communication with the outside world since February 24th.

In spite of problems with transport, the war has brought Ukraine closer to its western neighbours. Poland, with which Ukraine has many unresolved historical issues, has put aside its grievances and become one of Ukraine's main partners. Moldova, whose industrial region, Transnistria, has long been occupied by Russia, also helps Ukraine to the best of its ability. Ukrainians are making a real contribution to the development of the Moldovan economy, and this is reflected in the recent decision of the country's principal T.V. channel to transmit two programmes in Ukrainian each week.

The more Putin tries to "de-Ukrainianise" Ukraine, the more intensely the integration of Ukraine into Eastern and Western Europe takes place. Books in Ukrainian are already being printed in Lithuania, Poland, and the Czech Republic. Many restaurants in Eastern Europe now have menus in Ukrainian. What's more, new Ukrainian restaurants are appearing in many European towns and cities. Often, they are created by refugees from Ukraine the ones that, most likely, will not come back. But some of the profits from these restaurants may well return in the form of pick-up trucks for use by the Ukrainian army – hopefully with well-trained drivers.

Epilogue

In Ukraine, people treat oriental wisdom and culture with surprising tenderness. Sometime in the 1970s, there even arose a separate cult of Japanese culture and, of course, the cult of the samurai. Since then, from time to time, a saying attributed to samurai pops up in the conversations of Ukrainians: "If you sit on the riverbank for a very long time, then sooner or later the corpse of your enemy will float past you downstream". I don't know if such a saying really exists in Japan, but in Ukraine it is still loved.

While you were reading this book, I was not sitting on the banks of the river, I was writing a new diary – more precisely, the continuation of my diary of Russia's aggression. Of course, from the mass media, you already know the general picture of what is happening in Ukraine and, perhaps, if the body of my enemy has already floated by, I will have returned to writing the novel that I had just begun in February 2022. But, in any case, my diary will continue to follow Ukraine's struggle for freedom and reconstruction. I hope in due course to be able to share this with you.

Index